# THE WEHRMACHT

## 1935–1945

# WORLD WAR II DATA BOOK

# THE WEHRMACHT

## 1935–1945

## THE ESSENTIAL FACTS AND FIGURES FOR HITLER'S GERMANY

MICHAEL E. HASKEW

amber
BOOKS

First published in 2011 by
Amber Books Ltd
Bradley's Close
74–77 White Lion Street
London N1 9PF
United Kingdom
www.amberbooks.co.uk

ISBN: 978-1-907446-95-5

Project Editor: Michael Spilling
Design: Hawes Design
Picture Research: Terry Forshaw

Printed in China

PICTURE CREDITS
Amber Books: 116, 163, 176
Art-Tech/Aerospace: 2, 20/21, 48, 71, 155, 162, 174, 179
Cody Images: 13, 17, 18, 38/39, 42, 59, 96/97, 117, 128/129,
    139, 158/159, 169, 183
Library of Congress: 6/7
Ukrainian State Archive: 56/57, 109

All profile artworks courtesy Art-Tech.

# CONTENTS

# CHAPTER 1

# History of the German Army

*The disillusion and national humiliation which followed defeat in World War I cast a long shadow over the German nation. The punitive terms of the Treaty of Versailles contributed to political unrest and economic chaos during the decade which followed, facilitating the rise of the Nazi Party.*

■ German soldiers from the Kaiser's Imperial Army stare through a barbed wire fence, 1919.

# Out of the Ashes

*Although its size and potential for offensive operations were severely restricted by the Treaty, the German Army remained a potentially potent force within the country. Its allegiance or opposition to the actions of the post-war government influenced the course of events which followed.*

In the spring of 1918, the German high command, principally General Erich Ludendorff, Chief Quartermaster General and joint commander of the Army along with Field Marshal Paul von Hindenburg, the hero of the great victory in the East at Tannenberg in 1914, realized that its last and best hope for victory in the Great War lay in a final massive offensive on the Western Front. The United States had entered the war in April 1917, and it was apparent that the industrial might and sheer manpower the Americans could bring to bear would allow the Allies, or the Entente, to make good their losses during four years of fruitless trench warfare while Germany was being bled white and could not sustain heavy losses in men and materiel for an indefinite period.

Furthermore, Germany had been successful on the Eastern Front, forcing Russia out of the war and signing the Treaty of Brest-Litovsk in 1917. Peace with Russia freed 50 German infantry divisions for transfer to the West, and on 21 March 1918, the four-pronged Spring Offensive was launched. Often referred to as Operation 'Michael', the codename of the largest of the German ground efforts, the offensive was initially successful, gaining more territory than any large-scale attack by either

side since 1914. With the initial objective of reaching the Channel ports and splitting the British and French armies, German planners employed lightly-armed shock troops, called stormtroopers, who rapidly penetrated Allied trench lines.

In the end, however, the stormtroopers and the regular infantry units which followed them took heavy casualties and overstretched their supply lines. Unable to sustain their momentum, the Germans were eventually compelled to retire. Heavy Allied counter-attacks later recovered the majority of the lost ground.

Following the failure of the Spring Offensive, the defeat of Imperial Germany was inevitable. Its resources exhausted, Germany was forced to sue for peace. Kaiser Wilhelm II abdicated and fled to exile in the Netherlands, while German diplomats expected to achieve an honourable armistice as the guns fell silent on 11 November 1918.

## Vindictive Versailles

On 28 June 1919, the Treaty of Versailles was signed in the Hall of Mirrors at the great palace built during the reign of Louis XIV. In sharp contrast to the high hopes of the German delegation, Allied leaders were not in a conciliatory mood.

Their nations had suffered tremendously in the loss of lives and treasure, and retribution was to be exacted. Rather than negotiating at least somewhat favourable terms, the Germans found themselves on the receiving end of a harsh, punitive agreement which was essentially dictated to them, and they were given no choice but to sign the document.

With Allied armies poised along their western frontier ready to invade Germany itself, a strangling blockade barring the import of even basic foodstuffs, and an economy in tatters, the German delegation did so grudgingly, only minutes before the deadline to comply expired. Regardless, the German public was outraged by the harsh terms of the Treaty, giving rise to the theory that the Army itself had not lost the war in the field but had been stabbed in the back by moderates and leftists who sought to end the war. The careers of those politicians and military officers who had endorsed peace negotiations or become involved with the hated Treaty were damaged beyond repair.

According to the Treaty, the German nation was required to accept blame for the war. The country was also required to pay war reparations to the Allies of more than 130 billion marks, the equivalent of

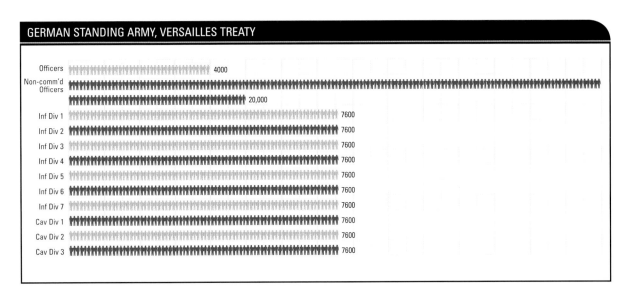

GERMAN STANDING ARMY, VERSAILLES TREATY

| | |
|---|---|
| Officers | 4000 |
| Non-comm'd Officers | |
| | 20,000 |
| Inf Div 1 | 7600 |
| Inf Div 2 | 7600 |
| Inf Div 3 | 7600 |
| Inf Div 4 | 7600 |
| Inf Div 5 | 7600 |
| Inf Div 6 | 7600 |
| Inf Div 7 | 7600 |
| Cav Div 1 | 7600 |
| Cav Div 2 | 7600 |
| Cav Div 3 | 7600 |

nearly $32 billion. Germany was stripped of its colonial empire, while its territory was reduced significantly. Chief among the territorial losses were the provinces of Alsace and Lorraine, returned to France, the establishment of the Polish Corridor, which separated East Prussia from the rest of the country and designated the port of Danzig a free city, the demilitarization of the Rhineland, and the occupation of the coal-rich region of the Saar by France for 15 years in compensation for the devastation of the French coal industry during the war.

The German armed forces were restricted to a standing army of only 100,000 men, including an officer cadre of no more than 4000 and 20,000 non-commissioned officers. Structurally, the Army was to include no more than seven infantry and three cavalry divisions, while the use of tanks, armoured cars, poison gas and military aircraft was prohibited and the numbers and types of artillery, small arms and automatic weapons were severely restricted. The reductions in armaments were to be accomplished to a supervised timetable.

Article 163 of the Treaty reads in part, 'Within three months from the coming into force of the present treaty the total number of effectives must be reduced to 200,000 and the number of units must not exceed twice the number of those laid down in Article 160 (10 divisions). At the expiration of this period, and at the end of each subsequent period of three months, a conference of military experts of the principal Allied and associated powers will fix the reductions to be made in the ensuing three months, so that by 31 March 1920, at the latest the total number of German effectives does not exceed the maximum number of 100,000 men …'

**Weimar and economic woes**
Only weeks after the signing of the Versailles Treaty, a republic was established in Germany to replace the old monarchy. Named for the city in which the government had met when civil unrest in Berlin had forced its relocation, the Weimar Republic was established in early 1919. Faced with the crippling reparations payments mandated by the Treaty and rising unemployment, which reached a peak of nearly 30 per cent on the eve of Hitler's rise to power in 1933, the Weimar government also had to contend with runaway inflation. The German war effort had been financed through heavy borrowing and inflationary monetary policies, and the downward spiral of the mark continued unabated throughout the mid-1920s. By 1923, the mark, whose value at the time of the Armistice had been greater than that of the French franc, had plummeted to one trillionth of its pre-World War I value against the Gold Standard. The result was widespread poverty and economic chaos in Germany. A wheelbarrow full of

GERMANY'S SITUATION IN EUROPE, 1920–21

Germany's situation in Europe, 1920–21

- - - - Poland's treaty boundary 1921

Western Allies

New States created 1919–20

● States undertaking minorities obligations under the peace treaties

● States making minorities declarations to the League of Nations

Neutral States

■ POSTWAR EUROPE: Under the terms of the post-World War I treaties, Germany became strategically squeezed in Europe. East Prussia was separated from the rest of the German state by the Polish Corridor, while in the West, Alsace-Lorraine, Saarland and Eupen-Malmedy were eventually transferred to France or Belgium. The Rhineland remained a German possession, but no military deployment was permitted here.

marks was required to purchase a loaf of bread. By the end of the 1920s, the catastrophe of the Great Depression further weighed on the German economy.

### Political instability

The rise of Bolshevik Russia and the anarchy which followed the end of World War I were catalysts for political unrest across Europe. Revolutionary voices gained large audiences of disillusioned young people, disadvantaged citizens, and soldiers who had returned home to find their families destitute, few prospects for jobs, and a government which, many believed, bore the

responsibility not only for losing the war but also for the economic catastrophe which followed.

Prior to the formation of the Weimar Republic, Friedrich Ebert, leader of the Social Democratic Party, had assumed the de facto office of Chancellor of Germany. Already, the left-wing Spartacist movement was inciting unrest among the people and more than 3000 German Navy sailors had mutinied, demanding money. Most distressing of all, the people were on the verge of starvation. In some areas, the infant mortality rate within one month of birth approached 40 per cent in 1920.

### The Kapp-Lüttwitz Putsch

Military and civil dissent was not confined to the left. While right-wing extremist groups such as the National Socialist German Workers (Nazi) Party were in their infancy during the early 1920s and the future Nazi leader and *Führer* of Germany, Adolf Hitler, was attempting to form his own political identity, elements within the hierarchy of the former Imperial German Army were enraged by the Treaty of Versailles.

Of particular concern to a number of German officers was the provision which called for the deactivation of much of the Army. In March 1920, when consternation over the Treaty had reached new heights, General Walther von Lüttwitz, commander of troops in Saxony, Thuringia and Hanover, and the right-wing agitator Wolfgang Kapp led an uprising which would bear their names. Troops seized control of Berlin and instituted a short-lived government, declaring martial law and clashing with labour organizations which had taken to the streets against them.

The coup lasted for just days; however, a general strike and the apparent inability of the government to summon troops under its control to suppress the rebels created even greater unrest from all quarters. The Kapp-Lüttwitz Putsch also resulted in a change in tactics by right-wing militarists. Rather than opposing the Weimar government openly, they would exert influence through the quiet support of the paramilitary *Freikorps* and other organizations whose intent was supposedly benign.

# The Freikorps

*The German soldiers who had marched home from the trenches in the autumn of 1918 were welcomed as heroes.*

In their minds and the minds of many in the civilian population, the Army had not been decisively defeated in battle, rather the military had been ill-

served by politicians and defeatists who failed to see the far-reaching consequences of a dictated peace. The armed forces had been stabbed

in the back. Further, the officer corps had traditionally been raised from the German aristocracy and maintained its monarchist mindset, which fostered difficult relations between the military and the liberal Weimar government from the outset.

## Communist threat

However, in the face of a continuing threat from the communist Spartacists and widespread civil discord, an uneasy period of cooperation between the government and the military ensued. True enough, the returning soldiers fractured to some extent, fighting in the streets with elements of both the left and right. Most had been in the military for some time, however, and did not relish the thought of an unproductive and rather aimless return to civilian life.

In response to the growing threat of communist revolution a large number of these Army veterans formed volunteer units called *Freikorps*. Advocated initially by Major Kurt von Schleicher, later to play an important role in the destabilization of the government and the rise of the Nazis, the *Freikorps* were recruited from among former soldiers, particularly those with right-wing political views who had formed their own *ad hoc* units, with the promise of pay and a degree of influence on the appointment of officers and other issues. Ranging in size from fewer than 100 men to fairly well-equipped units numbering several thousand, the *Freikorps*

fought the communists and defended the eastern borders of Germany against encroaching Polish forces.

Ebert himself was introduced to a *Freikorps* formation of 4000 former Army troops and accepted the offer of their commander to employ them in an effort to restore order, particularly when the Army had proven ineffective in suppressing the communists. Although the *Freikorps* had been organized and equipped by former Army officers, their ranks replete with veteran soldiers, and the Weimar government tacitly approved of its creation, they remained somewhat beyond the immediate control of the Army high command. Often, the commanders of individual

## GERMAN POPULATION, 1918–39 (MILLIONS)

| Year | Population |
|------|-----------|
| 1918 | 66.8 |
| 1919 | 62.9 |
| 1920 | 61.7 |
| 1921 | 62.4 |
| 1922 | 62.0 |
| 1923 | 62.4 |
| 1924 | 62.5 |
| 1925 | 63.1 |
| 1926 | 63.6 |
| 1927 | 64.0 |
| 1928 | 64.3 |
| 1929 | 64.7 |
| 1930 | 65.0 |
| 1931 | 65.4 |
| 1932 | 65.7 |
| 1933 | 66.0 |
| 1934 | 66.4 |
| 1935 | 66.8 |
| 1936 | 67.3 |
| 1937 | 67.8 |
| 1938 | 75.3 |
| 1939 | 86.9 |

units exerted a great deal of autonomy. The *Freikorps* served their purpose in quelling the communist threat to the Weimar government, and while the government actually financed much of the *Freikorps'* activities the Army benefited as well, successfully avoiding the potential repercussions of fighting directly against the civilian population.

■ *Freikorps* **soldiers stand in a town square somewhere in Germany, 1919.** *Freikorps* **members were involved in street battles with left-wing groups.**

# The Reichswehr

*On 6 March 1919, the provisional government of Germany established an armed forces structure which was to be a new creation, distinct from the administration of the former Imperial Army but nevertheless bound to it by tradition and the bonds of comradeship formed during years of war in the trenches.*

Known officially as the *Vorläufige Reichswehr*, or Provisional German Defence Force, the military was to include a land force, the *Vorläufige Reichsheer*, and a small navy, the *Vorläufige Reichsmarine*. The land component soon grew to more than 50 units, each roughly equivalent to brigade strength, with 400,000 men under arms.

Typical of the units of the *Vorläufige Reichswehr* was Brigade 2 Stettin, formed in June 1919 primarily from *Freikorps* troops in the area. Later merging with other units, it was incorporated into the 2nd Division of the *Reichswehr* in October 1920. Initially Brigade 2 consisted of

infantry, light infantry, cavalry, artillery and pioneer regiments.

By the autumn of 1919, the *Vorläufige Reichsheer* had given way to the *Übergangsheer*, or Transitional Army, which was constituted in the wake of the Treaty of Versailles and subject to its restrictions. Its 30 brigades were officially formed on 30 September and would in due course be scaled back according to the terms of the Treaty.

In accordance with Versailles, on 1 January 1921, the German armed forces were once again reconstituted and renamed. The new *Reichswehr* was to be maintained for defensive purposes only and was to consist of

the *Reichsheer* and *Reichsmarine*. In addition to its restricted size of 100,000 troops formed in three cavalry and seven infantry divisions, the *Reichsheer* was limited to only two groups of senior commanders since the high command of the German Army had been abolished. The divisions of the *Reichsheer* were formed through the integration of former brigades of the *Übergangsheer*.

The principal organizer of the *Reichswehr* was General Hans von Seeckt, who also actively supported the *Freikorps*, which became known to some as the 'Black *Reichswehr*', particularly for the illegal clandestine

## ORGANIZATION OF THE *REICHSHEER*, 1921

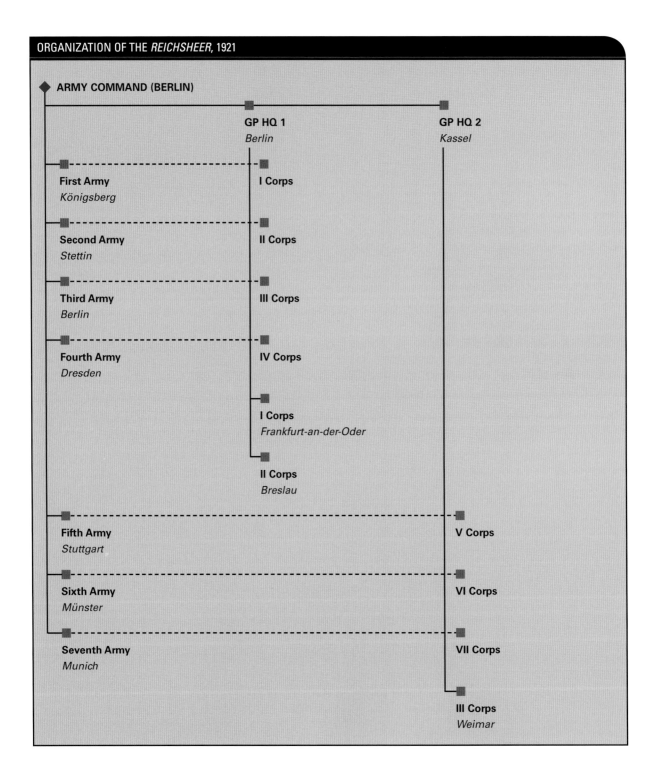

◆ ARMY COMMAND (BERLIN)

GP HQ 1
*Berlin*

GP HQ 2
*Kassel*

First Army
*Königsberg*

I Corps

Second Army
*Stettin*

II Corps

Third Army
*Berlin*

III Corps

Fourth Army
*Dresden*

IV Corps

I Corps
*Frankfurt-an-der-Oder*

II Corps
*Breslau*

Fifth Army
*Stuttgart*

V Corps

Sixth Army
*Münster*

VI Corps

Seventh Army
*Munich*

VII Corps

III Corps
*Weimar*

operations of 60,000 troops along the Polish frontier which were supported by the *Reichswehr* leadership and the government. Seeckt was hostile to the terms of the Versailles Treaty and vowed to lead the *Reichswehr* to battle against the Allies once again should certain provisions of the Treaty be enforced to excess. He was also an advocate of cooperation with the fledgling Soviet Union. Seeckt was among the earliest of German military leaders to actively circumvent the terms of the Versailles Treaty, concealing the existence of an operating general staff for the *Reichsheer* by euphemistically referring to it as the *Truppenamt*, or Troop Office.

Seeckt was largely responsible for the Army's indifferent response to the Kapp-Lüttwitz Putsch. While it might be plausible that the intent of the Army leadership as a whole was to remain neutral in regard to political events and that this position should be preserved within the *Reichswehr*, it must be noted that the *Reichswehr* actively suppressed the attempts of the Left to foment revolution and was unsympathetic to the Weimar democracy. Therefore, it is understandable that the autocratic traditions of the Army would remain inherent in the *Reichswehr* and explain, at least in part, the future establishment of a working relationship between the leadership of the Army and the Nazis.

The *Reichswehr* was organized into seven military districts, or *Wehrkreise*, across Germany and

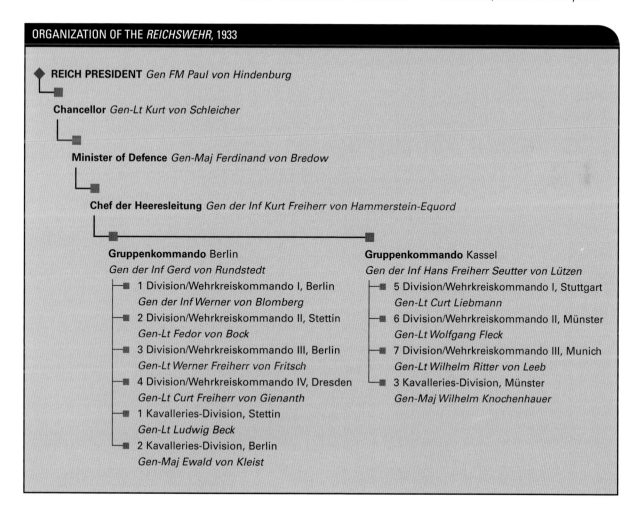

## ORGANIZATION OF THE *REICHSWEHR*, 1933

**REICH PRESIDENT** *Gen FM Paul von Hindenburg*

**Chancellor** *Gen-Lt Kurt von Schleicher*

**Minister of Defence** *Gen-Maj Ferdinand von Bredow*

**Chef der Heeresleitung** *Gen der Inf Kurt Freiherr von Hammerstein-Equord*

**Gruppenkommando** Berlin
*Gen der Inf Gerd von Rundstedt*
- 1 Division/Wehrkreiskommando I, Berlin
  *Gen der Inf Werner von Blomberg*
- 2 Division/Wehrkreiskommando II, Stettin
  *Gen-Lt Fedor von Bock*
- 3 Division/Wehrkreiskommando III, Berlin
  *Gen-Lt Werner Freiherr von Fritsch*
- 4 Division/Wehrkreiskommando IV, Dresden
  *Gen-Lt Curt Freiherr von Gienanth*
- 1 Kavalleries-Division, Stettin
  *Gen-Lt Ludwig Beck*
- 2 Kavalleries-Division, Berlin
  *Gen-Maj Ewald von Kleist*

**Gruppenkommando** Kassel
*Gen der Inf Hans Freiherr Seutter von Lützen*
- 5 Division/Wehrkreiskommando I, Stuttgart
  *Gen-Lt Curt Liebmann*
- 6 Division/Wehrkreiskommando II, Münster
  *Gen-Lt Wolfgang Fleck*
- 7 Division/Wehrkreiskommando III, Munich
  *Gen-Lt Wilhelm Ritter von Leeb*
- 3 Kavalleries-Division, Münster
  *Gen-Maj Wilhelm Knochenhauer*

existed for 14 years. It was formally succeeded by the *Heer*, or German Army, created in the spring of 1935. By that time, Hitler and the Nazis had been in power in Germany for more than two years and the Allies had acquiesced to numerous violations of the Versailles Treaty, both overt and covert. By 1939, just prior to the invasion of Poland, the *Heer* numbered more than 3.7 million men.

Meanwhile, the *Reichsheer* of the 1920s and early 1930s was actively engaged in training and even mounted military advisory missions and delegations to the Soviet Union and China. Although it was ostensibly prohibited from doing so, the deceptively-named *Truppenamt* was involved in military planning and evaluating strategy and tactics which would avoid the horrific stalemate of the trenches experienced during the Great War, facilitating mobilization and the logistical support of offensive forces. While such war planning activities were expressly forbidden by the Versailles Treaty, they went on in secret.

The rapid movement of the earlier *Freikorps* units throughout Germany during their suppression of civil unrest and communist agitation gave rise to the concepts of quick deployment, combined-arms operations and mobile warfare. These theories, in fact, trace their origin to this period, through the proving ground of the Spanish Civil War, and onto the world stage in 1939.

A number of the senior commanders of the *Heer* from 1939 to 1945 were veterans of World War I who had maintained their ties to the military through the *Freikorps* or *Reichswehr*. Among them was future General Heinz Guderian, whose *Blitzkrieg* tactics and aggressive use of tanks and armoured fighting vehicles revolutionized modern warfare, Erwin Rommel, an infantry officer who became famous during World War II as commander of the vaunted *Afrika Korps*, and Hasso von Manteuffel, a distinguished commander of armoured forces.

# Clandestine Militarism

*Although many historians have concentrated on the repudiation of the Treaty of Versailles and the clandestine rearmament and expansion of the German military which occurred under Hitler after 1933, it is evident that Germany never really did demilitarize.*

The Army's officer corps remained active in the military and political affairs of the country following the end of World War I. The existence of the *Freikorps* themselves could be construed as a violation of the Treaty, while the successor *Reichswehr* retained much of the tradition of the old Imperial Army.

'Of course, the army took advantage of any loophole that existed or could be constructed in the Versailles disarmament rules,' wrote E.J. Gumbel. 'Each company continued the tradition of an imperial regiment and got the corresponding numbers and colors. Since four companies make up a battalion, the battalion corresponded to a division and the regiment to an army corps. Thus, the *Reichswehr* threw a shadow, and the shadow was the larger of the two. The meaning of this shadow was the image of the Imperial Army.'

Seeckt personally maintained the tradition of the old Imperial Army and its aristocratic officer corps. Since each company was awarded the history and trappings of a regiment which would ordinarily number 3000 men, at least 10 times the size of a standard company, the *esprit de corps* of some of the Army's legendary field units would survive. Individual officers were consistently trained to assume the responsibilities of those holding higher ranks, while few tangible Treaty restrictions had been placed on non-commissioned officers and a nucleus of up to 40,000 sergeants and other ranks could be assigned duties within an Army infrastructure. In turn, this infrastructure was to become capable of supporting a field force many times the size of the legitimate *Reichswehr*.

The Treaty mandated that the volunteer *Reichswehr* would consist of officers and other ranks committed to long terms of service, 25 years for officers and 12 years for the rank and file, therefore restricting the number of troops which could be trained during an extensive period of time. This provision was circumvented with the manipulation of rosters and duties.

'The officers in the *Reichswehr*,' reasoned Gumbel, 'served longer in the same ranks, sometimes up to two and a half times the length of service in the Imperial Army. Thus, the average officer was actually a higher-ranking officer in the shadow army. Reserve officers were illegally trained and advanced in a legally nonexisting reserve. Fifty-eight thousand noncoms were able to train a much larger army which existed,

partly on paper, in the patriotic organizations forming an illegal reservoir, and in illegal paramilitary formations. The instructions in official manuals were based on the strengths of arms and munitions of a great modern military power and not on the legal 100,000-man army. Since the soldiers had to sign up for twelve years, 8000 could leave each twelve years and 8000 new soldiers could then be enrolled. In reality, various devices such as unforeseen illnesses were used to justify large, premature dismissals and new entrants. New soldiers were introduced under the identification of legal soldiers, so that the formal number remained constant.'

Seeckt also sanctioned the creation of large civil police forces. Numbering in the thousands, these units were heavily armed with rifles and machine guns and issued some of the few armoured vehicles available in Weimar Germany.

Rigorous training and recruiting efforts resulted in a paramilitary force which could be called upon to fill the ranks of a resurgent German Army.

While the Treaty forbade Germany from importing and exporting arms, the trade went on relatively unrestricted. Seeckt forged a cooperative effort between the *Reichswehr*, the Weimar government and prominent industrialists to facilitate the nation's rearmament. The production of arms in German factories was monitored by an Allied commission, but numerous loopholes were discovered and exploited.

The giant German arms manufacturer Krupp of Essen gained a controlling interest in the Swedish Bofors company through the exchange of patent rights and technical expertise for shares of

■ *Reichswehr* **troops undergo military training with some improvised armoured cars, 1923.**

## GENERAL HANS VON SEECKT

■ Hans von Seeckt (left) talks to a member of his staff.

*Seeckt was the consummate military staff officer, serving with efficiency in the Imperial German Army during World War I and receiving credit for planning the successful invasion of Serbia. As chief of the* Reichswehr, *Seeckt was largely responsible for maintaining the framework of a large, professional army and facilitated the growth and modernization of the* Heer *in defiance of the Versailles Treaty. Although the Army General Staff had been abolished at Versailles, Seeckt maintained the organization under the euphemistic name of the 'Troop Office'. He also made overtures to the Soviet Union, which provided clandestine training facilities for German troops.*

| | |
|---|---|
| BIRTH: | 22 April 1866 |
| DEATH: | 27 December 1936 |
| PLACE OF BIRTH: | Schleswig |
| PERSONAL RELATIONSHIPS: | Married Dorothea Fabian 1893 (no children) |
| SERVICE: | Kaiser Alexander Grenadier Regiment 1885 |
| | *Kriegsakademie* 1897 |
| | Chief of Staff III Corps 1913 |
| | Colonel 1915 |
| | Brigadier-General 1915 |
| | Chief of Staff Eleventh Army 1915 |
| | Chief of Staff Austro-Hungarian |
| | Seventh Army 1916 |
| | Lieutenant-General, last Chief of General Staff 1918 |
| | Chief of Staff *Reichswehr* 1919 |
| | Suppresses Beer Hall Putsch 1923 |
| | Dismissed from office 1926 |
| | Elected to *Reichstag* 1930 |
| | Military Advisor to China 1934 |

Bofors stock and produced some armaments outside the borders of Germany. Krupp also operated companies with apparently harmless names as cover for the production of weapons and the development of military technology. Some German weapons had been shipped to the Netherlands prior to the end of the war and stored there. By the mid-1920s, Allied commissioners

estimated that within a year German arms manufacturers could once again be producing weapons and ammunition at levels seen during World War I.

Concurrently, the growing popularity of the automobile allowed German car-makers to develop new types of vehicles with the capability of cross-country travel, and the manufacture of tractors and other

heavy equipment was necessary for the benefit of German agriculture. Growth in civilian air travel and the need for the transportation of goods by air led to the design of passenger and transport planes which could be converted to military use. In each case, such industries could be placed on a wartime footing and adapted to military production based on covert designs which had been conceived for military purposes with blueprints ready for manufacture and production schedules already drawn up.

In 1922, Germany and the Soviet Union concluded a secret military agreement at the same time as they signed the Treaty of Rapallo, in which each dropped territorial or financial claims against the other resulting from the 1917 Treaty of Brest-Litovsk. The Soviet Union was not a party to the Treaty of Versailles and, therefore, was not bound by its terms. According to the secret protocol, the German government would pay the Soviets an annual sum and experienced officers and non-commissioned officers of the *Reichswehr* would train soldiers of the Red Army.

In return, the Soviets were to provide facilities inside the Soviet Union where German troops could train with tanks, heavy guns, aircraft and other weapons prohibited by the Versailles Treaty away from the prying eyes of the world and particularly of the former Allies. Eventually, the seven battalions of the *Reichswehr* designated as 'transport' units would form the core of the panzer divisions which devastated Europe during World War II.

At the direction of Seeckt, Special Group Russia was created to bring about cooperation between the German and Soviet military organizations. As a result, two facilities, one for the training of airmen and another for testing and training with tanks and armoured vehicles, were established in the Soviet Union. Artillery shells, aircraft frames, small arms, and even poison gas were manufactured in Soviet

facilities for the future use of the German Army.

The secret augmentation of the German military was financed partially through private funds, channelled to the military by major industrialists or from other such sources. These contributions were often solicited directly by military personnel who pointed out that big business was destined to profit from the rearmament programme. Approximately one-quarter of the Weimar Republic military budget consisted of funds which could be diverted from their original purpose for use elsewhere, while some military expenses were listed under generally accepted civilian budget categories for which no further accounting was necessary. Between 1924 and 1928, the budget of the *Reichswehr* doubled, and by 1929 the German military enjoyed such strong financial support that it actually ended the year with a substantial surplus.

## Offensive primer

In 1921, General von Seeckt released an updated and expanded version of the *Reichswehr* field manual. Titled *Command of Combined Arms Tactics*, the treatise described the anticipated offensive capability of the Army. Enrolment in paramilitary, police or athletic organizations steadily increased, while *Reichswehr* training continued. Exercises were conducted with live ammunition when possible, automobiles or trucks were painted with signs which designated them as 'tanks' during training, and future pilots of the *Luftwaffe* trained in gliders.

The *Reichswehr* itself had been called upon to suppress rebellions fomented by both the left and the right, particularly during the tumultuous year of 1923 in which political disturbances flared in the provinces of Bavaria, Saxony and Thuringia. Most notably that year, Seeckt's troops quelled the putsch attempt in Munich which had been initiated by Adolf Hitler and the Nazi Party.

In 1926, Seeckt retired from active service with the *Reichswehr*, having advanced the rebirth of the German Army substantially despite continuing political turmoil which often erupted in violence and in direct contravention of the Treaty of Versailles. He had served the Weimar Republic as its military chief of staff while balancing the Army's general disdain for the government against the need for cooperation in the process of redevelopment.

'One thing no peace treaty, no foe can take from us is manly thought,' he declared. 'When fate again summons the German people to arms, and this day will inevitably come again, then it shall find a people of men, not weaklings, who will powerfully grip their trusted weapon. The form of this weapon is not so important, if hands of steel and hearts of iron employ it.'

When the *Reichswehr* re-emerged as the *Heer* in 1935, the foundation of one of the world's most powerful military machines had been laid. Its employment as an instrument of conquest and destruction in the hands of Adolf Hitler was yet to come.

# CHAPTER 2

# The German Army Before World War II

*Head of state in name only, the World War I hero Paul von Hindenburg was elected President of Germany on 26 April 1925. Manipulated by a group of close advisors, several of whom were consumed by their own ambitions, Hindenburg had entered the political arena reluctantly and found himself succumbing to the rise of the Nazi Party.*

*The embodiment of the Prussian military tradition and the honour of the German Army, he was in his 80s, frail and approaching senility.*

■ **Adolf Hitler salutes German soldiers preparing for the war with Poland, August 1939.**

# Hitler Ascendant

*On 30 January 1933, Adolf Hitler was appointed Chancellor of Germany. His Nazi Party held, in itself, a majority within the* Reichstag, *the German Parliament.*

That majority had, in part, been brought about by the political infighting and posturing among Hindenburg's ministers, including Hitler's predecessors in the office of Chancellor, the career diplomat Franz von Papen and General Kurt von Schleicher, the Catholic Centre Party leader Heinrich Brüning, who had served as Chancellor from 1930 to 1932, and Minister of War Wilhelm Groener, who was humiliated and driven from office.

Following a series of elections, votes of no confidence, the dissolution of the *Reichstag* and other intrigues, Hitler and von Papen were at odds over the office of Chancellor, which wielded the power of government in Germany due to the language in the nation's constitution which allowed President von Hindenburg to dissolve the *Reichstag*, enact emergency legislation without the consent of the legislative body which still maintained a limited power of veto, and to appoint the Chancellor. Hitler was offered the rather innocuous post of Vice-Chancellor and flatly refused any office other than that of Chancellor in the upcoming coalition government.

Rather than carrying his challenge to Hitler for the office of Chancellor to the brink, von Papen concluded that he might persuade Hindenburg, a close friend, to appoint Hitler Chancellor and then manage to keep the Nazi strongman under control. As long as Hindenburg remained President, von Papen believed that his own political acumen and the influence of the other ministers in the cabinet would force Hitler to cooperate.

However, Hindenburg was also useful to Hitler. The old general would serve to legitimize the Nazi Party and Hitler as a leader while also providing a link to the old officer corps of the German Army. Although the two despised one another, they were often seen in public together – displaying their solidarity in government to the German people. Posters portraying the two men with the slogan 'The Marshal and the Corporal' were seen across Germany. Meanwhile, Hitler outmanoeuvred von Papen and the other ministers, biding his time.

### Hindenburg no hinderance

On 2 August 1934, Hindenburg died at the age of 86. Hitler had visited Hindenburg on his deathbed, and the decrepit President was drifting in and out of consciousness. Believing that Hitler was Kaiser Wilhelm II, he addressed the Chancellor as 'Your Majesty' when he entered the room. Undoubtedly Hitler was pleased by this.

During his last days, Hindenburg had become a tool of the ultra-right. Following the burning of the *Reichstag* on 27 February 1933, which Hitler successfully blamed on the communists, Hindenburg issued

| HITLER'S CABINET, 30 JANUARY 1933 | |
|---|---|
| *Official* | *Position* |
| Adolf Hitler (NSDAP) | Chancellor |
| Alfred Hugenberg (DNVP) | Economics, Food and Agriculture Minister |
| Franz Gürtner (DNVP) | Justice Minister |
| Günther Gereke (*Christliches Landvolk*) | Employment Minister |
| Hermann Göring (NSDAP) | Minister Without Portfolio |
| Johann Ludwig von Krosigk (non-party) | Finance Minister |
| Constantin Freiherr von Neurath (non-party) | Foreign Minister |
| Paul Freiherr Eltz von Rübenbach (non-party) | Posts and Transport Minister |
| Franz Seldte (non-party) | Labour Minister |
| Franz von Papen (non-party) | Vice-Chancellor and Reich Commissioner for Prussia |
| Werner von Blomberg (non-party) | Defence Minister |
| Wilhelm Frick (NSDAP) | Interior Minister |

a decree which sharply curtailed the civil liberties of the German people, such as freedom of the press and freedom to assemble. A month later, Hindenburg dissolved the *Reichstag* and passed the Enabling Act, which essentially provided the cabinet with the ability to enact laws without *Reichstag* approval. In early March, the Nazi Party won 288 seats in the *Reichstag*, a substantial majority, with 44 per cent of the popular vote.

During his short tenure as Chancellor, von Papen had already overturned a law which banned the Nazi *Sturmabteilung* (SA), Hitler's private army of street thugs which had grown to more than two million men by the summer of 1934. Germany was swiftly and steadily marching toward a Nazi dictatorship. Hitler had achieved his short-term goal, taking control of the government by legitimate means.

Immediately following Hindenburg's death, Hitler declared the office of President vacant and proclaimed himself *Führer und Reichskanzler*, undisputed leader of the German people. A plebiscite was held two weeks after Hindenburg died, and the Nazis reported that 90 per cent of the German people approved of the consolidation of power in the hands of Hitler, although the actual results were likely short of the stated mandate given that the Nazis maintained lower corresponding numbers in the *Reichstag*.

## Hitler's vision
Years earlier, while serving time in prison following the failed Munich Beer Hall Putsch of 1923, Hitler had described the political course which the nation would pursue with the Nazis in power. The Treaty of Versailles would be repudiated once and for all. German-speaking peoples in neighbouring countries, including

### GOVERNMENT OFFICIALS IN THE NAZI PARTY, 1936

| Individual | Position/Office |
|---|---|
| Hitler, Adolf | *Führer* and Reich Chancellor |
| Hess, Rudolf | Deputy *Führer* |
| Bormann, Martin | Staff of *Führer*'s Deputy |
| Schwarz, Franz | Treasurer |
| Buch, Walter | Supreme Party Court |
| Grimm, W. | Supreme Party Court |
| Frick, Wilhelm | Leader of *Reichstag* Delegation |
| Ley, Robert | German Labour Front; Political Organizations (Cadres) |
| Goebbels, Joseph | Head of Propaganda |
| Dietrich, Otto | Press Chief |
| Amann, Max | *Reichsleiter*, Press |
| Bouhler, Philipp | Nazi Literature |
| Darré, Walther | Agrarian Policy; Reich Agriculture Minister; Reich Peasant Leader |
| Frank, Hans | Reich Law Officer |
| Rosenberg, Alfred | Foreign Policy Office |
| von Epp, Franz | Head of Colonial Office |
| von Schirach, Baldur | Youth Leader |
| Lutz, Victor | SA |
| Hierl, Konstantin | Reich Labour Service |
| Hühnlein, A. | National Socialist Motor Corps |
| Himmler, Heinrich | *Reichsführer-SS* and Head of German Police |

### NAZI GOVERNMENT AND KEY MINISTRIES, 1 SEPTEMBER 1936

| Position/Ministry | Official |
|---|---|
| *Führer* & Chancellor | Adolf Hitler |
| Agriculture | Walther Darré |
| Aviation | Hermann Göring |
| Defence | Werner von Blomberg |
| Economics | Walther Funk |
| Finance | Johann Ludwig von Krosigk |
| Foreign Affairs | Constantin Freiherr von Neurath |
| Interior | Wilhelm Frick |
| Justice | Franz Gürtner |
| Labour | Franz Seldte |
| Post and Communication | Paul Freiherr Eltz von Rübenbach |
| Public Enlightenment and Propaganda | Joseph Goebbels |
| Religion | Hans Kerrl |
| Science, Education and Culture | Bernhard Rust |

Austria, Poland, Czechoslovakia and territories occupied by the Allies following World War I, would be united in the greater German Reich, and Germany would expand eastward, seizing *Lebensraum*, living space, for its growing population

In due time, the German Army became an instrument of conquest and the primary means of perpetuating Nazi hegemony.

### *Reichswehr* to *Wehrmacht*

It was well known that much of the officer corps of the German Army, limited in strength and numbers as the *Reichswehr* had been by the terms of the Treaty of Versailles, did not favour the democratic Weimar Republic and sought the return of the monarchy or the establishment of a right-wing government. The efforts of General von Seeckt and others like him, perhaps unwittingly, facilitated the rise of the Nazis. Seeckt spearheaded the effort to maintain a cadre of professional soldiers who led the *Reichswehr* during a critical time in the history of Germany and found themselves politically manoeuvred into a marriage of convenience with Hitler.

The re-emergence of Germany as a great military power was well underway when Hitler assumed complete control of the government. As for the pragmatic generals, most were willing to go along with the curtailment of civil liberties and the growing persecution of the Jews, which commenced during the early days of the Nazi regime, as long as the honour of Germany was to be restored, the Army was to play a key role in the future of the nation, and

order was to be maintained after years of chaotic street fighting and weak central government.

Only three days after assuming the post of Chancellor, Hitler reiterated his goals for the new Germany and informed an assemblage of *Reichswehr* generals that the secret rearmament of the country was to continue. In October 1933, Germany withdrew from the League of Nations, and within months the military leaders were instructed to

augment the ranks of the Army to 300,000, three times the level authorized by the Versailles Treaty.

The swastika, symbol of the Nazi Party, was pervasive. Banners hung from public buildings, and flags were paraded through the streets or waved from poles in public areas. Nazi regalia also became prevalent on the uniforms of German soldiers, as a new *Reichskokarde* insignia was instituted in March 1933 along with the incorporation of the German

## SWASTIKA FLAGS: TYPES AND VARIATIONS

| Image | Flag | Example |
|---|---|---|
| | 45° black swastika, set on a white disc | NSDAP flag |
| | 45° black swastika, set in a white lozenge | Hitler Youth flag |
| | 45° black swastika, set in a white outline | Tail marking on *Luftwaffe* aircraft |
| | 45° black swastika, outlined by white and black lines, set on a white disc | German War Ensign |
| | upright black swastika, outlined by white and black lines, set on a white disc | Adolf Hitler's personal standard |
| | 45° swastikas in gold, silver, black, or white; often set on or being held by an eagle | Numerous military badges and flags |
| | upright swastika with curved arms, described in white outline on black background, forming a circle | Emblem of *Waffen-SS Nordland* Division |

eagle and the swastika in a new decal which emblazoned the familiar coal-scuttle helmet. By February 1934, a shield of black, white and red was included on helmets, and in the autumn of 1935 the German eagle, its wings spread and its talons clutching the Nazi swastika, became standard on the breast of the uniform of the new *Wehrmacht*. The masterful blending of the old and new order brought the Army and the Nazi Party into closer cooperation.

Pro-Nazi officers were appointed to positions of authority in the *Reichswehr*, including General Werner von Blomberg, who succeeded Schleicher as Minister of Defence on 14 March 1933, General Ludwig Beck, who was named to head the *Truppenamt* that same year, and General Werner von Fritsch, who was promoted to chief of the Army High Command in February 1934. Each of these officers played a key role in the expansion of the German Army during the mid-1930s but was destined to run afoul of Nazi ideologues.

### Instrument of power

A shrewd and pragmatic politician, Hitler realized early in his gambit for power in Germany that the support of the *Reichswehr* and the nation's industrial elite was vital. While successfully winning over such notables as Gustav Krupp and the steel tycoon Fritz Thyssen, he enlisted the support of the economic and financial expert Hjalmar Schacht, who financed the growth of the German military through a series of bond issues and the confiscation of the assets of Jews and other so-

called enemies of the state. Meanwhile, during the decade of the 1930s German military spending increased exponentially from a few million to nearly $8 billion.

Much of the anticipated military expansion was achieved during the execution of the Four Year Plan, which was directed by the Air Ministry chief Hermann Göring beginning in the autumn of 1936. Designed to decrease unemployment and essentially place the nation's economy on a wartime footing, the Four Year Plan included ambitious public works projects such as the *Autobahnen*, which were planned to link Germany's major cities with kilometres of new highway and potentially facilitate the rapid movement of troops, control of agriculture, steel production, and other essential functions.

Armament production was significantly increased in 1936, and related spending was doubled over the prior year, outpacing the combined government expenditures for construction and transportation. In 1931 and 1932, unemployment in Germany peaked at a staggering six million; however, with Hitler's massive public works projects, the return of military conscription, and the compulsory service in state-run labour organizations, the figure plunged to an average of about 100,000 by the end of the decade.

As for the Army, Schleicher had succeeded in deftly undermining the chancellorships of both Groener and von Papen. By the time he assumed the office of Chancellor himself in December 1932, retaining the post of Defence Minister, his underhanded

tactics had caught up with him. He served only seven weeks as Chancellor before Hindenburg compelled him to resign and appointed Hitler to the coveted office. Still, Schleicher had managed to elevate the importance of the Army within the German government to new heights. Convinced like so many other leading politicians and soldiers that Hitler could be manipulated and controlled, he supported Hindenburg's decision to appoint the Nazi leader to high office.

### Blomberg

One of the primary links in the political chain which was to bind Hitler, Blomberg was quickly appointed as Defence Minister by the ageing president. From the outset, this aspect of the plan backfired. Blomberg rapidly became an ardent admirer of Hitler. Blomberg's new-found fascination with the Nazi leader and the loyalty of the old commanders to Hindenburg facilitated effective control of the *Reichswehr*. Hitler courted the high-ranking generals, intimated that he would not interfere with the running of the Army and encouraged its continued strengthening.

Blomberg instituted the Nazi salute and dismissed Jews from the Army. Instrumental in melding the tradition of the *Reichswehr* with the new order of the Third Reich, he further directed military personnel to render the stiff-arm Nazi salute to party officials who were in uniform but were not actually serving in the armed forces.

# 'Night of the Long Knives'

*Eventually, only a single major obstacle prevented Hitler from gaining the support of the majority of the Army leadership.*

The *Sturmabteilung* (SA) had been formed in 1921, during the early days of the Nazi Party, as a paramilitary force which protected party meetings and rallies from disruption by communists and other rival political factions. The leader of the SA, Ernst Röhm, was a brutal street thug who vigorously advocated a socialist revolution and recruited other rabble-rousers to the Nazi cause. A voracious homosexual, Röhm was a veteran of World War I, bore the scars of previous brawls and duels on his cheeks, and was one of Hitler's oldest comrades in the Nazi movement.

Known as the Stormtroopers or Brownshirts because of their conspicuous uniforms, the SA had grown steadily in size during the 1920s and 1930s, and by 1934 numbered in the millions, dwarfing the manpower of the *Reichswehr*. Although Hitler had moved to consolidate power for the Nazis, Röhm remained ardently revolutionary, at one time even putting forward a plan to absorb the *Reichswehr* into the ranks of the SA to form a new army of the people. Röhm further began to criticize Hitler openly and even talked of deposing the *Führer*. In the spring of 1934, Röhm considered his power base strong enough to announce, 'The SA … will not tolerate the German revolution going to sleep or betrayed

at its half completed stage by non-combatants.'

Within months, Hitler concluded that Röhm and the SA, in its present form, had outlived their usefulness and even posed a threat to his consolidation of power once the aged Hindenburg was dead. The captains of industry were distressed by the SA terror campaign and continuing violence in the streets, while Blomberg was wary of Röhm

and the intent of the SA to take pre-eminence over the Army. Blomberg warned Hitler that he could not provide assurances of complete cooperation from the Army unless the SA was reined in.

Finally, Röhm's powerful rivals within the party, Göring and Heinrich Himmler, the head of the black-shirted *Schutzstaffel* (SS), which had been formed in 1925 as a personal security force for Hitler, advised the

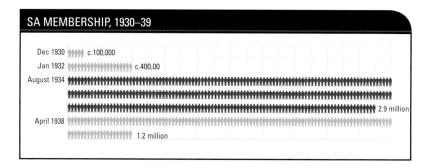

**SA MEMBERSHIP, 1930–39**

| | |
|---|---|
| Dec 1930 | c.100,000 |
| Jan 1932 | c.400,00 |
| August 1934 | |
| | 2.9 million |
| April 1938 | |
| | 1.2 million |

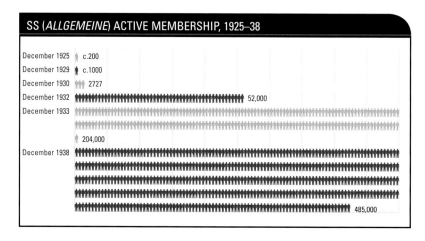

**SS (*ALLGEMEINE*) ACTIVE MEMBERSHIP, 1925–38**

| | |
|---|---|
| December 1925 | c.200 |
| December 1929 | c.1000 |
| December 1930 | 2727 |
| December 1932 | 52,000 |
| December 1933 | |
| | 204,000 |
| December 1938 | |
| | 485,000 |

*Führer* to move against the leaders of the SA.

On the night of 30 June 1934, Röhm and virtually all of the high-ranking SA leaders were arrested by the SS on the pretext of inciting a putsch. Although Hitler hesitated to order the execution of Röhm, the SA commander was eventually shot along with dozens of others. Hitler conveniently utilized the so-called 'Night of the Long Knives' to settle other old political scores. Among those killed was his former rival Schleicher, who was murdered in his home along with his wife while his 16-year-old stepdaughter was also in the house. With the blood purge of the SA, Hitler made good on his promise some years earlier that the *Reichswehr* was to be one of the twin pillars, along with the Nazi

Party, which would restore the honour of Germany.

### The Sacred Oath

For years both military personnel and those in the civil service had been required to swear an oath of fidelity to the German people and the nation. On 20 August 1934, just weeks after the death of Hindenburg and the 'Night of the Long Knives', the traditional oath of allegiance was altered. In retrospect, the changes were chilling. Rather than swearing allegiance to their 'people and country', German soldiers were instructed to repeat the following: 'I swear by Almighty God this sacred oath: I will render unconditional obedience to the *Führer* of the German Reich and people, Adolf Hitler, Supreme Commander of the *Wehrmacht*, and, as a brave

soldier, I will be ready at any time to stake my life for this oath.'

There was now no question as to the institutional loyalty of the Army to Hitler. That loyalty had been bought with the blood of the SA. As the Nazis embarked on a path toward war, officers and soldiers of the German Army found themselves bound by an oath sworn personally to Hitler. Those who disagreed with the *Führer*'s aims did so at their peril and at the risk of violating that oath. Indeed, the oath presented quite an issue for many officers who engaged in plots to assassinate Hitler or remove him from power during the 12 years of the Third Reich. Nevertheless, the Hitler Oath, as it became known, further cemented the Army to the Nazi movement and bound the military establishment to Hitler as a matter of honour.

# Covert and Overt Military Expansion

*On 21 May 1935, the* Reichswehr *officially became known as the* Wehrmacht, *the German Armed Forces, which was to be composed of an army, the* Heer, *a navy, the* Kriegsmarine, *and an air force, the* Luftwaffe.

On that same day, Hitler addressed the *Reichstag* and told the world that Germany had been compelled to respond to the terms of the unjust Versailles Treaty and to rearm in the face of its former enemies, principally Great Britain and France, maintaining superior military strength while Germany was in fact defenceless, particularly following the failure of the League of Nations World Disarmament Conference in late 1932.

'… The German government has announced the extent of the reconstruction of the German Army,' Hitler railed. 'Under no circumstances will it depart therefrom. It sees neither on land, nor in the air, nor at sea any threat to any other nation in fulfilling its programme … I cannot better conclude my speech to you … than by repeating our confession of faith in peace: Whoever lights the torch of

war in Europe can wish for nothing but chaos. We, however, live in the firm conviction our times will see not the decline but the renaissance of the West. It is our proud hope and our unshakeable belief Germany can make an imperishable contribution to this great work.'

The covert rearmament of Germany had been underway for some time. By 1934, the original seven military districts of the

*Reichswehr* had been expanded to 21, and these were to be the basis for a new German Army of 21 divisions. On 16 March 1935, Hitler openly repudiated the Treaty of Versailles, announcing the reintroduction of compulsory military service, which was extended to a term of two years on 24 August 1936. Further plans were announced to expand the *Heer* with the addition of eight more divisions. The *Heer* would later be raised to 36 divisions in 12 army corps, with the number of men under arms increasing from 280,000 to 550,000. At the end of October 1935, the large provincial police forces, which had been raised ostensibly as civil units, were absorbed by the Army as well.

During the seventh Nazi Party Congress and the carefully choreographed rally at Nuremberg in 1935, troops of the *Heer* paraded with heavy guns and tracked vehicles and engaged in mock battles to the delight of the huge crowd which had gathered. The demonstration included infantry, artillery and the fast-moving tanks which were destined to ravage Europe. The filmmaker Leni Riefenstahl directed a documentary titled *Day of Freedom: Our Armed Forces*, which was released in December of that year.

By October 1936, only 17 months after Hitler had made the German rearmament programme public, the *Heer* had reached its projected strength of 36 divisions. These included 21 infantry divisions, three armoured divisions, a cavalry brigade, a mountain brigade and a parachute infantry company. In the autumn of 1937, two more army corps were formed, and in 1938 four additional corps were constituted as the five divisions of the Austrian Army were incorporated into the *Heer* following the *Anschluss* which took place in March of that year.

The composition of the *Heer* itself evolved during the course of World War II as its ranks were depleted

### INCREASES IN MILITARY EXPENDITURE OF THE GREAT EUROPEAN POWERS

|  | 1931/32 | 1938/39 |
|---|---|---|
| Great Britain | £107.5m | £397.4m |
| France | 13.8bn francs | 29.1bn francs |
| USSR | 1.4m roubles | 27m roubles |
| Germany | 0.61bn RM | 17.24bn RM |
| Italy | 5.01bn lire | 15.02bn lire |

### MILITARY CAPABILITY: 1932 AND 1939 COMPARED

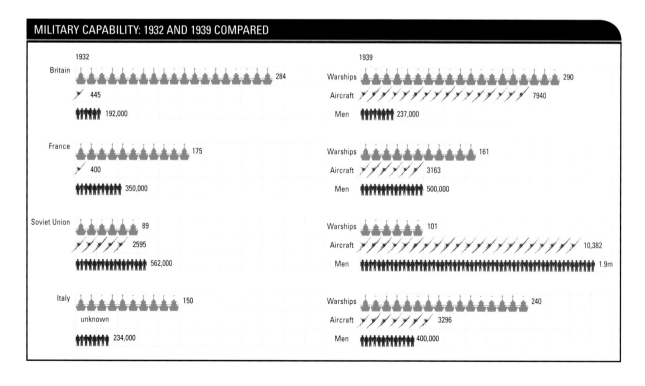

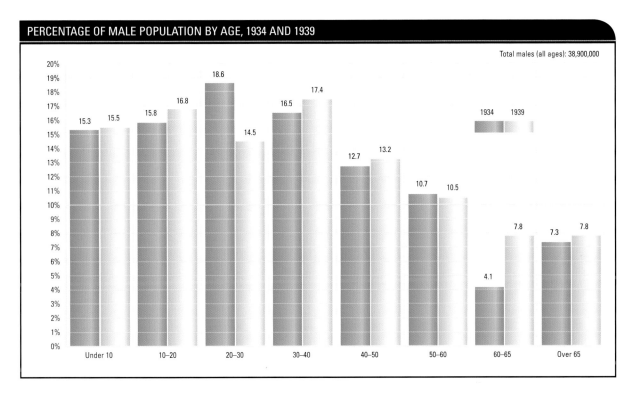

PERCENTAGE OF MALE POPULATION BY AGE, 1934 AND 1939

through combat casualties which were difficult to make good. In time, contingents of foreign soldiers fought with the German Army. Among these were the Spanish Blue Division which served on the Eastern Front and pro-Nazi units raised in France, Belgium, Norway and Denmark. By the spring of 1944, a number of the soldiers manning the fortifications of the Atlantic Wall who would confront the Allied landings on D-Day were Poles or other Eastern Europeans – even Soviet prisoners of war – who had been pressed into service.

Particularly on the Eastern Front, the German Army was obliged to advance or defend across vast expanses of territory. Out of necessity, large sections of the front line were often occupied by ill-trained, poorly led and under-equipped Romanian or Hungarian troops. When the Red Army counter-attacked and surrounded the German Sixth Army at Stalingrad in November 1942, the inferior Romanian and Hungarian formations north and south of the city were decimated. The turning point of the war in the East, and perhaps of the entire war, Stalingrad was a disaster for the German Army.

Through six long years of fighting, the *Heer* was by far the largest branch of the *Wehrmacht* and sustained the lion's share of casualties. From the invasion of Poland through to the end of the war nearly 1.8 million German soldiers died, while approximately 1.65 million more were listed as missing in action and presumed dead (these figures also include personnel of the *Waffen*, or Armed, SS). From the ruins of Stalingrad, more than 90,000 Germans marched into captivity in the Soviet Union. Only about 5000 of these lived through their ordeal and returned to Germany, most sometime during the 1950s. In 1945, no fewer than 560,000 German prisoners of war were being held by the US Army in a horrendously overcrowded camp at Bad Kreuznach.

**Valuable experience**
Among the challenges which confronted the new *Heer* during its years of expansion in the 1930s, and indeed had been a difficult proposition since covert rearmament was undertaken, was the shortage of

officers and non-commissioned officers who could train and lead the large number of recruits entering the Army. In response, a great number of veterans who had been forced to leave the military in 1919 under the terms of the Versailles Treaty were called back into the service as administrative personnel to free active soldiers for combat training or other duties. Some of these veterans were still fit for active service and were placed in command of combat units.

## Reaching out

In 1938, Hitler extended his reach for experienced Army veterans to include those who were over the previous age limit and those who lived outside Germany, while all officers became subject to remaining in the service for an indefinite period of time. At the end of the year, the German Army numbered two million men, and an annual quota of 500,000 recruits was being achieved. Nevertheless, the expanding Army was hindered not only by a shortage of experienced officers but also by a lack of modern arms and equipment. Much of the Army's equipment was of World War I vintage but was being upgraded steadily after 1936 under the auspices of the Four Year Plan.

Although German military capability was limited by the number of modern weapons available, annual displays of fire and manoeuvre during the Nuremberg rallies served notice to the world that Germany was rapidly re-emerging as a military titan. In 1937, an observer from the *New York Times* wrote, 'There was seen today perhaps one twentieth of

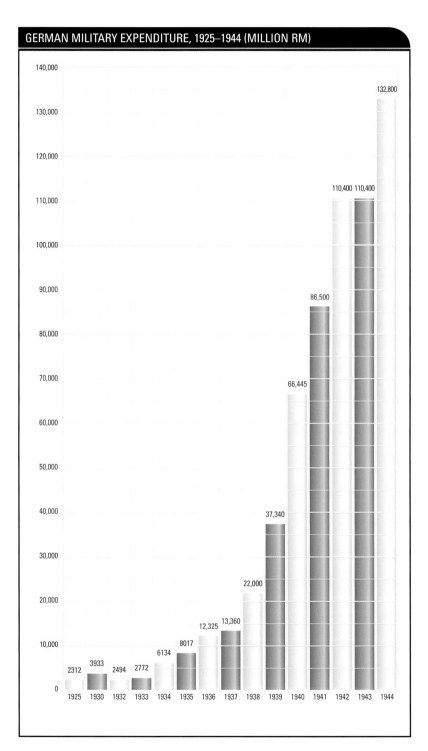

GERMAN MILITARY EXPENDITURE, 1925–1944 (MILLION RM)

what the German peacetime establishment could produce at need. If it is a sample of the rest, it portrays a strength no other European nation can match.'

## Army strength

When the German Army invaded Poland in 1939, its strength on paper included 103 divisions, seven of which were armoured plus at least four light armoured under the cavalry designation, four divisions of motorized infantry, three mountain divisions and a pair of independent panzer brigades. However, about half this strength was actually operational while the remainder consisted of units which were still in training or the early stages of formation. Meanwhile, the

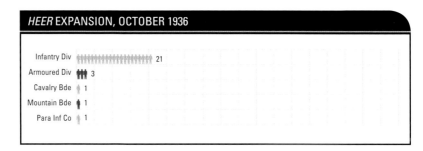

| GERMAN REARMAMENT, 1932–39 | | | | |
|---|---|---|---|---|
| Year | Army (peacetime conscripts) | Military Aircraft | Major Warships | Military Expenditure |
| 1932 | 100,000 soldiers | 36 | 26 | RM 0.61 billion |
| 1939 | 730,000 soldiers | 8295 | 88 | RM 17.24 billion |

**HEER EXPANSION, OCTOBER 1936**

| Infantry Div | 21 |
| Armoured Div | 3 |
| Cavalry Bde | 1 |
| Mountain Bde | 1 |
| Para Inf Co | 1 |

commitment of some troops to the Spanish Civil War, the formation of the *Waffen-SS*, and the transfer of some personnel to the *Luftwaffe* depleted available manpower somewhat.

# Reorganizing for War

*As it steadily grew in numbers during the mid-1930s, the Army was restructured under a new concept called the* Kriegsheer, *or War Army, with a formal standing force called the* Feldheer, *Field Army, whose purpose was to maintain national security at all times and to function as the first strike capability of the armed forces on the ground.*

The *Feldheer* could, in theory, prosecute wars of short duration and defend the country's borders. A second, reserve army called the *Ersatzheer* (Replacement Army) existed to maintain high standards of readiness among troops which could be called upon as replacements for casualties or to reinforce the *Feldheer* in the event of a conflict of extended duration. The soldiers of the *Ersatzheer* could also function as

occupation troops to hold territory gained in battle.

The *Ersatzheer* and *Feldheer* were closely linked as each field unit of regimental size or greater was assigned a corresponding replacement unit, sharing the same number but slightly smaller in size. For example, a *Feldheer* division would technically be supported by an *Ersatzheer* regiment. In addition to providing replacements for casualties,

the *Ersatzheer* also maintained responsibility for some administrative duties and the extended care of some wounded soldiers.

When mobilization came in 1939, the *Heer* was well organized and prepared for the logistical challenges presented. Each of Germany's 19 military districts, or *Wehrkreise*, was the equivalent of a corps headquarters with corresponding infrastructure for its subordinate

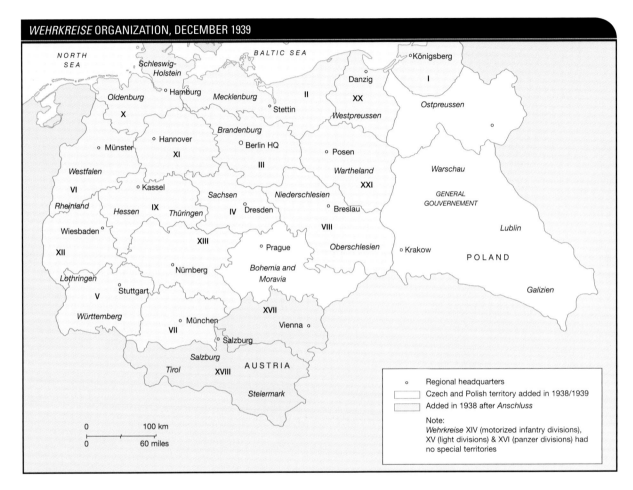

**WEHRKREISE ORGANIZATION, DECEMBER 1939**

NORTH SEA

BALTIC SEA

Schleswig-Holstein

° Königsberg

Oldenburg

° Hamburg

Mecklenburg

° Danzig

I

Ostpreussen

X

° Stettin

II

XX

Westpreussen

Brandenburg

° Hannover

° Berlin HQ

° Posen

° Münster

XI

III

Wartheland

Warschau

Westfalen

° Kassel

Sachsen

Niederschlesien

XXI

GENERAL GOUVERNEMENT

VI

IX

Rheinland

Hessen

Thüringen

IV

° Dresden

° Breslau

Wiesbaden °

XIII

VIII

Lublin

XII

° Prague

Oberschlesien

° Krakow

POLAND

Lothringen

° Nürnberg

Bohemia and Moravia

Galizien

° Stuttgart

V

XVII

Württemberg

° München

Vienna °

VII

° Salzburg

Salzburg

AUSTRIA

Tirol

XVIII

Steiermark

° Regional headquarters

Czech and Polish territory added in 1938/1939

Added in 1938 after *Anschluss*

Note:
*Wehrkreise* XIV (motorized infantry divisions), XV (light divisions) & XVI (panzer divisions) had no special territories

0    100 km
0    60 miles

## ■ *WEHRKREISE*

The *Wehrkreis* system geographically streamlined the process of recruiting, training and assigning soldiers. By 1943 there were 19 *Wehrkreise*, and they corresponded with the peacetime corps areas, designated by Roman numerals. The headquarters of each *Wehrkreis* had an active field component and also a deputy component that remained in the home territory and was responsible for administering new intakes of soldiers and controlling the application of reserves.

divisions. Among these were several districts located within the former boundaries of Austria and Czechoslovakia. Also included in each *Wehrkreis* were the offices which handled security, civil service matters, conscription and other administrative functions. With most divisions already in a high state of readiness, full mobilization could generally be achieved by a combat division of the *Heer* in as little as half a day.

In the 12 months prior to the initiation of hostilities, older reservists

were called up first and assigned to existing units. Successively ordered to report in waves, soldiers were incorporated into the Army in a manner which was least disruptive to civilian life and the continuation of essential war-related industries. Such was the standard practice until late in the war when heavy casualties and the rapidly deteriorating military situation made manpower a premium in the armed forces.

By September 1939, four waves of mobilization had already been undertaken. The first wave included manpower for 35 divisions, each numbering nearly 18,000 personnel of the regular Army, while the second wave consisted of 16 divisions made up primarily of reservists, the third wave of 21 divisions of men whose training was incomplete, and the fourth wave of 14 divisions grouped in reinforcement battalions. During the war years, 31 more waves were generated, some of which failed to produce numbers substantial enough to raise complete divisions and

included old men and boys who filled the ranks of the *Volkssturm* ('Home Guard') or Hitler Youth units raised in the waning days of the Third Reich. Exemptions from the service for individuals such as the sole wage earner for a large family or for a family's only surviving son were discontinued as the course of the war turned against Germany.

Theoretically, the *Feldheer* included army groups which consisted of two armies, each with a pair of divisions.

However, the exigencies of war and immediate requirements of the commanders in the field often resulted in deviation from the standard blueprint. As the number of German troops in the field increased, an original plan for 10 army commands was expanded substantially and a network of support units, such as anti-aircraft, pioneer, transport or armoured, was available for assignment to a particular formation.

## MOBILIZATION WAVES, 1939

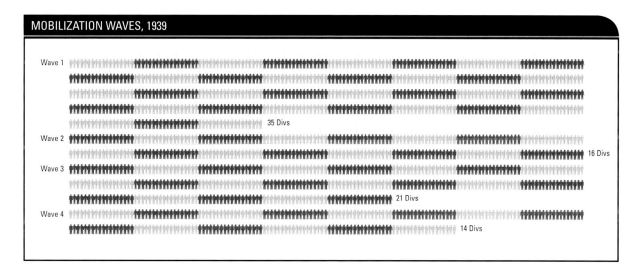

Wave 1 ... 35 Divs

Wave 2 ... 16 Divs

Wave 3 ... 21 Divs

Wave 4 ... 14 Divs

---

# Command Transition

*While the tradition of the German Army and its aristocratic officer corps supplied the foundation of the* Wehrmacht, *the increasing influence of Nazi ideology transformed the fighting force into something quite different from its Imperial heritage.*

On the eve of World War II, it is probable that many old line officers and veterans of the Kaiser's military would scarcely have

recognized the modern structure and sheer power of the *Heer*. Along with the conceptualization of innovative strategy and tactics,

modern weapons such as the tank, light and easily portable machine guns, and versatile artillery were rapidly developed. The command and control of the *Heer* evolved as well.

Senior officers of the *Heer* acknowledged the expansion of the armed forces under the Nazis and the resources which had been dedicated to the future of the Army; however, by the late 1930s many were also aware that they had essentially lost the ability to direct that Army. Hitler had seen to it that officers who openly criticized his policies of expansion were demoted or purged from the *Heer* altogether.

## Rhineland occupation

Foremost among those who were marginalized were Blomberg, Fritsch and Beck. When Hitler sent the *Heer* into the demilitarized Rhineland in 1936 and threatened to trigger retaliation by the much stronger French Army, the *Führer* had described the Defence Minister's conduct as the rantings of a 'hysterical young maid'. Fritsch had backed Blomberg, also concerned that the French would crush the small force of only three *Heer* battalions, roughly 3000 troops, which entered the Rhineland and marched to the French border in open defiance of Versailles. Fritsch was concerned that Hitler was moving too aggressively and supported Blomberg.

Within months, Blomberg had been disgraced. Following his marriage to his secretary, Eva Gruhn, who was 32 years his junior, Blomberg became a victim of the conniving Göring and Himmler who informed Hitler that the Berlin police had discovered that Gruhn had posed for pornographic photographs. Göring also trumped up

a charge that Gruhn had actually worked as a prostitute. Hitler demanded that Blomberg have the marriage annulled, and when he refused to do so Blomberg was compelled to resign his position when Göring threatened to take the scandal public.

Days later, Fritsch was falsely accused of being a homosexual and committing illegal acts with a boy called 'Bavarian Joe' near the Potsdam railway station in suburban Berlin. Fritsch was a bachelor and had never shown great interest in marrying. In truth, he preferred to concentrate on his career. Although Fritsch was forced to resign in February 1938, a court of inquiry found him innocent of the charges. The damage had already been done, and Fritsch took a field command. He was killed in action during the Polish campaign in September 1939. Beck believed that Germany could not possibly be ready for war until 1940 and objected to Hitler's threat of armed conflict to resolve issues surrounding the occupation of Czechoslovakia. Beck managed to retain his position until August 1938. By the time of his resignation, he was virtually without influence.

Throughout that year, Hitler replaced those senior commanders he believed to be anti-Nazi or simply too cautious. With the exit of Blomberg and Fritsch, Hitler took to himself the position of Supreme Commander of the German Armed Forces while no fewer than 60 senior officers were either dismissed from the Army, forced to retire, or relegated to roles of less significance. Field Marshal Walther

von Brauchitsch and General Friedrich Fromm were installed as Commander-in-Chief of the *Heer* and commander of the *Ersatzheer* respectively. General Franz Halder replaced Beck as Chief of the Army General Staff.

Command and control of the German armed forces was concentrated in Hitler as the head of the *Oberkommando der Wehrmacht* (OKW), which was founded in 1938 and constituted a high command for the entire armed forces, including the senior command structures of the *Heer*, *Luftwaffe* and *Kriegsmarine*. The responsibilities of OKW included war and defence planning and coordinated operations of the three branches of the *Wehrmacht*. With the outbreak of World War II, OKW was split into two administrative sections. A forward command supervised operations in progress, while the rear headquarters remained in the capital of Berlin to handle administrative issues and concerns.

## High-profile sacking

Throughout the course of the war, Hitler was well known for sacking generals and sometimes later reappointing them to senior command roles. One of the first military men to fall victim to the *Führer's* wrath was von Brauchitsch, who was relieved in December 1941 following the failure of the *Heer* to capture Moscow during the first winter of fighting on the Eastern Front. Two ardent Nazis served Hitler within OKW until the bitter end in 1945. Field Marshal Wilhelm Keitel was essentially an adjutant to Hitler although he was nominally the chief of OKW for more than six years. Colonel-General Alfred Jodl was a trusted advisor to Hitler who ran the operations branch of OKW. Both men were tried and executed as war criminals at Nuremberg after the war. At the *Heer* level, the principal organizational structure was the high command, otherwise known as the general staff, which operated through its headquarters, *Oberkommando des Heeres* (OKH).

The theoretical operation of the OKH during wartime was similar to that of the OKW, with a forward and rear echelon headquarters arrangement responsible for coordinating operations in the field and for administrative support respectively. However, Hitler's creation of the OKW essentially subordinated the decision-making capacity of the OKH to Hitler and the OKW, although this was only accomplished after considerable disagreement between the generals of the OKH and the Führer. Hitler's long mistrust of the military elite was readily apparent as he sought to isolate and disenfranchise the infrastructure of the OKH.

**Creeping influence**

While the OKH was still nominally the command structure through which *Heer* formations in the field received their operational orders, logistical support and other directives, Hitler maintained a field headquarters close to that of the OKH, perhaps to intervene should he sense a lack of resolve or aggressiveness in the generals. By December 1941, responsibility for the German armies

---

**HITLER'S DECREE ON TAKING COMMAND OF THE *WEHRMACHT*, 4 FEBRUARY 1938**

*As of now, I am personally assuming direct command of the entire Wehrmacht. The former Department of the Wehrmacht in the Reich Ministry of War, with all its assignments, comes directly under my command as the High Command of the Wehrmacht and as my military staff. The former Chief of the Department of the Wehrmacht becomes Chief of Staff of the High Command of the Wehrmacht with the title 'Chief of the High Command of the Wehrmacht.' His rank is equivalent to that of a Reich Minister. The High Command of the Wehrmacht assumes control of the affairs of the Reich Ministry of War, the Chief of the Wehrmacht exercises, in my name, the authority hitherto vested in the Reich Minister of War. The obligation of the High Command of the Wehrmacht in time of peace is the unified preparation in all spheres of the defence of the Reich according to my directives.*
*Berlin, 4 February 1938*

*The Führer and Reich Chancellor: ADOLF HITLER*

---

in the field had passed solely to the OKW with the exception of the war on the Eastern Front.

Hitler maintained continuous influence with OKH via the existence of a command element which he directly controlled, bypassing the General Staff. After 1943 this included the command of *Heer* panzer troops. Often during the latter years of the war it was Hitler alone who controlled the deployment of panzer divisions, either offensively or defensively. On several occasions, the *Führer's* personal order was necessary to commit panzer units – to the detriment of German forces in the field. One significant example was his denial of a request from Field Marshal Erwin Rommel to release the panzer divisions held in reserve near the Pas de Calais following the D-Day landings of 6 June 1944. Therefore, an armoured counter-attack against the Allied beachhead

in Normandy was not possible for some time. A single *Heer* armoured division, 21st Panzer, counter-attacked alone from the vicinity of Caen on D-Day and reached the coast before being compelled to retire due to lack of reinforcements.

Within the command structure of the OKH during the war were the general staff, the personnel office, the command structure of the *Ersatzheer*, the headquarters of army groups, and the staffs of individual armies. By 1944, up to 11 army group commands had been fielded, and nearly 30 individual armies were operating. However, following the 20 July 1944 attempt on the *Führer's* life at his *Wolfsschanze* (Wolf's Lair) headquarters in East Prussia, Fromm was removed from command of the *Ersatzheer* and replaced by Himmler, effectively removing command of the reserve army from OKH and vesting it in the SS.

## OKW ORGANIZATION, 1938

◆ **OKW**

**Wehrmacht-Führungsamt (WFA)** *Operational orders*
 └■ Abteilung Landesverteidigungsführungsamt (WFA/L) *Operational planning*

**Amt Ausland/Abwehr** *foreign intelligence*

- Chief of Staff
- Zentralabteilung *central department*
- Abteilung Ausland *foreign*
  - Gruppe I: Außen- und Wehrpolitik *foreign and defence policy*
  - Gruppe II: Beziehung zu fremden Wehrmächten *relations with foreign militaries*
  - Gruppe III: Fremde Wehrmächte, Meldesammelstelle des OKW *foreign militaries*
  - Gruppe IV: Etappenorganisation der Kriegsmarine
  - Gruppe V: Auslandspresse *foreign media*
  - Gruppe VI: Militärische Untersuchungsstelle für Kriegsvölkerrecht *research service for international laws of war*
  - Gruppe VII: Kolonialfragen *colonial matters*
  - Gruppe VIII: Wehrauswertung *defence analysis*
- Abteilung Nachrichtenbeschaffung *intelligence*
  - Gruppe H: Geheimer Meldedienst Heer *army intelligence service*
  - Gruppe M: Geheimer Meldedienst Marine *naval intelligence service*
  - Gruppe L: Geheimer Meldedienst Luftwaffe *air intelligence service*
  - Gruppe G: Technische Arbeitsmittel *technical equipment*
  - Gruppe Wi: Geheimer Meldedienst Wirtschaft *economic intelligence service*
  - Gruppe P: Presseauswertung *media analysis*
  - Gruppe I: Funknetz Abwehr Funkstelle *radio communications*

- Abteilung Sonderdienst *special service*
  - Gruppe I: Minderheiten *minorities*
  - Gruppe II: Sondermaßnahmen *special measures*
- Abteilung Abwehr *counter-intelligence*
  - Führungsgruppe W: Abwehr in der Wehrmacht *counter-intelligence in the military*
  - Gruppe Wi: Abwehr Wirtschaft *economic counter-intelligence*
  - Gruppe C: Abwehr Inland *inland counter-intelligence*
  - Gruppe F: Abwehr Ausland *foreign counter-intelligence*
  - Gruppe D: Sonderdienst *special service*
  - Gruppe S: Sabotageabwehr *counter-sabotage*
  - Gruppe G: Gutachten *evaluation*
  - Gruppe Z: Zentralarchiv *central archives*
- Auslands(telegramm)prüfstelle *foreign communications*
  - Gruppe I: Sortierung *sorting*
  - Gruppe II: Chemische Untersuchung *chemical testing*
  - Gruppe III: Privatbriefe *private mail*
  - Gruppe IV: Handelsbriefe *commercial mail*
  - Gruppe V: Feldpostbriefe *military mail*
  - Gruppe VI: Kriegsgefangenenbriefe *POWs' mail*
  - Gruppe VII: Zentralkartei *central register*
  - Gruppe VIII: Auswertung *analysis*
  - Gruppe IX: Kriegsgefangenen-Brief-Auswertung *analysis of POWs' mail*

**Wirtschafts und Rüstungsamt** *supply matters*

**Amtsgruppe Allgemeine Wehrmachtangelegenheiten**
*miscellaneous matters.*
- Abteilung Inland *inland*
- Allgemeine Abteilung *general*
- Wehrmachtsfürsorge- und versorgungsabteilung *supplies*
- Wehrmachtsfachschulunterricht *education*
- Wissenschaft *science*
- Wehrmachtsverwaltungsabteilung *administration*
- General zu besonderen Verfügung für Kriegsgefangenenwesen
  *prisoners of war*
- Abteilung Wehrmachtverlustwesen (WVW) *casualties*
  - Wehrmachtauskunftstelle für Kriegerverluste und Kriegsgefangene
    (WaSt) *information centre for war casualties and prisoners of war*

During the course of World War II, Hitler dominated the OKW and controlled the OKH, quelling dissent and even encouraging division and rivalry among his subordinates in order to suppress any organized opposition. Therefore, neither could function in a fully cooperative and efficient manner. As the war progressed, Hitler, who once seemed incapable of error, began to exhibit flawed judgement. By the time it became apparent that he was leading the *Heer* and the nation to ruin it was too late to alter the course of events. On more than one occasion, however, most notably the plot of 20 July 1944, it was his own generals who conspired to assassinate the *Führer*. For most officers, however, it was convenient for the Army to stay out of the political arena, turning a blind eye to the suspension of civil liberties in Germany, the persecution of the Jews and other minorities, and the quashing of internal opposition in any form.

In retrospect, the highest echelons of the German Army had been seduced by Hitler's uncanny successes in re-establishing German prestige among nations, building the armed forces to the status of a world military power, claiming territory without firing a shot, pacifying the Soviet Union with a non-aggression pact in the summer of 1939, and causing Great Britain and France to wallow indecisively in the face of his bold moves. When the German juggernaut rolled across the Polish frontier on 1 September 1939, the *Heer* had at last been unleashed as an offensive weapon of awesome destructive power.

# CHAPTER 3

# Command Structure

The command structure of the German Army
embodied a long tradition of competence and efficiency.
On the eve of World War II, Oberkommando des Heeres
(OKH) served as the primary organization through which
the Army General Staff executed its operational plans.

While the General Staff had been recognized
as the cadre of officers with the most effective grasp of
strategy and tactics, it was nevertheless relegated to a
subordinate role as Hitler asserted his own grand
design and created the Oberkommando
der Wehrmacht (OKW).

■ Hitler and some of his senior generals gather round a map at
OKW headquarters.

# Manipulation of Power

*While Hitler exerted control of the OKW and the OKH, those dissident elements within the General Staff were placed in a particular quandary.*

Unlike those whose anti-Hitler sentiments had been widely known, other high-ranking officers of the *Heer* were obliged to accept the fact that the General Staff had been reduced from an executive role actually influencing the strategic direction of German military operations to an agency of implementation, simply carrying out the orders of the *Führer* as his directives rippled through the ranks.

For a number of officers who remained associated with the General Staff, their conduct became a curious blend of the performance of duty tinged with the realization that opposition to Hitler must be covert. Therefore, opposition to Hitler existed within the highest echelons of the German Army from the beginning of the Nazi era, and Hitler's mistrust of the General Staff as a whole was well founded.

Those officers who had questioned Hitler's judgement lost credibility during the 1930s as he succeeded in reclaiming territory which had been taken from Germany following World War I and expanded the borders of the nation without firing a shot while Great Britain and France failed to challenge his aggressive actions. The prestige of the *Führer* had reached such heights and his popularity had grown to such an extent among the German people that open opposition or substantive differences of opinion

were at best hazardous to the career of an individual officer or group of officers and at worst subjected those who dissented to harsh punishment. Regardless, some officers were convinced that the most effective form of opposition to Hitler might actually come from within.

One such was Admiral Wilhelm Canaris, who led the *Abwehr*, or Intelligence, branch of OKW from 1935. The paradox of Canaris' career is that while he was responsible for safeguarding the Third Reich against enemy espionage he was also a member of the domestic opposition to the *Führer*. Canaris opposed Hitler's

policy of expansion, quietly intervened to save Jews and prisoners of war from execution, persuaded the Spanish dictator General Franco not to allow German troops to cross Spanish territory to attack the British fortress at Gibraltar, and conspired with high-ranking officers of Army Group C on the Eastern Front to assassinate Hitler. Canaris was arrested following the 20 July 1944 attempt to kill the *Führer* and was eventually hanged on 9 April 1945. In his book *To The Bitter End*, Hans Bernd Gisevius, a friend of Canaris, wrote that the Admiral 'hated not only Hitler and Himmler,

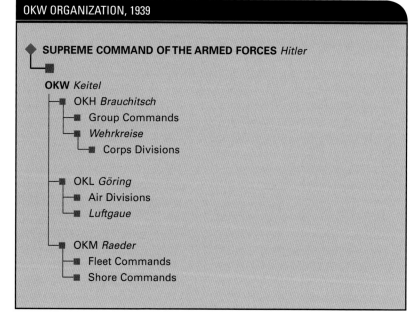

OKW ORGANIZATION, 1939

**SUPREME COMMAND OF THE ARMED FORCES** *Hitler*

**OKW** *Keitel*
- OKH *Brauchitsch*
  - Group Commands
  - *Wehrkreise*
    - Corps Divisions

- OKL *Göring*
  - Air Divisions
  - *Luftgaue*

- OKM *Raeder*
  - Fleet Commands
  - Shore Commands

but the entire Nazi system as a political phenomenon …'.

## Hitler's lackey

Despite a substantial opposition to Hitler, those senior officers of the German Army who witnessed the *Führer*'s spectacular early successes were more often willing participants in the Nazi plan of conquest. As they became aware of Hitler's intent to plunge Europe into its second major war in 25 years, some feebly argued that Germany could not possibly be prepared to wage such a war until 1942 at the earliest. Hitler's timetable, however, was accelerated, and the invasion of Poland took place on 1 September 1939.

These officers considered themselves bound by their personal oath to Adolf Hitler and further obligated to perform their duties on the basis of the *Führer* Principle, which stated, 'The *Führer*'s word is above all written law'. Rooted in Social Darwinism, the *Führer* Principle was not uniquely Nazi. However, it did find robust application during the 12 years of the Third Reich. Some high-ranking Nazis who stood trial at Nuremberg after the war actually asserted the doctrine in their own defence.

Following the Blomberg and Fritsch scandals, which removed two of the last impediments to Hitler's assumption of full control of the German armed forces, the *Führer* appointed Field Marshal Wilhelm Keitel as Commander-in-Chief of OKW. Keitel, a career Army officer, had previously served as chief of the Armed Forces Office, appointed by his former friend Defence Minister

---

**WEHRMACHT HIGH COMMAND**

◆ **FÜHRER** *Adolf Hitler*
  ├─■
  
  **C-in-C Wehrmacht** *Gen FM Werner von Blomberg; Adolf Hitler (from 1938)*
  ├─■ OKW *Adolf Hitler*
  ├─■ OKH *Gen FM Walther von Brauchitsch; Adolf Hitler (from 1941)*
  ├─■ OKL *Gen FM later Reichsmarschall Herman Göring*
  └─■ OKM *Gr Adm Erich Raeder, Gr Adm Karl Dönitz (from 1943)*

---

Blomberg. A veteran of World War I who had been wounded in action and subsequently managed to rise rapidly through the ranks of the inter-war *Reichswehr*, he had been alienated from Blomberg, who failed to press Keitel's idea of a unified command structure for all of the German armed forces. Hitler, however, seemed to be moving toward such a command structure, and Keitel cooperated willingly.

As the chief of OKW, Keitel structured the organization with an Economics Section under Major-General Georg Thomas, an Intelligence Section under Canaris, and an Operations Section led by Colonel-General Alfred Jodl. In time, Keitel became a devoted follower of the *Führer*. He proved unwavering in his support for Hitler with virtually blind obedience and was quoted at Nuremberg as saying that the *Führer* Principle was paramount in 'all areas and it is completely natural that it had a special application in reference to the military'.

Keitel did attempt to stand up to Hitler on one notable occasion, however. As plans for Operation 'Barbarossa', the invasion of the

Soviet Union, were being formulated, the Field Marshal objected that the plan was too ambitious an undertaking. Hitler flew into a rage, but when Keitel offered to resign, Hitler refused, saying that only he, as supreme commander of the German armed forces, could decide when and if the head of OKW should step aside. From that time on, Keitel was a slavish servant to the *Führer*, so much so that some officers whispered a joke that he should be referred to as '*Lakeitel*' or 'Lackey'.

As the war dragged on, Hitler continually exploited his relationship with Keitel, issuing orders such as the '*Nacht und Nebel*', 'Night and Fog', directive of December 1941, which mandated that enemies of the Nazi state were to 'disappear' without a trace, as well as decrees for the killing of prisoners of war and the immediate execution of captured Communist Party commissars.

Several weeks before the invasion of the Soviet Union began, Hitler declared that the war in the East was to be one of annihilation. Keitel issued the Barbarossa Decree, which sanctioned the ruthless suppression of partisan activities and authorized units of the *Heer* to utilize extreme measures in the process. Furthermore, officers were directed to use 'collective measures' against the local population where attacks against German forces occurred if the actual culprits could not be located. Officers were also empowered to execute hostile persons without trial or formal adherence to any law or legal process. Officers of the *Heer* were assured that they were authorized to exercise such authority without fear of prosecution for actions which would normally be violations of German law. Generals and senior commanders who protested summary executions and acts of brutality committed by both Army and *Waffen-SS* personnel were often relieved of duty or otherwise silenced. Each of these orders originated with Hitler; however, the implementation of them rested with Wilhelm Keitel and the signature on the actual paper order was his.

While Keitel had considered himself a loyal officer of the German Army, he had fatally linked that loyalty to the person of Adolf Hitler. In doing so, he undermined the effectiveness of the Army General Staff and OKH, precipitated an indelible stain on the honour of the Army and the officer corps, and was hanged as a war criminal.

## FIELD MARSHAL WILHELM BODEWIN GUSTAV KEITEL

*A senior Nazi and member of Hitler's inner circle throughout World War II, Keitel served as chief of the* Oberkommando der Wehrmacht *(OKW) and conducted the armistice negotiations with the French government in the Forest of Compiègne in 1940. Keitel was a career soldier and was wounded in action during World War I. Acknowledged as a capable staff officer, his blind allegiance to Hitler facilitated numerous errors in the strategic and tactical prosecution of the German war effort. Field Marshal Keitel was tried at Nuremberg and convicted of war crimes and crimes against humanity. He was hanged on 16 October 1946.*

■ **Keitel talks with Italian leader Benito Mussolini, 1943.**

| | |
|---|---|
| BIRTH: | 22 September 1882 |
| DEATH: | 16 October 1946 |
| PLACE OF BIRTH: | Helmscherode, Braunschweig |
| FATHER: | Carl Keitel |
| MOTHER: | Apollonia Vissering |
| PERSONAL RELATIONSHIPS: | Married to Lisa Fontaine (six children) |
| SERVICE: | Cadet Officer 1901 |
| | Wounded in action 1914 |
| | Joined *Freikorps* 1919 |
| | Head of Army Organization Department 1929 |
| | Brigadier-General 1934 |
| | Head of Armed Forces Office 1935 |
| | Major-General 1936 |
| | General of Artillery 1937 |
| | Armed Forces High Command 1938 |
| | Colonel-General 1938 |
| | Chief of OKW 1938 |
| | Field Marshal 1940 |
| | Convicted and executed at Nuremberg 1946 |

# The Führer's Orders

*In the spring of 1940, the German armed forces moved against Norway and Denmark. Historically, such an operation would have been planned by the General Staff of the Army and executed through OKH.*

However, Operation 'Weserübung' (Weser Exercise) was controlled from the outset by OKW. Soon afterward, OKW issued orders to move an entire division of the *Heer* from Norway to Finland, establishing a new theatre of war for the armed forces which was completely outside the control or influence of the General Staff or OKH.

When the invasion of the Soviet Union began on 22 June 1941, and 120 German divisions attacked the Red Army along a 1600km (1000-mile) front, Hitler could not refrain from interfering with ongoing operations. He accomplished this through orders issued via OKW. Just as he had done in France weeks earlier, ordering his ground troops to halt and allowing thousands of British and French soldiers to escape from Dunkirk, he grew restless as German forces neared the Soviet capital of Moscow. Hitler diverted troops of Field Marshal Fedor von Bock's Army Group Centre to the north and south of the Soviet capital, rendering Bock's planned armoured thrust to capture Moscow impossible and depriving him of the initiative necessary to potentially win the war in the East.

From the autumn of 1940 until the end of the war, the *Feldheer* in the West, also known as the *Westheer*, was under the control of *Oberbefehlshaber West*, or OB West, which answered directly to OKW. In

its subordinate role, OB West was mainly responsible for the implementation of orders issued directly by Hitler and transmitted through OKW. The OB West area of operations primarily included the coastal defences of the Atlantic Wall, which opposed the Allied landings in Normandy on 6 June 1944, and the occupied territories of the Low Countries. At the end of the war, the remnants of the OB West command were concentrated in Bavaria.

Indicative of Hitler's continuing suspicions of the Army General Staff and the high-ranking commanders whose careers were traced to the officer elite of the Junker class, he replaced the commanders of OB

West no fewer than six times. Field Marshal Gerd von Rundstedt was appointed and then sacked on three occasions. He commanded OB West from October 1940 to April 1941 and was replaced by Field Marshal Erwin von Witzleben from May 1941 to March 1942. Rundstedt was reinstated and commanded OB West from March 1942 to July 1944 and was followed by Field Marshal Günther von Kluge from early July to mid-August of that year. Field Marshal Walther Model held the post for only two weeks in August and September 1944, and Rundstedt again commanded OB West from September 1944 until March 1945. The final commander of OB West was

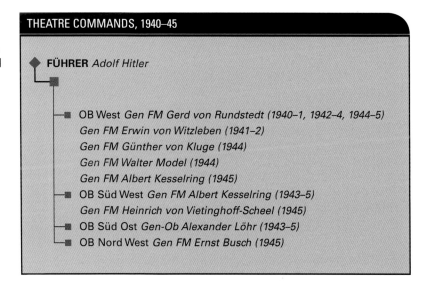

THEATRE COMMANDS, 1940–45

**FÜHRER** *Adolf Hitler*

- OB West *Gen FM Gerd von Rundstedt (1940–1, 1942–4, 1944–5)*
  *Gen FM Erwin von Witzleben (1941–2)*
  *Gen FM Günther von Kluge (1944)*
  *Gen FM Walter Model (1944)*
  *Gen FM Albert Kesselring (1945)*
- OB Süd West *Gen FM Albert Kesselring (1943–5)*
  *Gen FM Heinrich von Vietinghoff-Scheel (1945)*
- OB Süd Ost *Gen-Ob Alexander Löhr (1943–5)*
- OB Nord West *Gen FM Ernst Busch (1945)*

Field Marshal Albert Kesselring, who served until the end of the war.

'Hitler's distrust of the generals caused him to interfere extensively in the conduct of operations,' wrote Walter Görlitz in his *History of the German General Staff*. 'The policy ... which left the subordinate commander freedom for individual decisions within the framework of general directives, and which had become an essential part of Germany's traditional military method, was particularly in place in those great Russian spaces. Hitler, however, a victim of the illusion that he could move armies around as though they were battalions on parade, now adopted the practice of leaving commanders virtually no latitude at all. There was already a severe difference of opinion between General Staff and Supreme War Lord as to the real objectives of the campaign. Hitler ... introduced into it a further element of disastrous uncertainty.'

# Officers and Soldiers

*The German soldier, whether infantry, armour, artillery or assigned to some other specialized unit, was indeed part of a great war machine, trained, organized and intended for conquest. Quite a small percentage of those who wore the uniform of the* Heer *were officers.*

While the *Heer* grew exponentially during the 1930s, the character of its officer corps also evolved markedly. The tradition of Prussian and then German aristocratic senior commanders began to fade for several reasons, including Hitler's mistrust of the elitist old line officers, the expansion itself which demanded more officers to lead the increasing number of units, and the inculcation of Nazi ideology throughout the ranks of an army which eventually subordinated itself to the *Führer*. As the war progressed, individuals who might not otherwise have been able to achieve officer rank did actually do so, either based on merit as observed on the battlefield or due to attrition as casualties mounted.

Officers of the *Heer* were grouped into three classifications based upon experience and particularly the circumstances under which an individual officer had risen to his rank. Prior to the outbreak of World War II, the reserve officer corps consisted primarily of non-commissioned officers who had served with distinction and were commissioned as reserve officers when they were discharged from active duty, or of men who had been conscripted and carried out their duties capably during their first year of service, showing promise as officers. A sufficient level of education was a prerequisite for the second group, and such qualified reservists were designated as officer cadets, receiving rigorous training as infantry platoon leaders during their second year of service. Reservists were required to participate in yearly training exercises.

The other two groups of officers were within the framework of the standing *Heer* or had retired from it. General Staff corps officers included those who were deemed capable of high command and were chosen from among their peers for specialized training to fill such roles. The regular officers were those who were active with the *Heer* and held various command and staff positions throughout the hierarchy. As the war progressed, the number of regular officers was increased by the recall of many of those who had retired prior to 1939 and the permanent commissioning of some non-commissioned officers who had been promoted in the field.

The requirement for manpower led to conscripts being retained for service following the end of their initial compulsory enlistment period. Relatively few of these men either volunteered or were recognized as conscripts with the necessary qualities to become reserve officers.

These few were trained as officers, received reserve commissions, and were obliged to serve for the duration.

In wartime, soldiers were routinely commissioned following a few months of specific training based upon their combat experience and demonstrated leadership capabilities, although the standard training period for officer candidates remained up to 20 months. Some officer candidates were also given credit for active duty regardless of combat experience due to the increasing need for field officers as casualty rates climbed.

The officer corps of the *Heer* was divided into four basic groups, one consisting of junior officers such as lieutenants, another of all captains, and a third of field grade officers including majors, lieutenant-colonels and colonels. The fourth group included all general officers, who, along with lower-ranking officers of the General Staff, wore distinctive wide red stripes running the length of their trousers.

Although the elite status of the German officer corps was eroded somewhat during the Nazi era, the pre-war life of an officer included good pay, accommodation and food. Officers were also given a uniform allowance upon commissioning but thereafter were required to purchase their own uniforms.

While wartime training periods were often shortened due to the need for officers in combat zones, the standard regular officer training regimen included 10 months of basic

## *HEER* RANK SYSTEM

| German Rank | Translation | German Rank | Translation |
|---|---|---|---|
| Schütze | Rifleman | Gefreiter | Junior Cadet |
| Soldat | Soldier | Obergefreiter | Corporal |
| Grenadier | Infantryman | Stabsgefreiter | Staff Corporal |
| Fusilier | Rifleman | Unteroffizier | Junior NCO |
| Musketier | Rifleman | Unterfeldwebel | Junior Sergeant |
| Jäger | Chasseur | Fähnrich | Officer Candidate |
| Reiter | Cavalryman | Feldwebel | Sergeant |
| Kanonier | Gunner | Oberfeldwebel | First Sergeant |
| Panzerschütze | Tank Soldier | Hauptfeldwebel | Chief Sergeant |
| Panzergrenadier | Armoured Infantryman | Stabsfeldwebel | Staff Sergeant |
| Pionier | Engineer | Leutnant | Second Lieutenant |
| Funker | Radio Operator | Oberleutnant | First Lieutenant |
| Fahrer | Horse Rider | Hauptmann | Captain |
| Kraftfahrer | Motor Driver | Major | Major |
| Musikerschütze | Musician | Oberstleutnant | Lieutenant-Colonel |
| Sanitätssoldat | Medical Orderly | Oberst | Colonel |
| Oberschütze | Chief Rifleman | Generalmajor | Major-General |
| Oberreiter | Chief Cavalryman | Generalleutnant | Lieutenant-General |
| Obergrenadier | Chief Infantryman | General der... | General of... |
| Oberjäger | Chief Chasseur | General der Infanterie | General of Infantry |
| Oberkanonier | Chief Gunner | General der Artillerie | General of Artillery |
| Panzeroberschütze | Chief Tank Soldier | General der Kavallerie | General of Cavalry |
| Oberpanzergrenadier | Chief Armoured Infantryman | General der Panzertruppen | General of Armoured Troops |
| Oberpionier | Chief Engineer | General der Pioniere | General of Engineers |
| Oberfunker | Chief Radioman | General der Gebirgstruppen | General of Mountain Troops |
| Oberfahrer | Chief Rider | Generaloberst | Colonel-General |
| Oberkraftfahrer | Chief Motor Driver | Generalfeldmarschall | Field Marshal |
| Musikoberschütze | Chief Musician | | |
| Sanitätsobersoldat | Chief Medical Orderly | | |

infantry and non-commissioned officer training under the direction of the Replacement Army, seven months in the field to include affiliation with a serving unit, training in an appropriate staff setting or combat arms school, and three months of advanced, specialized training in infantry, armour, artillery or support branches. The training curriculum for reserve officer candidates was similar; however, it involved more extensive supervision by the Replacement Army.

Continually favouring offensive action, the *Heer* stressed the concept of leading from the front. In doing so, it paid a terrible price. By the end of World War II, at least 80 German generals had been killed in action, while dozens more had been wounded. From September 1939 to March 1942, more than 16,000 German officers died, the vast majority in action on the Eastern Front.

## NCO backbone

The non-commissioned officer was the backbone of the Army in the field and included career soldiers or those identified from the ranks of draftees who completed training and chose to apply for non-commissioned officer rank. The latter were designated as a reserve component to differentiate them from those who had chosen a military career rather than having been conscripted. NCOs were divided into two groups, senior and junior, senior non-commissioned officers being distinguished by a cord worn on sidearm. Young men over 16 years of age were allowed to apply for non-commissioned officer training and to

| TABLE OF COMPARATIVE RANKS FOR THE *WEHRMACHT/WAFFEN-SS* | | | |
|---|---|---|---|
| *Heer* | *Luftwaffe* | *Kriegsmarine* | *Waffen-SS* |
| Grenadier | Flieger | Matrose | SS-Schütze |
| Obergrenadier | | | SS-Oberschütze |
| Gefreiter | Gefreiter | Matrosengefreiter | SS-Sturmmann |
| Obergefreiter | Obergefreiter | Matrosenobergefreiter | SS-Rottenführer |
| Stabsgefreiter | Hauptgefreiter | Matrosenhauptgefreiter | |
| | Stabsgefreiter | Matrosenstabsgefreiter | |
| Unteroffizier | Unteroffizier | Maat | SS-Unterscharführer |
| Unterfeldwebel | Unterfeldwebel | Obermaat | SS-Scharführer |
| Fähnrich | | Fähnrich zur See | |
| Feldwebel | Feldwebel | Feldwebel | SS-Oberscharführer |
| Oberfeldwebel | Oberfeldwebel | Stabsfeldwebel | SS-Hauptscharführer |
| Hauptfeldwebel | | Oberfeldwebel | SS-Stabsscharführer |
| Oberfähnrich | | Oberfähnrich zur See | |
| Stabsfeldwebel | Stabsfeldwebel | Stabsoberfeldwebel | SS-Sturmscharführer |
| Leutnant | Leutnant | Leutnant zur See | SS-Untersturmführer |
| Oberleutnant | Oberleutnant | Oberleutnant zur See | SS-Obersturmführer |
| Hauptmann | Hauptmann | Kapitänleutnant | SS-Hauptsturmführer |
| Major | Major | Korvettenkapitän | SS-Sturmbannführer |
| Oberstleutnant | Oberstleutnant | Fregattenkapitän | SS-Obersturmbannführer |
| Oberst | Oberst | Kapitän zur See | SS-Standartenführer |
| | | Kommodore | SS-Oberführer |
| Generalmajor | Generalmajor | Vizeadmiral | SS-Brigadeführer |
| Generalleutnant | Generalleutnant | Konteradmiral | SS-Gruppenführer |
| General der ... | General der ... | Admiral | SS-Obergruppenführer |
| Generaloberst | Generaloberst | Generaladmiral | SS-Oberstgruppenführer |
| Generalfeldmarschall | Generalfeldmarschall | Grossadmiral | Reichsführer-SS |
| | Reichsmarschall | | |

enter the Army at the age of 17, while those active soldiers who applied were required to have served at least a year from the date of their conscription. Service terms of four years and six months or of 12 years were initially available depending upon the age of the soldier, and training included four months of basic instruction followed by six months of specific training for armour, infantry, artillery, mountain troops or other service branches.

Late in the war, the training regimen was modified, accelerating

the basic period which was to take place within an active arm of the *Heer* rather than in a school setting. This was followed by five months as a squad commander or perhaps a shorter period for other specialized assignments. Wartime demands eventually reduced the training of some non-commissioned officers to less than three months, particularly for those who were already combat veterans.

The *Landser*, or ordinary German footsoldier, was usually a conscript who received his notification to report for service from the local civil police organization. Volunteers did receive one major benefit, the choice of their branch of service. The conscript reported for registration and underwent two physical examinations to determine his fitness for service. Assignment to a specific unit or a return home until called then followed. The call-up was usually communicated by mail and included orders for reporting along with instructions for transportation.

## Training

During the war, soldiers were assigned to a unit within the Replacement Army before moving on to the *Feldheer*. Training consisted of a 16-week regimen of physical fitness and basic command and fire and manoeuvre techniques. The soldier became familiar with a variety of weapons and was cognisant of field operations up to platoon level. Demanding training and harsh

discipline were hallmarks of the *Heer* during World War II, and the tacit endorsement of strict rules and regulations by OKW and the General Staff was well known. As the war progressed, such measures were considered vital for the maintenance of discipline in the ranks and to ensure that soldiers would obey orders. Offences such as disobedience or desertion were punishable by immediate execution, and at times even officers who were perceived to have failed in their duties were summarily shot.

The training was rigorous, continuing a proven track which had been effective during the years of the *Reichswehr* and the clandestine build-up of the German military. Lengthy forced marches with full combat loads, live fire drills, and relentless rounds of conditioning exercises resulted in some recruits dying from sheer exhaustion. Injuries were common. The typical day lasted

from sunrise until well after dark. Despite the *Heer*'s image as a modern mechanized force, approximately 80 per cent of its transport was horse-drawn throughout the entire war. Soldiers who joined the artillery or supply branches were therefore trained to care for their unit's horses. Infantry training was a requirement for personnel of all branches of the *Heer*. Basic artillery school, for example, included a further three months of training once the infantry component was completed.

Published in 1945, the US Army technical manual on the German military organization notes the opening clause of the Military Service Law issued by Hitler on 21 May 1935. 'Military service is honorary service to the German

## CATEGORIZATION OF RESERVE MANPOWER

Information from US War Department Technical Manual, *TM-E 30-451: Handbook on German Military Forces* published in March 1945:

Reserve status. All men not doing their active military service are classified into the following categories:

| Reserve Status | Description |
|---|---|
| Reserve I: | Those under 35 who have completed their regular period of active service and been discharged. There are only very few fit men in this group today. |
| Reserve II: | Those under 35 who have been through a period of short-term training. This applied before the war to some of the older classes. |
| Ersatzreserve I: | Fit men under 35 who have not been trained. |
| Ersatzreserve II: | Unfit and limited-service men under 35 who have not been trained. |
| Landwehr I: | Trained men between 35 and 45 (actually from 31 March of the year in which the 35th birthday occurs until the 31 March following the 45th birthday). |
| Landwehr II: | Untrained men between 35 and 45. |
| Landsturm I: | Trained men between 45 and 55 (actually from the 31 March following the 45th birthday until the 31 March following the 55th birthday). |
| Landsturm II: | Untrained men between 45 and 55. (The two categories of Landsturm applied in peacetime only to East Prussia; they now include men up to 61.) |

## INDIVIDUALS PROHIBITED FROM MILITARY SERVICE

The following categories of men are described as 'unworthy to bear arms' and therefore 'excluded from military service':

- Those sentenced to penal servitude (*Zuchthaus*).
- Those who do not possess the honorary civil rights.
- Those subjected to 'security and improvement' measures (concentration camp for supposed habitual criminals).
- Those deprived of their 'worthiness to bear arms' by a court martial.
- Those sentenced for activities inimical to the state.
- Jews also are excluded from military service, but in wartime are required to do other types of service.

Information from US War Department Technical Manual, *TM-E 30-451: Handbook on German Military Forces* published in March 1945

## GERMAN SOLDIER'S TEN COMMANDMENTS (PRINTED IN PAY BOOK)

1.  While fighting for victory, the German soldier will observe the rules of chivalrous warfare. Cruelties and needless destruction are below his values.

2.  Combatants will be wearing uniform or will wear specially introduced and clearly identifiable badges. Fighting in civilian clothes or without such badges is prohibited.

3.  No enemy who has surrendered will be executed, including partisans and spies. They will be duly punished by courts.

4.  POWs will not be ill-treated or mocked. Arms, maps and records will be taken away from them, but their personal belongings will not be touched.

5.  Dum-Dum bullets are prohibited; also no other bullets may be transformed into Dum-Dums.

6.  Red Cross institutions are sacrosanct. Injured enemies are to be treated humanely. Medical personnel and army chaplains should not be hindered in performing their medical or clerical activities.

7.  The civilian population is sacrosanct. No looting nor egregious destruction is permitted by the soldier. Landmarks of historical value or buildings serving religious purposes, art, science, or charity are to be especially respected. Deliveries in kind made, as well as services rendered by the population, may only be claimed if ordered by superiors and only against compensation.

8.  Neutral territory will never be entered nor passed over by aircraft, nor shot at; it will not be the focus of warmaking of any kind.

■ A young German soldier poses for the camera during the invasion of France, May 1940. He is armed with a Kar 98 rifle and has a stick grenade tucked in his belt.

9.  If a German soldier is made a POW he will give his name and rank if he is asked for them. Under no circumstances will he reveal the unit to which he belongs, nor will he give any information about German military, political and economic conditions. Neither promises nor threats may induce him to do so.

10. Offences against the a/m matters of duty will be punished. Enemy offences against the principles under 1 to 8 are to be reported. Reprisals are only permissible on order of higher commands.

people. Every German is liable to military service. In time of war, in addition to liability to military service, every German man and every German woman is liable to service to the Fatherland,' it read.

From 1935 on, German men were subject to military service from their 18th birthday until the end of the month of March following their 45th birthday. Later, conscription was extended to cover those aged 17 to 61, and during the last days of the Third Reich boys as young as 12 were defending the smouldering ruins of Berlin. Individuals who were deemed as somewhat short of immediate fitness for service were classified in one of several reserve components and subject to activation as needed. Certain classes of the population, such as Jews, were excluded from service. However, as the need for manpower increased the standards for physical fitness were lowered, convicts serving prison terms were pressed into the ranks, and convalescing soldiers who might have previously been sent on leave were returned to their units.

During World War II, the strength of the *Heer* at its peak approached 10 million men. Between 1939 and 1945, the *Heer* suffered more than 4.2 million dead and nearly 400,000 taken prisoner, bearing by far the lion's share of the burden of the fight for Germany. The combat prowess of the German soldier in World War II was grudgingly acknowledged by his adversaries, and historians have noted that as a whole the German Army acquitted itself with tremendous courage in the face of a continually deteriorating strategic

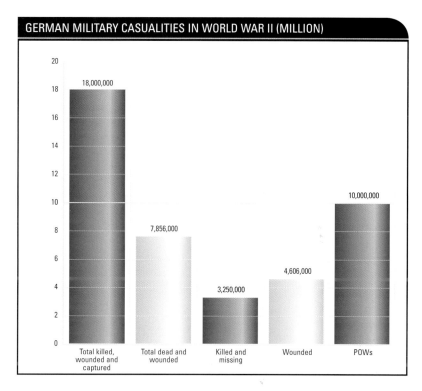

**GERMAN MILITARY CASUALITIES IN WORLD WAR II (MILLION)**

and tactical situation after 1942. Although some *Heer* units are known to have committed atrocities against prisoners of war and civilians alike, most common soldiers of the German Army acquitted themselves honourably in combat.

In his acclaimed book *Frontsoldaten*, Stephen G. Fritz points out, 'As perpetrators, whether out of conviction or not, these common men existed as part of a great destructive machine, ready and willing to kill and destroy in order to achieve the goals of a murderous regime. In the role of victims, they lived daily with the physical hardships, the psychological burdens, and the often crushing anxieties of death and killing that constitute the everyday life of all combat soldiers.'

■ **Every German campaign, even the successful ones, added significantly to the death toll on the German Army. Tens of thousands died in Poland, France, and the Balkans, but the real price was paid on the Eastern Front.**

For all his ineptitude as a military strategist, particularly his strategic blunders committed in 1940 and later, Adolf Hitler was nevertheless the catalyst for the growth and development of a fighting machine which was, up to that time, the most formidable in the world. The *Heer*, in turn, was the premier component of that machine, fighting across fronts which extended from the Caucasus to the deserts of North Africa and from the English Channel to the Arctic Circle.

# Organized for Conquest

*When the* Feldheer *deployed for combat, its strategic perspective was divided into theatres both large and small, but each created on the same basic principle of separating the front-line units and combat commands from the support and administrative units to their rear.*

Division- or corps-sized formations were placed before the enemy on the strategic map with reserves drawn up to provide reinforcements if necessary. The front-line troops and reserves were grouped in an area designated as the combat zone. Directly behind, in the communications zone, were the rear areas of individual armies, while the rear area of an entire army group was still further back. Collectively, the combat and communications zones were known as a theatre of operations.

Behind the theatre of operations was the occupied territory, or zone of military administration, which could range in size from a few kilometres to an entire country. Furthest from the front was the German homeland, divided into its military districts which maintained direct communication with the *Feldheer* and the Replacement Army to facilitate the transport of supplies and troops to the front. The theatre concept proved flexible and effective, easily adapted to the size and strength of the forces at hand.

The organizational structure of the *Feldheer* was continually changing during World War II as divisions, corps and even armies were realigned among commands, transferred from one area of operations to another, or reconstituted as replacement troops filled the depleted ranks of units which had taken combat losses. At times, some *Heer* units were so depleted that they retained their designation as divisions or regiments although their effective strength was far below the proper level.

### Army group in action

The largest operational unit within the *Feldheer* was the army group, which consisted of two or more armies with organic components of infantry, armour, artillery and often a cooperating *Luftwaffe* contingent. The strength of an army group was usually several hundred thousand men, and those which consisted entirely of German troops were known as *Heeresgruppen*.

One example of the evolving composition and deployment of *Feldheer* forces was *Heeresgruppe Nord*, Army Group North, which was nominally under the control of OKH throughout World War II. Army Group North was formed in September 1939 under the command of Field Marshal Fedor von Bock. During the invasion of Poland, its organic elements included Third and Fourth Armies with the 10th Panzer Division and the 73rd, 206th and 208th Infantry Divisions in reserve.

In October 1939, after the conclusion of the Polish campaign, Army Group North was transferred to the Western Front, redesignated as Army Group B, and was made up of Fourth and Sixth Armies. By the time the *Wehrmacht* executed 'Case Yellow', unleashing 136 divisions for the invasion of France and the Low Countries on 10 May 1940, Bock's Army Group B included the three corps of General Georg von Küchler's Eighteenth Army and the six corps of the Sixth Army under General Walter von Reichenau. The total strength of Army Group B in the spring and summer of 1940 included 29 divisions. Of these 23 were infantry, three panzer, two motorized infantry and one cavalry.

| WEHRMACHT UNIT DEFINITIONS | |
|---|---|
| *Unit* | *Translation* |
| Heeresgruppe | Army Group |
| Armeegruppe | Army Group |
| Armee | Army |
| Korps | Corps |
| Division | Division |
| Brigade | Brigade |
| Regiment | Regiment |
| Abteilung/Bataillon | Battalion |
| Kompanie | Company |
| Zug | Platoon |
| Gruppe | Group |
| Halb-Zug | Half-platoon |
| Trupp | Troop |
| Kampfgruppe | Battle Group |

## INFANTRY ARMIES' DEPLOYMENT, 1939–45

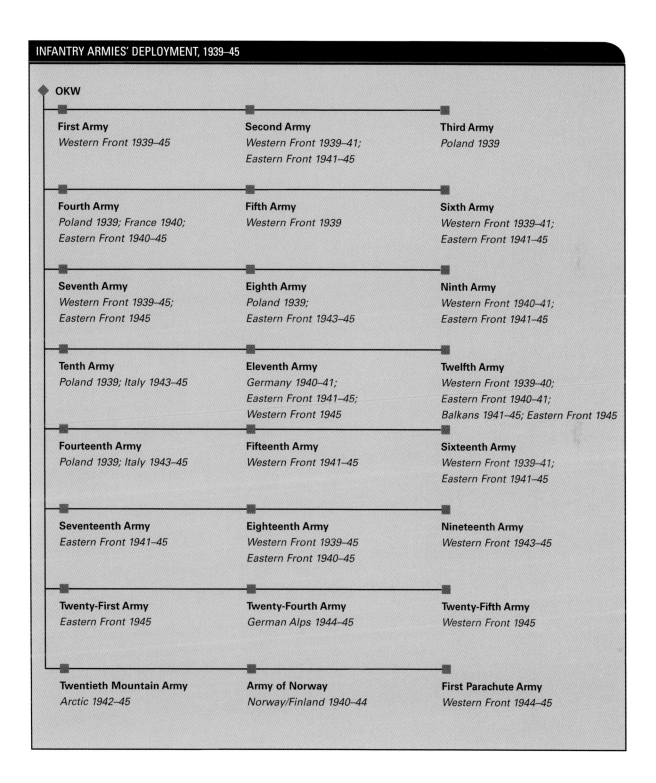

◆ **OKW**

**First Army**
*Western Front 1939–45*

**Second Army**
*Western Front 1939–41;*
*Eastern Front 1941–45*

**Third Army**
*Poland 1939*

**Fourth Army**
*Poland 1939; France 1940;*
*Eastern Front 1940–45*

**Fifth Army**
*Western Front 1939*

**Sixth Army**
*Western Front 1939–41;*
*Eastern Front 1941–45*

**Seventh Army**
*Western Front 1939–45;*
*Eastern Front 1945*

**Eighth Army**
*Poland 1939;*
*Eastern Front 1943–45*

**Ninth Army**
*Western Front 1940–41;*
*Eastern Front 1941–45*

**Tenth Army**
*Poland 1939; Italy 1943–45*

**Eleventh Army**
*Germany 1940–41;*
*Eastern Front 1941–45;*
*Western Front 1945*

**Twelfth Army**
*Western Front 1939–40;*
*Eastern Front 1940–41;*
*Balkans 1941–45; Eastern Front 1945*

**Fourteenth Army**
*Poland 1939; Italy 1943–45*

**Fifteenth Army**
*Western Front 1941–45*

**Sixteenth Army**
*Western Front 1939–41;*
*Eastern Front 1941–45*

**Seventeenth Army**
*Eastern Front 1941–45*

**Eighteenth Army**
*Western Front 1939–45*
*Eastern Front 1940–45*

**Nineteenth Army**
*Western Front 1943–45*

**Twenty-First Army**
*Eastern Front 1945*

**Twenty-Fourth Army**
*German Alps 1944–45*

**Twenty-Fifth Army**
*Western Front 1945*

**Twentieth Mountain Army**
*Arctic 1942–45*

**Army of Norway**
*Norway/Finland 1940–44*

**First Parachute Army**
*Western Front 1944–45*

## GERMAN ARMIES, 1939–45

| Army | Date Formed | Notes |
|---|---|---|
| First Army | August 1939 | Stationed in Western Europe for duration of war |
| First Parachute Army | July 1944 | Consolidated various *Luftwaffe* combat units in the West |
| Second Army | October 1939 | Renamed Army Command East Prussia in April 1945 |
| Third Army | August 1939 | Became Sixteenth Army after Poland campaign |
| Fourth Army | August 1939 | Destroyed in March 1945, and remnants used to form Twenty-First Army |
| Fifth Army | August 1939 | Became Eighteenth Army in November 1940 |
| Sixth Army | October 1939 | Destroyed at Stalingrad in February 1943. Re-formed in March 1943 |
| Seventh Army | August 1939 | Served until its surrender in April 1945 |
| Eighth Army | August 1939 | Redesignated Second Army after Poland campaign |
| Ninth Army | May 1940 | Surrendered in April 1945 |
| Tenth Army | August 1939 | Redesignated Sixth Army after Poland campaign. Re-formed in August 1943 |
| Eleventh Army | October 1940 | Redesignated Army Group Don in November 1942. Re-formed in February 1945 |
| Twelfth Army | October 1939 | Redesignated Armed Force South East in June 1941, Army Group East in December 1942, then Twelfth Army in February 1945 |
| Fourteenth Army | August 1939 | Redesignated Twelfth Army after Poland campaign. Re-formed in November 1943 |
| Fifteenth Army | January 1941 | Served in West for duration of the war |
| Sixteenth Army | October 1939 | Remained unchanged for duration of the war |
| Seventeenth Army | December 1940 | Effectively destroyed in May 1944 |
| Eighteenth Army | November 1940 | Active to May 1945 |
| Nineteenth Army | August 1943 | Largely destroyed in January/February 1945 |
| Twentieth Mountain Army | June 1942 | Formed from Army of Lapland |
| Twenty-First Army | April 1945 | Created from Fourth Army |
| Twenty-Fourth Army | December 1944 | Did not reach operational status until April 1945 |
| Twenty-Fifth Army | January 1945 | Deployed in West |
| Army of Norway | December 1940 | Disbanded in December 1944 |
| Army of Lapland | January 1942 | Redesignated Twentieth Mountain Army in June 1942 |

In preparation for the invasion of the Soviet Union, a new Army Group North was constituted on the Eastern Front and consisted largely of units drawn from Army Group C. Under Field Marshal Wilhelm Ritter von Leeb, Army Group North advanced on Leningrad and was poised to take the city by direct assault when Hitler ordered the advance halted so that its civilian population could be starved into submission by siege. In the end, the 900-day siege of Leningrad was unsuccessful and tied down large numbers of German troops for nearly three years. During the opening months of Operation 'Barbarossa', this second constitution of Army Group North included the Eighteenth Army, Fourth Panzer Army, Sixteenth Army and attached specialized units.

Army Group North was deployed on the Eastern Front for the remainder of the war, and in October 1941 included the Sixteenth and Eighteenth Armies along with the troops of the Spanish Blue Division, Fascist soldiers from Franco's Spain who had volunteered to serve with the *Feldheer*. A year later, under the command of von Küchler, Army Group North was augmented by the Eleventh Army. During seven months of combat along the Baltic in 1944, the army group was commanded by Field Marshal Walter Model, Colonel-General Georg Lindemann, Colonel-General Johannes Friessner, and Field Marshal Ferdinand Schörner.

In the waning months of the war, Army Group North operated in Prussia with the Sixteenth and Eighteenth Armies reinforced by various detachments and battle groups. Fighting in Latvia in January 1945, it was renamed Army Group Courland, while the remnants of the former Army Group Centre was redesignated as yet another Army Group North.

Army Group B was actually the designation of three different formations during the war. In addition to Bock's command of 300,000 troops which fought in Belgium and the Netherlands in May 1940, a second Army Group B was formed in the East prior to the *Wehrmacht* offensive against the Red Army in the summer of 1942. This command consisted primarily of troops of the former Army Group South and included the ill-fated Sixth Army under General Friedrich Paulus, which was annihilated by the Red Army during the six-month Battle of Stalingrad.

After the Stalingrad debacle, this Army Group B was combined with Army Group Don to form another Army Group South.

Army Group B's third incarnation took shape in northern Italy in 1943 under Field Marshal Erwin Rommel. The army group was transferred to France after D-Day, and command passed to Field Marshal Günther von Kluge and later to Field Marshal Model. Elements of Army Group B participated in the fighting in Normandy, Operation 'Market Garden' (the Allied airborne and ground invasion of the Netherlands), and in the Ardennes offensive, popularly known as the Battle of the Bulge.

While in Italy, Army Group B had included at various times the German Second Army, the Italian Eighth Army, the Hungarian Second Army, and for a time the II SS Panzer Corps. Its composition on the Western Front included Panzer Group West, First Army, Seventh Army, Fifteenth Army, Fifth and Sixth Panzer Armies, and First Parachute Army.

Axis army groups which included German formations along with those of other nations, particularly the Italian Army in North Africa and the Romanian and Hungarian armies on the Eastern Front, were often designated as *Armeegruppen*. Prior to 1943, the term *Armeegruppe* was more loosely defined to include reinforced formations or even large groupings of particular divisions. Later, when Axis forces of more than one nation operated cooperatively, the headquarters of the German component of the *Armeegruppe* was usually in overall command.

## GERMAN ARMY GROUPS, 1939–45

| Army Group | Date Formed | Notes |
|---|---|---|
| Army Group A | October 1939 | Participated in Western Campaign 1940, Somme, Dunkirk; redesignated *Oberbefehlshaber West*, October 1940; a second Army Group A was formed in July 1942 on the Eastern Front and a third in Jan 1945 |
| Army Group B | July 1942 | Formed with the breakup of Army Group South and was at Stalingrad; an earlier Army Group B was formed in the West in 1940 and a third in Italy in 1943 |
| Army Group C | August 1939 | Assaulted the Maginot Line during May 1940 offensive in the West; relocated to East Prussia and renamed Army Group North in April 1941; reconstituted November 1943 in Southwest Italy |
| Army Group D | October 1940 | Formed in France from disbanded Army Group C; commander was elevated to commander-in-chief in the Western theatre in April 1941 |
| Army Group E | January 1943 | Engaged in anti-partisan operations in the Balkans |
| Army Group F | August 1943 | Formed in Bayreuth and engaged in anti-partisan activities in the Balkans |
| Army Group G | May 1944 | Formed in the West and fought in the Vosges Mountains; elements fought in the Battle of the Bulge |
| Army Group H | November 1944 | Netherlands garrison duty and defence of the Rhine |
| Army Group Africa | February 1943 | Formed under General Erwin Rommel and active through the remainder of the North African campaign |
| Army Group Don | November 1942 | Formed primarily to mount an offensive to relieve encircled Stalingrad; in the spring of 1943 Army Group Don was assimilated into Army Group South |
| Army Group Courland | January 1945 | Formerly Army Group North, the formation defended the Courland Pocket in the final months of the war |
| Army Group Liguria | October 1943 | Consisting of just four divisions, it was formed by Mussolini's puppet regime in Northern Italy following the fall of his Fascist government |
| Army Group Centre (*Heeresgruppe Mitte*) | June 1941 | From Operation 'Barbarossa' to the Königsberg Pocket, Army Group Centre served on the Eastern Front; a second Army Group Centre was formed by Hitler in January 1945 when the original formation was renamed Army Group North |
| Army Group North (*Heeresgruppe Nord*) | September 1939 | Served on the Eastern Front during the invasion of Poland and the Soviet Union; renamed Army Group Courland in January 1945 |
| Army Group North Ukraine (*Heeresgruppe Nordukraine*) | April 1944 | Created when Army Group South was renamed; fought defensive operations on the Eastern Front |
| Army Group South (*Heeresgruppe Süd*) | August 1939 | Three active formations bore this name, the first formed prior to the invasion of Poland, the second in October 1940 and operating on the Eastern Front prior to being divided in the summer of 1942, and the third in February 1943 from Army Group Don |
| Army Group Southeast (*Heeresgruppe Sudost*) | December 1942 | Active in the Balkans |
| Army Group South Ukraine (*Heeresgruppe Südukraine*) | March 1944 | Active on the Eastern Front and absorbed into Army Group South in September 1944 |
| Army Group Tunisia (*Heeresgruppe Tunis*) | February 1941 | Concurrent with Army Group Africa, commanded by General Erwin Rommel |
| Army Group Upper Rhine (*Heeresgruppe Oberrhein*) | November 1944 | Disbanded in January 1945 following brief command of Heinrich Himmler |
| Army Group Vistula (*Heeresgruppe Weichsel*) | January 1945 | Engaged in the defence of Berlin, including the final German offensive actions of World War II |

# Echelons of Command

*A standard* Wehrmacht *army-sized formation numbered 60,000–100,000 men, formed of at least one corps and including attached units detailed for specific operations.*

An army corps consisted of one or more divisions along with attached units, reserves and any additional support troops necessary. Corps headquarters served as 'bridge' command structures between the strategic direction of armies and the tactical deployment of smaller units such as divisions or battle groups. The corps generally consisted of 40,000 to 60,000 men, including combat and support personnel.

The composition of the divisions of the *Feldheer* during World War II depended upon their type and purpose. Infantry divisions, by definition, were composed of different units from panzer divisions. Accordingly, a division most often consisted of up to four regiments

along with attached units, a total of 10,000 to 20,000 men. Its headquarters provided tactical field direction for fighting regiments under its command.

Activated in October 1934, during the early phase of the German Army's expansion under the Nazi regime, the 1st Infantry Division traced its beginning to the pre-war *Reichswehr* and was originally known by a series of euphemistic names to camouflage its true purpose as an infantry formation which violated the terms of the Versailles Treaty. A Wave One unit, the 1st Division included soldiers who were called up in the first wave of German military conscription.

The 1st Division participated in the Polish campaign as part of XXVI Corps in Third Army, commanded by General

von Küchler. The division then briefly transferred to France and then returned to the Eastern Front for the duration of the war. Participating in the advance of Eighteenth Army on Leningrad, the division fought in the area of Lake Ladoga and transferred to the First Panzer Army in the winter of 1943. Later operating with the Third and Fourth Armies, the 1st Division fought the Red Army in the vicinity of Königsberg in East Prussia until the end of the war.

The exigencies of combat influenced the composition of the 1st Division significantly. During the Polish campaign, it consisted of three infantry regiments, the 1st, 22nd, and 43rd, an artillery regiment with an attached battalion, and machine-gun,

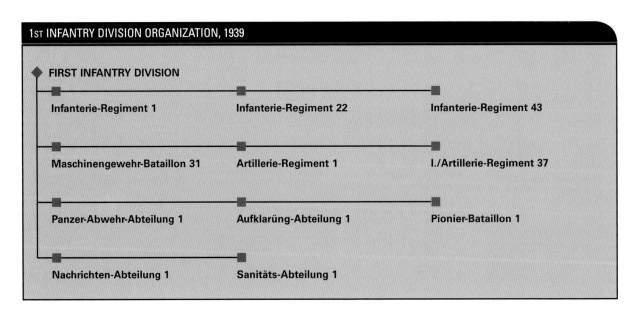

**1ST INFANTRY DIVISION ORGANIZATION, 1939**

**FIRST INFANTRY DIVISION**

| Infanterie-Regiment 1 | Infanterie-Regiment 22 | Infanterie-Regiment 43 |
|---|---|---|
| Maschinengewehr-Bataillon 31 | Artillerie-Regiment 1 | I./Artillerie-Regiment 37 |
| Panzer-Abwehr-Abteilung 1 | Aufklarüng-Abteilung 1 | Pionier-Bataillon 1 |
| Nachrichten-Abteilung 1 | Sanitäts-Abteilung 1 | |

anti-tank, pioneer, reconnaissance, signals and medical battalions. By 1944, the division included Füsilier Regiment 22, which combined the capabilities of heavy infantry and reconnaissance troops, Grenadier Regiments 22 and 43, which were composed of ordinary footsoldiers, Artillery Regiment 1 along with an additional artillery battalion, and various support formations. From its inception until the end of the war, the 1st Division had no fewer than 12 different commanders.

Below division level, the regiment consisted of 2000 to 6000 men who engaged in direct combat with the enemy and deployed organic units along with attached formations as necessary. At times, the regiment included independent battalions or *Abteilungen*. In theory, the 500- to 1000-man *Abteilung* was the smallest unit within the *Heer* which was capable of sustained combat operations without the direct support of other units. An operational *Abteilung* regularly included infantry, armour, artillery, pioneer and infantry-related heavy weapons support, such as machine guns and mortars, to accomplish an assigned tactical mission.

The 100- to 200-man company served at the tactical level and usually included four or five platoons, which were the primary combat formations of the *Heer*'s infantry. Each platoon was initially divided into squads of 13 men. Later, when this proved unwieldy, the size of the squad was reduced to 10 men. Interestingly, while Hitler closely controlled the highest levels of command through OKW and OKH, subordinate commanders in the

field were often allowed considerable independence. Junior officers and NCOs of the German Army were well known for their initiative in combat.

## The *Kampfgruppen*

Combat operations often necessitated the formation of self-contained units known as *Kampfgruppen*, battle groups. These were substantial combinations of units which provided comprehensive ground capabilities and ranged from corps to battalion or company size. Each typically included infantry, armour, artillery and anti-tank elements along with support troops such as pioneers and medical detachments. Formed in the field and composed of the units at hand, the *Kampfgruppe* was usually a temporary combat organization which bore the name of its commanding officer and was ordered to carry out a specific mission. A standard formation of *Heer* tactical guidelines and field operations, the *Kampfgruppe* was somewhat similar to the combat command structure employed by the US Army during World War II although no actual Allied tactical formation mirrored its composition.

During the retreat of Axis forces across North Africa following their defeat at El Alamein in November 1942, German and Italian troops were pushed across hundreds of kilometres of desert. With Allied forces advancing from east and west, the Axis troops under Field Marshal Erwin Rommel and Colonel-General Hans-Jürgen von Arnim were in danger of being cut off from one another during their fighting withdrawal toward the Tunisian coast. Several *Kampfgruppen* were dispatched to hold vital

mountain passes through which the Allies would advance.

One such battle group was *Kampfgruppe Fullriede*, formed in February 1943 under the command of Lieutenant-Colonel Fritz Fullriede. Defending the Fondouk passes along a front of 65km (40 miles), Fullriede had at his disposal 12 companies of infantry (nine German and three Italian), 14 Italian field guns, three small German artillery pieces, and the 334th Armoured Car Battalion, which fielded several light anti-aircraft guns and two formidable 88mm (3.5in) guns. Augmented by a special-forces platoon from the famed *Brandenburg* Regiment, Fullriede launched a successful counter-attack against US forces which had previously driven his forward elements from defensive positions and captured a village.

Further reinforced by the 190th Reconnaissance Battalion, Fullriede deployed a pair of self-propelled 75mm (2.95in) guns and cleared another mountain pass. Holding these routes open for days with little replenishment of supplies or reinforcements, *Kampfgruppe Fullriede* retired on 9 April after nearly two months of constant combat.

The formations of the *Feldheer* proved adept at swift movement and exploitation of breakthroughs in enemy lines during offensive operations, particularly the *Blitzkrieg*, which combined air, armour, infantry, and artillery in the conquest of Poland, vast swathes of the Soviet Union, and much of Western Europe from 1939 to 1941. Once on the defensive, the *Feldheer* was resilient, its tactical commanders resourceful, its soldiers determined and battle-hardened.

# CHAPTER 4

# The Panzerwaffe

*The development of the* Panzerwaffe, *or armoured forces, of the German Army prior to World War II presents one of the most remarkable military achievements of the twentieth century.*

*The Germans had experienced the shock of the armoured vehicle and its decisive capability on the battlefield a generation earlier, and the lesson was not lost on those who recognized the potential for mobile firepower.*

*Visionary commanders within the* Heer *put theory into practice with the* Blitzkrieg *of 1939–41, although the armoured fist was ultimately to fail – the tanks too few in number to win a costly war of attrition.*

■ German troops riding on the hull of a Panzer III watch Soviet soldiers surrender somewhere in western Russia during Operation 'Barbarossa'.

# Engine of Modern War

*The first tanks to serve in battle with the German military in World War I were massive, unwieldy beasts only capable of quite slow speed, manned by at least 18 soldiers, and sometimes responsible for asphyxiating their own crews with noxious gases from their primitive engines.*

Only 20 of an original order for 100 of the Sturmpanzerwagen A7V were delivered by 1918; however, these armoured fighting vehicles proved to be the progenitors of the swift, robust panzers which swept through Poland and France early in World War II and became, perhaps more than any other weapon, the symbol of the military might of the *Feldheer*.

Between the world wars, Germany was forbidden to produce or to field tanks, armoured cars or any other fighting vehicles of consequence by the terms of the Treaty of Versailles. Undeterred, the *Reichswehr* high command, itself an illegal entity, conspired to establish training facilities outside Germany. By the mid-1920s, German

soldiers were in training abroad, at Kazan in the Soviet Union, where they learned to operate Soviet, British and French machines far from the prying eyes of inspectors sent to monitor military activities inside the Fatherland.

**Secret operations**

By 1928, the first tanks produced in Germany were secretly in operation with the seven so-called transportation battalions of the *Reichswehr*. These battalions had initially been organized to carry supplies but adapted rapidly to their future combat role. There were sceptics within the *Reichswehr*, however, and one officer said to Captain Heinz Guderian, a young motor transport staff officer: 'To hell with fighting, you are supposed to carry flour.'

Guderian, however, was soon the standard-bearer not only for the continuing development of tanks within the German Army but also of the tactics for their successful deployment on the modern battlefield. Guderian later commanded Motor Transport Battalion No. 3 in Berlin, taking advantage of his location to advocate increasing emphasis on the panzers, lecturing on tank warfare, and drilling his soldiers with dummy

## PANZER UNIT DEFINITIONS

| Unit | Translation |
| --- | --- |
| Divisionen | Divisions |
| Panzer-Divisionen | Armoured Divisions |
| Panzer-Verbande Stegemann | Armoured Formation *Stegemann* |
| Leichte Divisionen | Light Divisions |
| Brigaden | Brigades |
| Panzer-Brigaden | Armoured Brigades |
| Regimenter | Regiments |
| Panzer-Regimenter | Armoured Regiments |
| Führer-Panzer-Regimenter | *Führer* Armoured Regiments |
| Panzer-Lehr-Regiment | Armoured Demonstration Regiment |
| Panzer-Regimentsstab 80 | 80th Armoured Regimental Staff |
| Abteilungen/Bataillone | Battalions |
| Panzer-Abteilungen | Armoured Battalions |
| Panzer-Abteilungen (Fkl.) | Remote-Controlled Armoured Battalions |
| Panzer-Abteilung z.b.V. 40 | Armoured Battalion 40 (for special purposes) |
| schwere Panzer-Abteilungen (Tiger) | Heavy Armoured Battalions (Tiger tanks) |
| schwere Panzer-Abteilungen (Panther) | Heavy Armoured Battalions (Panther tanks) |
| Sturm-Panzer-Abteilungen | Assault Armoured Battalions |
| Minenräum-Abteilung 1 | 1st Mine Clearance Battalion |
| Kompanien | Companies |
| Panzer-Kompanien | Armoured Companies |

tanks constructed of plywood and cardboard. He visited other countries and reported on the advances in equipment and military doctrine which he observed.

By 1931, the nucleus of the tank forces, or *Panzerwaffe*, which would dominate the battlefield at the end of the decade, had come into being, and the following summer, exercises which included infantry, cavalry and dummy tanks were conducted under the command of Major-General Oswald Lutz, recently elevated to the office of Inspector of Motorized Troops. Lutz was a forward-thinking officer, who replaced the elderly General Otto von Stülpnagel. Lutz's predecessor had once told Guderian bluntly, 'You are quite too impetuous. Believe me, in our lifetime neither of us will ever see German tanks in operation.'

## Promotion and reform

Lutz promoted Guderian to Chief of Staff of Motorized Troops, and the two began to reshape the *Heer*, confronting the old line officers who refused to embrace the Army of the future and initiating the manufacture of the first tanks which could be mass-produced.

In December 1932, Krupp engineers put forward a design for a 5.5-tonne (5.4-ton) tank with a crew of two and armed with a pair of 7.92mm (0.31in) MG13 machine guns. The lightly armed and armoured Panzerkampfwagen (PzKpfw) I Ausf. A (*Ausführung*, meaning model or design) entered service in 1934.

Perhaps the most significant event in the evolution of the panzer force was the fortuitous visit of the *Führer*

---

### GENERAL HEINZ GUDERIAN

■ **Guderian was one of the primary architects of armoured warfare.**

*Heinz Guderian is considered the foremost proponent of armoured warfare in the German armed forces during the years between the world wars. As an early advocate of the development of the* Blitzkrieg, *he is often referred to as the father of the devastating combined-arms tactic which swept across Poland, France and the Low Countries from 1939–40 and into the Soviet Union in 1941. Guderian was often at odds with Hitler, which cost him his command on the Eastern Front in December 1941 and again in March 1945 as Chief of the General Staff. In addition to* Achtung Panzer!, *the German primer on armoured warfare, Guderian also authored* Panzer Leader, *a memoir of his military career.*

| | |
|---|---|
| BIRTH: | 17 June 1888 |
| DEATH: | 17 May 1954 |
| PLACE OF BIRTH: | Kulm, Germany |
| PERSONAL RELATIONSHIPS: | Married Margarete Goerne 1913; sons Heinz and Kurt |
| SERVICE: | Lieutenant 1908 |
| | Signals and Staff officer 1914-18 |
| | Remains with *Reichswehr* 1919 |
| | Lieutenant-Colonel 1931; Chief of Staff to Inspectorate of Motorized Troops |
| | Colonel 1933 |
| | Commands 2nd Panzer Division 1935 |
| | Brigadier-General 1936 |
| | Published *Achtung Panzer!* 1937 |
| | Major-General 1938 |
| | General 1939; Commands XIX Panzer Corps |
| | Inspector General of Armoured Troops 1943 |
| | Chief of Staff of the *Heer* 1944 |
| | Surrendered to US troops 10 May 1945 |
| | Released from US custody as prisoner of war 1948 |

to the Army proving ground at Kummersdorf in the winter of 1934. The roar of the engines and the apparent speed with which Guderian's tanks performed in open terrain so impressed Hitler that he exclaimed, 'This is what I want, and this is what I shall have.'

On 15 October 1935, seven months after Hitler had reintroduced military conscription and publicly repudiated the Treaty of Versailles, the first three panzer divisions of the new *Heer* were created. Although its composition was to be altered numerous times in the years to come, at inception the 1st Panzer Division consisted of a light engineer

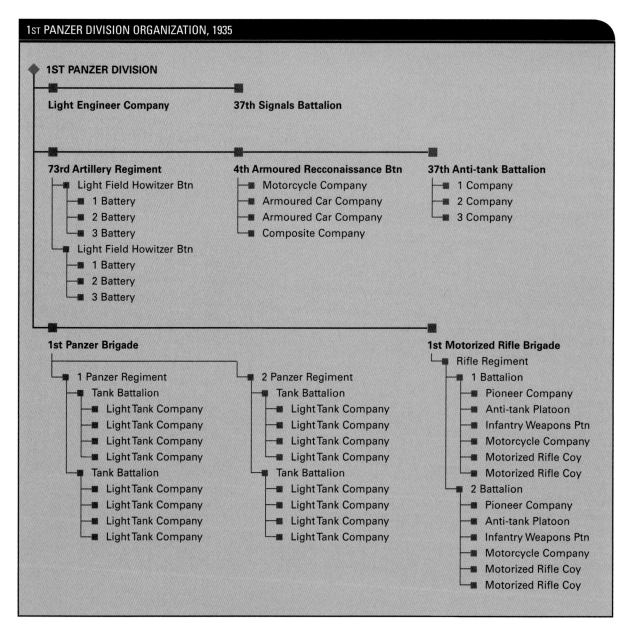

**1ST PANZER DIVISION ORGANIZATION, 1935**

**1ST PANZER DIVISION**

**Light Engineer Company**    **37th Signals Battalion**

**73rd Artillery Regiment**
- Light Field Howitzer Btn
  - 1 Battery
  - 2 Battery
  - 3 Battery
- Light Field Howitzer Btn
  - 1 Battery
  - 2 Battery
  - 3 Battery

**4th Armoured Recconaissance Btn**
- Motorcycle Company
- Armoured Car Company
- Armoured Car Company
- Composite Company

**37th Anti-tank Battalion**
- 1 Company
- 2 Company
- 3 Company

**1st Panzer Brigade**
- 1 Panzer Regiment
  - Tank Battalion
    - Light Tank Company
    - Light Tank Company
    - Light Tank Company
    - Light Tank Company
  - Tank Battalion
    - Light Tank Company
    - Light Tank Company
    - Light Tank Company
    - Light Tank Company
- 2 Panzer Regiment
  - Tank Battalion
    - Light Tank Company
    - Light Tank Company
    - Light Tank Company
    - Light Tank Company
  - Tank Battalion
    - Light Tank Company
    - Light Tank Company
    - Light Tank Company
    - Light Tank Company

**1st Motorized Rifle Brigade**
- Rifle Regiment
  - 1 Battalion
    - Pioneer Company
    - Anti-tank Platoon
    - Infantry Weapons Ptn
    - Motorcycle Company
    - Motorized Rifle Coy
    - Motorized Rifle Coy
  - 2 Battalion
    - Pioneer Company
    - Anti-tank Platoon
    - Infantry Weapons Ptn
    - Motorcycle Company
    - Motorized Rifle Coy
    - Motorized Rifle Coy

company, elements of the 37th Signals Battalion (one company with radios and the other supplied with telephone equipment), the 73rd Artillery Regiment, including two battalions of light field howitzers grouped into three batteries, the 4th Armoured Reconnaissance Battalion, composed of two armoured car companies, a motorcycle company and a composite company, the three companies of the 37th Anti-tank Battalion, the 1st Motorized Rifle Brigade and the 1st Panzer Brigade.

The two regiments of the 1st Panzer Brigade each included two tank battalions composed of four light tank companies, while the 1st Motorized Rifle Brigade fielded one rifle regiment of two battalions. Each battalion consisted of a combined company of pioneer, anti-tank and infantry weapons platoons, a motorcycle company and two motorized rifle companies.

## 1938 Establishment

The composition of a panzer division varied based upon available equipment, and by 1938 its primary elements included the two potent regiments of the panzer brigade, each with two or three tank battalions. Within the battalions were the headquarters and up to three companies which usually contained three tank platoons. Each tank platoon fielded as many as five tanks. Therefore, the actual armoured strength of the panzer regiment on the eve of World War II consisted of up to 400 tanks. A number of these tanks were contained within the headquarters units of the regiments, battalions and companies for defence purposes, to temporarily replace combat losses or to exploit breakthroughs in enemy lines.

During the first year of the war, support functions were enhanced, while an anti-aircraft battalion was added to the divisional table of organization and equipment, the contingent of pioneers was increased to battalion strength, and reconnaissance capabilities were improved. Some of these changes were the direct result of combat experience during the Polish campaign.

# The Architect

*When the* Feldheer *roared into action in Poland and months later stormed across France to the English Channel, its bold, aggressive victories validated the vision of the 51-year-old Heinz Guderian who had taken command of the 2nd Panzer Division in 1935 as a colonel and subsequently attained the rank of general during the years of military expansion in pre-war Germany.*

By the mid-1930s, Guderian had become familiar with the innovative armoured theories of the British officers J.F.C. Fuller and Basil Liddell Hart, the French Colonel Charles de Gaulle, and the Soviet General Mikhail Tukhachevsky. Each of these recognized the potential offensive capabilities of the armoured force, and Guderian grasped the concept as well. Although he could never legitimately claim sole authorship of the combined-arms tactics which became known to the world as *Blitzkrieg*, or 'Lightning War', he undoubtedly championed its implementation by the *Feldheer*.

Guderian penned the landmark book *Achtung Panzer!* in 1937, and years later authored another work, *Panzer Leader*, in which he wrote that in 1929 he 'became convinced that tanks working on their own or in conjunction with infantry could never achieve decisive importance. My historical studies, the exercises carried out in England and our own experience with mock-ups had persuaded me that the tanks would never be able to produce their full effect until weapons on whose support they must inevitably rely were brought up to their standard of speed and of cross-country performance. In such formation of all arms, the tanks must play a primary role, the other weapons being subordinated to the requirements of the armour. It would be wrong to include tanks in infantry divisions: what was needed were armoured divisions which would include all the supporting arms needed to fight with full effect.'

From this conviction, he had formulated the basis of the panzer division. The logical follow-on was that of the tactics which could take full advantage of the firepower and mobility of the tank. Guderian was an early advocate of radio communication, which would facilitate swift, coordinated movement. *Blitzkrieg* involved cooperative artillery bombardment, tactical air strikes to disrupt communications and the concentration of enemy troops, while panzer reconnaissance formations probed for weaknesses in the enemy's defensive front.

Once a weak point was located, the panzers would hit hard, advance rapidly without halting to consolidate gains or secure flanks, and penetrate deeply into the enemy's rear. Motorized infantry and anti-tank units would follow closely to cover the flanks and consolidate territorial gains. The key element of the *Blitzkrieg*, however, was the rapid movement of the tanks. Guderian admonished his tank commanders not to wait for slower infantry to come forward in support, ignore flank security, and press home their attacks with relentless speed.

German military doctrine had long stressed the tactic of encirclement along with the Napoleonic manoeuvre of penetration into enemy rear areas. Therefore, *Blitzkrieg* was in keeping with traditional German offensive thinking, and the mobility and combat prowess of the panzers would, to a degree, demonstrate the capabilities of a modern, armoured cavalry. In his book *Blitzkrieg*, the author Len Deighton writes, 'Perhaps it is unique in military history for one man to influence the design of a weapon, see to training the men who use it, help plan an offensive, and then lead his force into battle. Heinz Guderian did just that.'

### Poland prostrate

In the spring of 1939, the *Heer* had constituted five panzer divisions with a sixth nearing combat readiness. These divisions included 10 panzer regiments, forming five brigades of four battalions each. At least four other panzer regiments remained independent, either designated to form the nucleus of new panzer divisions or for other reasons. The light PzKpfw I was by far the most plentiful offensive weapon, while the motorized infantry relied on trucks and halftracks for transportation.

Heavier tanks were already in production in the late summer of 1939; however, only a relative few of these were available by September. Conceptually, these heavier tanks were designed to perform more specific functions than the early armoured vehicles of the *Feldheer*. The PzKpfw I had proven adequate during its combat debut in support of Generalissimo Francisco Franco's Nationalist forces in the Spanish Civil War, but its light armour was only capable of withstanding small-arms fire and its two machine guns were unable to effectively engage heavier tanks such as the French Char B1 bis with its turret-mounted 47mm (1.85in) cannon and hull-mounted 75mm (2.95in) howitzer. The PzKpfw II was armed with a 20mm (0.79in) cannon, while the PzKpfw III was conceived to take on enemy tanks with a 37mm (1.45in) main weapon and the PzKpfw IV, with a range of more than 160km (100 miles), to drive deeply into the enemy rear areas, blasting fixed fortifications and enemy armoured vehicles with its 75mm (2.95in) gun.

When the *Wehrmacht* initiated 'Case White', the invasion of Poland, on 1 September 1939, its *Blitzkrieg* theory was put to the test, and the results were spectacular, particularly with the panzers operating in open country and executing their textbook encirclement tactic. For the invasion, the *Heer* fielded 15 'mechanized' divisions which offered varying degrees of mobility. Six of these were panzer divisions, while four were motorized infantry, four were light divisions, and a single panzer division was composed of both *Heer* and *Waffen-SS* units. The light divisions were essentially smaller panzer divisions which consisted principally of one regiment of tanks and complementary motorized infantry.

### Uneven contest

Against slashing panzers supported by the air attacks of Junkers Ju-87 Stuka dive-bombers, the Poles could muster roughly 500 armoured vehicles formed into two brigades. Most of the Polish tanks were licence-built British models such as the light Vickers Armstrong or Carden-Loyd tankettes. The stiffest resistance was encountered in the streets and suburbs of the Polish capital of Warsaw, where the mobility of the 4th Panzer Division was

neutralized and the fighting was at times house to house. Guderian's XIX Panzer Corps dashed eastward and reached its objective of Brest-Litovsk

on the northern shoulder of the offensive in a remarkable 15 days. The XXII Panzer Corps, under General Ewald von Kleist, linked up

## ARMY GROUP NORTH: PANZER STRENGTH, SEPTEMBER 1939

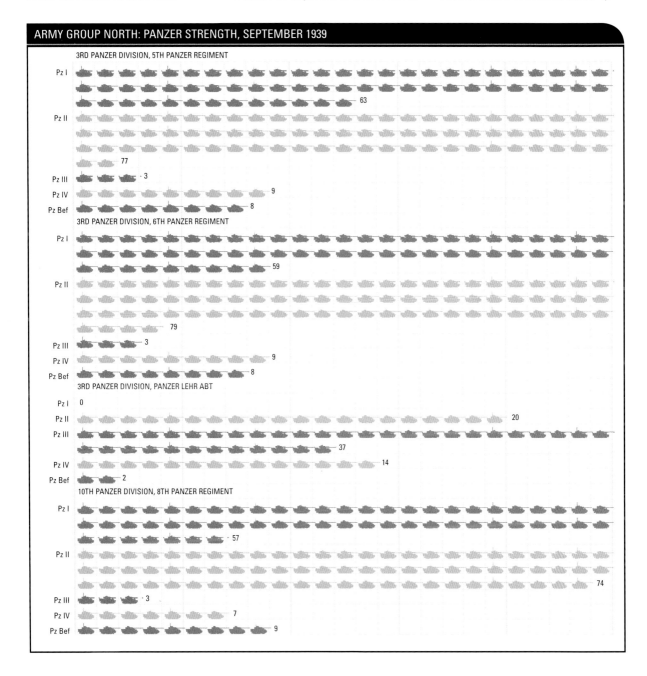

## ARMY GROUP SOUTH: PANZER STRENGTH, SEPTEMBER 1939 (1)

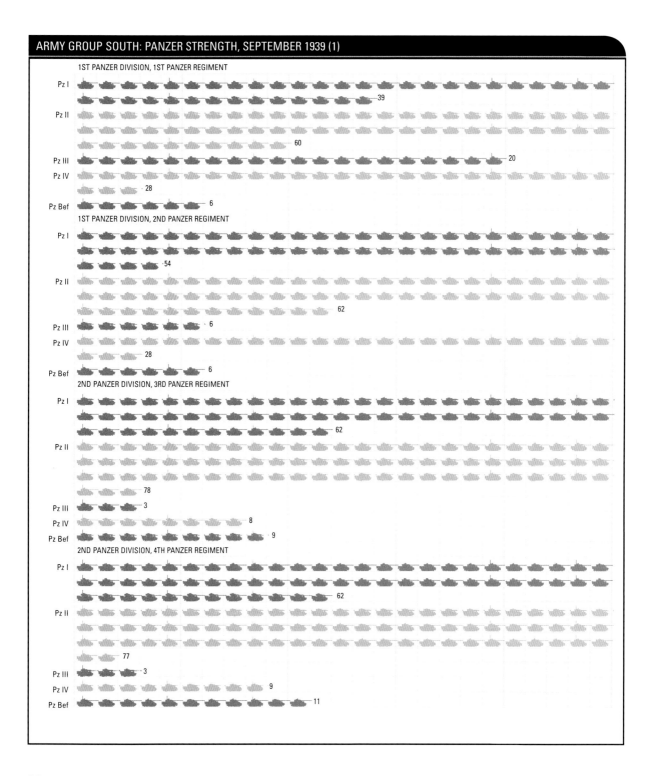

**1ST PANZER DIVISION, 1ST PANZER REGIMENT**

Pz I — 39

Pz II — 60

Pz III — 20

Pz IV — 28

Pz Bef — 6

**1ST PANZER DIVISION, 2ND PANZER REGIMENT**

Pz I — 54

Pz II — 62

Pz III — 6

Pz IV — 28

Pz Bef — 6

**2ND PANZER DIVISION, 3RD PANZER REGIMENT**

Pz I — 62

Pz II — 78

Pz III — 3

Pz IV — 8

Pz Bef — 9

**2ND PANZER DIVISION, 4TH PANZER REGIMENT**

Pz I — 62

Pz II — 77

Pz III — 3

Pz IV — 9

Pz Bef — 11

## ARMY GROUP SOUTH: PANZER STRENGTH, SEPTEMBER 1939 (2)

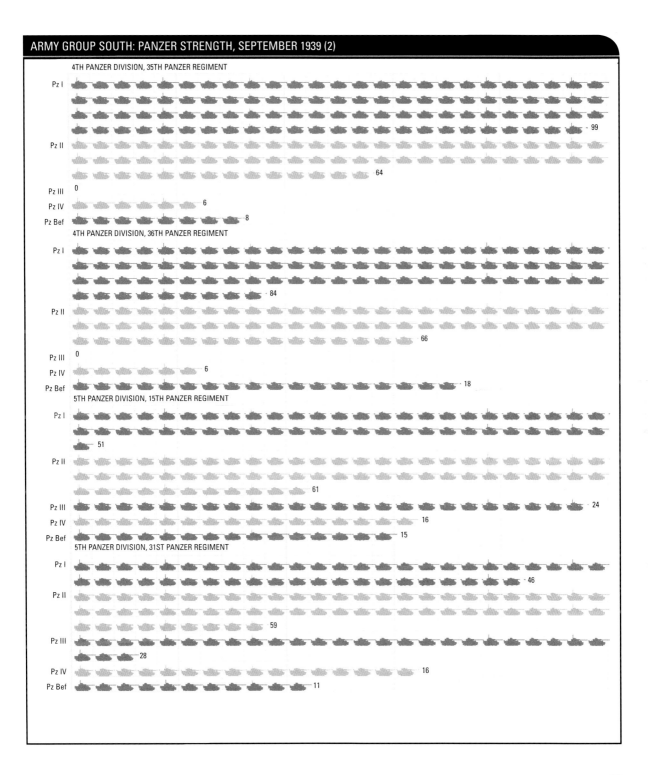

4TH PANZER DIVISION, 35TH PANZER REGIMENT

Pz I — 99

Pz II — 64

Pz III — 0

Pz IV — 6

Pz Bef — 8

4TH PANZER DIVISION, 36TH PANZER REGIMENT

Pz I — 84

Pz II — 66

Pz III — 0

Pz IV — 6

Pz Bef — 18

5TH PANZER DIVISION, 15TH PANZER REGIMENT

Pz I — 51

Pz II — 61

Pz III — 24

Pz IV — 16

Pz Bef — 15

5TH PANZER DIVISION, 31ST PANZER REGIMENT

Pz I — 46

Pz II — 59

Pz III — 28

Pz IV — 16

Pz Bef — 11

## INVASION OF POLAND

**Invasion of Poland**
**1–28 September 1939**

→ German advance
→ Russian advance
⇢ Polish retreat
⊣ German field work
〜 Polish defensive lines
— Polish positions
— German–Russian demarcation line

■ **1–28 SEPTEMBER 1939**
The invasion of Poland saw five German armies, amassing a total of some 60 divisions, cross the border on 1 September 1939. The panzer divisions of the newly-created *Panzerwaffe*, supported by light armoured divisions and motorized infantry divisions, formed the spearhead of the German drive on Warsaw, reaching the outskirts of the city within a week.

The campaign was not a true *Blitzkrieg* operation as envisaged by Guderian and others; rather, it was a massive double pincer movement, the inner pincer designed to close on the Vistula River, while the outer pincer, comprising faster-moving forces, was targeted on the Bug River. Poland's fate was sealed when the Soviets invaded from the east on 17 September 1939.

with Guderian east of Warsaw in mid-September, and the victory was complete. Although most of the panzer formations had been underequipped at the time of the invasion of Poland, their performance validated the concept of *Blitzkrieg*, even though the tanks had not operated with the complete independence that Guderian had envisioned. Rather than advancing totally unimpeded, they had been assigned at corps level to the command structures of two field army groups composed primarily of infantry.

**Reorganization**
During the seven months between the victory in Poland and the assault on France and the Low Countries, the *Feldheer* panzer force was reorganized. In addition to the six panzer divisions which had taken part in the Polish campaigns, the 1st to the 5th and the 10th, which was only part-formed at the time, four of the light divisions were augmented to constitute the 6th to the 9th Panzer Divisions. Meanwhile the 10th Panzer Division was topped up and an additional motorized infantry regiment joined the 4th Panzer Division.

# Armoured Operations: May 1940–July 1943

*Before dawn on 10 May 1940, more than 2000 German tanks, comprising 10 panzer divisions, launched 'Case Yellow' and stormed westward against France, Belgium, the Netherlands and Luxembourg.*

As he had done in Poland, Heinz Guderian led the XIX Panzer Corps, consisting of the 1st, 2nd and 10th Panzer Divisions and the Motorized Infantry Regiment *Grossdeutschland*, which roared through the Ardennes Forest, crossed the river Meuse at Sedan, and were slowed only briefly by French counter-attacks which were brushed aside.

In fact, Hitler's concern for the open flanks of the widening panzer corridor did more to slow Guderian's advance than the French forces which opposed him. Regardless, by 20 May the 2nd Panzer Division had reached the English Channel at Abbeville and captured Boulogne and Calais. In less than two weeks, Guderian had advanced further than the German Army had in four years of fighting during World War I. In seven days of fighting, the panzer spearheads of the *Feldheer* covered a distance of 257km (160 miles) and reached the Channel coast.

**Crossing the Meuse**
North of Guderian, the 7th Panzer Division under General Erwin Rommel crossed the river Meuse at Dinant on 13 May and reached the vicinity of Abbeville during the first week of June. Along the way, 7th Panzer earned the nickname of the 'Ghost Division' for its rapid movement, sometimes covering distances of up to 48km (30 miles) in a 24-hour period. Rommel also personally commanded German troops in the repulse of a strong Allied counter-attack at Arras. During the battle, he ordered that 88mm (3.5in) anti-aircraft guns be depressed to fire at oncoming British tanks with

## PANZER *ABTEILUNG*, 25TH PANZER REGIMENT, MAY 1940

*The panzer regiment in 1940 was very little changed from the panzer regiment of 1939. Although production of medium tanks was being stepped up, there were still too few Panzer IIIs and IVs in service to replace the lightweight Panzer Is and IIs that still served in large numbers. However, large numbers of Czech-built Panzer 35(t) and Panzer 38(t) tanks were being deployed, especially in the new panzer divisions formed after the end of the Polish campaign.*

**Abteilung Stab Kompanie**

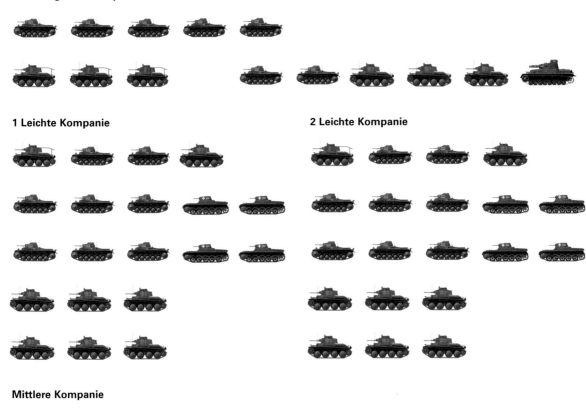

**1 Leichte Kompanie**

**2 Leichte Kompanie**

**Mittlere Kompanie**

| GERMAN FIELDED TANK STRENGTH, 10 MAY 1940 | | | | | | | | |
|---|---|---|---|---|---|---|---|---|
| Unit | Pz I | Pz II | Pz III | LTM 35 | LTM 38 | Pz IV | Bef Pz | Total |
| 1. Panzer Division | 52 | 98 | 58 | – | – | 40 | 8 | 256 |
| 2. Panzer Division | 45 | 115 | 58 | – | – | 32 | 16 | 266 |
| 3. Panzer Division | 117 | 129 | 42 | – | – | 26 | 27 | 341 |
| 4. Panzer Division | 135 | 105 | 40 | – | – | 24 | 10 | 314 |
| 5. Panzer Division | 97 | 120 | 52 | – | – | 30 | 16 | 315 |
| 6. Panzer Division | – | 60 | – | 118 | – | 31 | 14 | 223 |
| 7. Panzer Division | 34 | 68 | – | – | 91 | 24 | 8 | 225 |
| 8. Panzer Division | – | 58 | – | – | 116 | 23 | 15 | 212 |
| 9. Panzer Division | 30 | 54 | 41 | – | – | 16 | 12 | 153 |
| 10. Panzer Division | 44 | 113 | 58 | – | – | 32 | 18 | 265 |
| 40. Panzer-Abteilung | 29 | 18 | – | – | – | 3 | 4 | 54 |
| Total tanks | 583 | 938 | 349 | 118 | 207 | 281 | 148 | 2624 |
| Total available | 1077 | 1092 | 381 | 143 | 238 | 290 | 244 | 3465 |

devastating effect. Rommel went on to command German forces in North Africa and earn the nickname of the 'Desert Fox'.

At the end of May, thousands of Allied troops were trapped in a great pocket around the French port city of Dunkirk. The panzers were poised for the final victory. However, Hitler ordered the armoured spearheads to halt and allowed the *Luftwaffe* to bomb and strafe the Allied soldiers during a massive evacuation effort which has been called the 'Miracle of Dunkirk'. More than 300,000 Allied troops were evacuated to safety in England. It was one of Hitler's greatest military blunders, and many of the soldiers who were rescued in 1940 fought the Third Reich later.

### An ill wind in the East

By the autumn of 1940, the number of panzer divisions had been doubled in preparation for Operation 'Barbarossa', the invasion of the Soviet Union. Interestingly, the number of tanks did not increase;

divisional strength was effectively cut in half in the standard table of organization and equipment. Thus, the number of tanks in a standard panzer division of the *Feldheer* was reduced to between 150 and 200. This change had been brought about in order to provide more flexibility of movement as over 4000 tanks were allocated for deployment to the Eastern Front.

More than 160 German divisions attacked the Soviet Union on a 1600km (1000-mile) front on 22 June 1941. Army Group Centre, the strongest of three massive *Feldheer* army groups poised to attack

eastward, included the XXXIX and LVII Panzer Corps. The XXXIX fielded four divisions, the 7th and 20th Panzer and the 14th and 20th Motorized, while the LVII included the 12th, 18th and 19th Panzer Divisions. Three divisions, the 7th and 19th Panzer and 20th Motorized, began Operation 'Barbarossa' with a combat strength of 783 tanks.

### Heavy losses

Seven weeks into the campaign, they were down to 320 operational tanks with 267 lost and 196 in various stages of repair. At the same time, total operational *Feldheer* armoured

| PANZER GROUP 3 STRENGTH, JUNE 1941 | | | | | |
|---|---|---|---|---|---|
| Unit | Pz II | Pz 38(t) | Pz IV | Pz Bef 38(t) | Pz Bef |
| 7th Pz Div, 25th Pz Rgt | 53 | 167 | 30 | 7 | 8 |
| Unit | Pz I | Pz II | Pz 38(t) | Pz IV | Pz Bef 38(t) |
| 12th Pz Div, 29th Pz Rgt | 40 | 33 | 109 | 30 | 8 |
| 19th Pz Div, 27th Pz Rgt | 42 | 35 | 110 | 30 | 11 |
| 20th Pz Div, 21st Pz Rgt | 44 | 31 | 121 | 31 | 2 |

## ARMY GROUP SOUTH STRENGTH, JUNE 1941

| Unit | Pz I | Pz II | Pz III | Pz IV | Pz Bef |
|------|------|-------|--------|-------|--------|
| 9th Pz Div, 33rd Pz Rgt | 8 | 32 | 71 | 20 | 12 |
| 11th Pz Div, 15th Pz Rgt | 0 | 45 | 51 | 16 | 14 |
| 13th Pz Div, 4th Pz Rgt | 0 | 45 | 71 | 20 | 13 |
| 14th Pz Div, 36th Pz Rgt | 0 | 45 | 71 | 20 | 11 |
| 16th Pz Div, 2nd Pz Rgt | 0 | 45 | 70 | 20 | 9 |

## ARMY GROUP CENTRE STRENGTH, JUNE 1942

| Unit | Pz II | Pz III | Pz 38(t) | Pz IV | Pz Bef |
|------|-------|--------|----------|-------|--------|
| 1st Pz Div, 1st Pz Rgt | 2 | 26 | 10 | 10 | 4 |
| 5th Pz Div, 31st Pz Rgt | 26 | 55 | 0 | 13 | 9 |
| 17th Pz Div, 39th Pz Rgt | 17 | 36 | 0 | 16 | 2 |
| 18th Pz Div, 18th Pz Rgt | 11 | 26 | 0 | 8 | 2 |
| 19th Pz Div, 27th Pz Rgt | 6 | 12 | 35 | 4 | 0 |

strength on the Eastern Front had been reduced by 53 per cent, with a total loss rate of 30 per cent.

Although further offensive action would occur in the summer of 1942 and 1943, the failure to take Moscow in late 1941 and the harsh Russian winters which followed took their toll on German forces in the Soviet Union. The debacle at Stalingrad and the war of attrition on the Eastern Front eventually inflicted such heavy losses on the panzer formations that there was no hope of victory.

### Gully of death

In the summer of 1943, the German Army gathered itself for a decisive offensive against the Kursk Salient, 451km (280 miles) from Moscow. Six months after the Sixth Army had been destroyed at Stalingrad, the *Heer* and *Waffen-SS* massed 781,000 soldiers in 54 divisions, 20 of them panzer and panzergrenadier divisions, to

surround and annihilate Red Army forces in the salient which bulged deep into the German front line.

Nearly 3000 German tanks, many of them PzKpfw V Panthers and PzKpfw VI Tigers fresh from the factories of the Fatherland, would battle 5100 Soviet tanks and nearly two million soldiers of the Red Army in a series of clashes which constitute one of the largest battles in history and by far the largest contest of armoured forces. The fighting commenced on 5 July 1943, and lasted for more than six weeks.

The most prominent single action around Kursk was the Battle of Prokhorovka, during which Soviet armour prevented a German breach of the main Red Army defensive lines at tremendous cost. Although the battle was a Soviet victory, estimates of Red Army tank losses vary widely from 200 to nearly 900. In any case, the losses were tremendous. German estimates of their own tanks destroyed in battle have been as low as 60, while the Soviets have asserted that they destroyed more than 400 enemy tanks. Regardless, the losses sustained by German forces could not be easily replaced, while Soviet industry turned out replacement vehicles at an astonishing pace.

### Tank battle

Attached to Colonel-General Hermann Hoth's Fourth Panzer Army, the Panzergrenadier Division *Grossdeutschland* attacked the southern shoulder of the Kursk Salient and later blunted Soviet counter-attacks in conjunction with the efforts of three SS panzergrenadier divisions, the 1st LSSAH, 2nd *Das Reich* and 3rd *Totenkopf*. More than 800 Soviet tanks, roughly two-thirds of over 1100 committed, were destroyed, while

## III PANZER CORPS STRENGTH, JUNE 1943

| Unit | Pz II | Pz III | Pz IV | Pz Bef | Flmmpz |
|------|-------|--------|-------|--------|--------|
| 6th Pz Div, 11th Pz Rgt | 13 | 52 | 32 | 6 | 14 |

| Unit | Pz II | Pz III (50) | Pz III (75) | Pz IV | Pz Bef |
|------|-------|-------------|-------------|-------|--------|
| 7th Pz Div, 25th Pz Rgt | 12 | 43 | 12 | 38 | 5 |
| 19th Pz Div, 27th Pz Rgt | 2 | 27 | 11 | 38 | 14 |

two Soviet armies and a pair of tank corps were shattered in the south. The *Grossdeutschland* Division had begun Operation 'Citadel', as the Kursk offensive was codenamed, with 118 tanks. Just five days into the fighting, only three Tigers, six Panthers and 11 PzKpfw III and IV tanks were operating, although some of those lost were later repaired and returned to service.

■ **A company of Tigers from one of the newly-formed Tiger battalions awaits orders to move forward during the Kursk offensive, July 1943. The Tigers tended to lead the attack, forming the front end of a wedge that would also include Panzer IIIs and IVs. The frontal armour of the Tiger was virtually impenetrable for Soviet tank guns unless at point-blank range.**

## PANZER LOSSES, ARMY GROUP CENTRE, JULY 1943

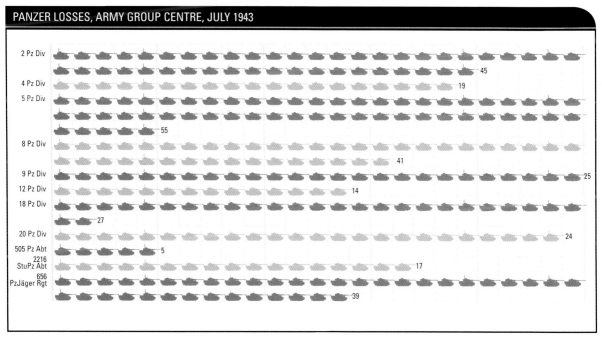

2 Pz Div — 45
4 Pz Div — 19
5 Pz Div
8 Pz Div — 55
9 Pz Div — 41
12 Pz Div — 25
18 Pz Div — 14
20 Pz Div — 27
505 Pz Abt — 24
2216 StuPz Abt — 5
656 PzJäger Rgt — 17, 39

## KURSK: OPERATION 'CITADEL'

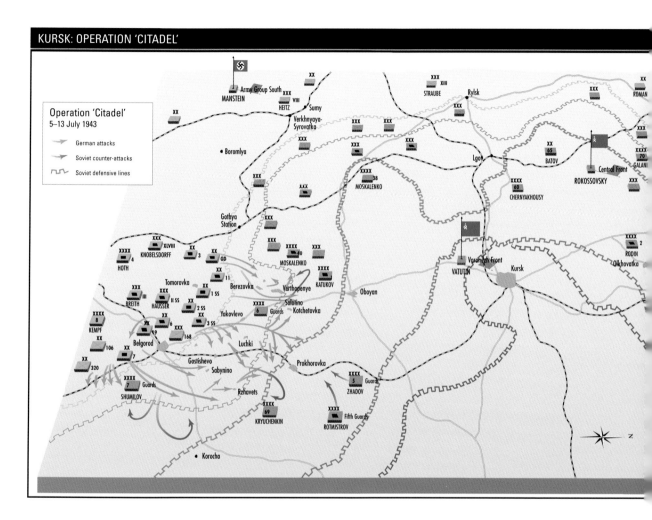

Operation 'Citadel'
5–13 July 1943

→ German attacks
→ Soviet counter-attacks
〜 Soviet defensive lines

## PANZER LOSSES, ARMY GROUP CENTRE, JULY 1943

| Unit | Pz III | Pz IV | Pz VI | StuG | StuPz IV | Ferdinand | Pz Bef | Total |
|------|--------|-------|-------|------|----------|-----------|--------|-------|
| 2nd Panzer Division | 13 | 29 | – | – | – | – | 3 | 45 |
| 4th Panzer Division | 3 | 15 | – | – | – | – | 1 | 19 |
| 5th Panzer Division | 11 | 43 | – | – | – | – | 1 | 55 |
| 8th Panzer Division | 14 | 24 | – | – | – | – | 3 | 41 |
| 9th Panzer Division | 7 | 18 | – | – | – | – | – | 25 |
| 12th Panzer Division | – | 13 | – | – | – | – | 1 | 14 |
| 18th Panzer Division | 14 | 12 | – | – | – | – | 1 | 27 |
| 20th Panzer Division | 3 | 20 | – | – | – | – | 1 | 24 |
| 505th Panzer Abteilung | – | – | 5 | – | – | – | | 5 |
| 2216th StuPz Abteilung | – | – | – | – | 17 | – | | 17 |
| 656th PzJäger Regiment | – | – | – | – | – | 39 | | 39 |

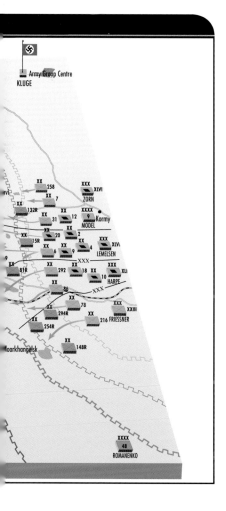

Army Group Centre
KLUGE

**■ KURSK OFFENSIVE**

The German attacks on both sides of the salient were crippled by the lack of good infantry formations to support the panzers. Even during the spectacular victories of 1941–42, the German infantry had sustained huge casualties – as early as May 1942, almost all units in the Soviet Union were understrength, reporting a total shortage of 635,000 men.

By mid-1943, the situation had worsened, forcing the use of panzer and panzergrenadier units in roles that should have been carried out by infantry. (The problem had even more widespread effects because the *Luftwaffe* was frequently called upon to provide emergency assistance for the hard-pressed infantry instead of attacking key targets behind the Soviet front line.)

During the Kursk offensive, German commanders were repeatedly forced to divert armoured units to support weak infantry formations. The effect of this was most serious in the southern sector, where it may have been instrumental in preventing a decisive breakthrough by Fourth Panzer Army.

At the same time, the XLVIII Panzer Corps was down to only 38 Panthers of its original complement of 200 by 10 July. A significant number of these were undergoing repairs due to mechanical difficulties.

Estimates of German losses during Operation 'Citadel' top 54,000 casualties, including more than 9000 killed. More than 250 German tanks and self-propelled guns were lost in roughly two weeks, with Army Group South sustaining at least 170 of these during the opening week of the fighting. The Soviets suffered nearly 178,000 casualties during the same period along with about 2600 tanks and armoured vehicles, approximately 50 per cent of the total number committed. Following Operation 'Citadel' and the subsequent Soviet counteroffensive, the armoured strength of the *Feldheer* on the Eastern Front never recovered. From mid-1943 until the end of the war, the German armed forces were compelled to fight on the defensive.

# Panzer Formations

*During World War II, the* Feldheer *formed at least 30 numbered panzer divisions along with a number of others which were named in honour of individuals or the areas in which they were raised, trained or served.*

In addition, 15 independent panzer brigades, seven reserve divisions, five light divisions, and 40 motorized or panzergrenadier divisions were formed. The composition of these formations varied greatly due to the availability of troops and equipment, the exigencies of war, and the transition from offensive to defensive operations.

Although the composition of the *Feldheer* panzer division evolved

## NUMBERED PANZER DIVISIONS, 1939–45

- 1st Panzer Division
- 2nd Panzer Division
- 3rd Panzer Division
- 4th Panzer Division
- 5th Panzer Division
- 6th Panzer Division (previously 1st Light Division)
- 7th Panzer Division (previously 2nd Light Division)
- 8th Panzer Division (previously 3rd Light Division)
- 9th Panzer Division (previously 4th Light Division)
- 10th Panzer Division
- 11th Panzer Division
- 12th Panzer Division (previously 2nd Motorized Infantry Division)
- 13th Panzer Division (previously 13th Infantry Division, 13th Motorized Infantry Division; later Panzer Division Feldherrnhalle 2)
- 14th Panzer Division (previously 4th Infantry Division)
- 15th Panzer Division (previously 33rd Infantry Division; later 15th Panzergrenadier Division)
- 16th Panzer Division (previously 16th Infantry Division)
- 17th Panzer Division (previously 27th Infantry Division)
- 18th Panzer Division (later 18th Artillery Division)
- 19th Panzer Division (previously 19th Infantry Division)
- 20th Panzer Division
- 21st Panzer Division (previously 5th Light Division)
- 22nd Panzer Division
- 23rd Panzer Division
- 24th Panzer Division (previously 1st Cavalry Division)
- 25th Panzer Division
- 26th Panzer Division (formerly 23rd Infantry Division)
- 27th Panzer Division
- 116th Panzer Division Windhund (previously 16th Infantry Division, 16th Motorized Infantry Division, and 16th Panzergrenadier Division)
- 155th Reserve Panzer Division (previously Division Nr. 155, Division Nr. 155 (mot.), Panzer Division Nr. 155)
- Panzer Division Nr. 178 (previously Division Nr. 178)
- 179th Reserve Panzer Division (previously Division Nr. 179, Division Nr. 179 (mot.), and Panzer Division Nr. 179)
- 232nd Panzer Division (previously Panzer Division Tatra, Panzer Training Division Tatra)
- 233rd Reserve Panzer Division (previously Division Nr. 233 (mot.), Panzergrenadier Division Nr. 233, and Panzer Division Nr. 233; later Panzer Division Clausewitz)
- 273rd Reserve Panzer Division

## NAMED PANZER DIVISIONS, 1939–45

- Panzer Division Clausewitz (previously Division Nr. 233 (mot.), Panzergrenadier Division Nr. 233, and Panzer Division Nr. 233, 233rd Reserve Panzer Division)
- Döberitz, Schlesien, and Holstein are approximately synonymous with Clausewitz.
- Panzer Division Feldherrnhalle 1 (previously 60th Infantry Division, 60th Motorized Infantry Division, and Panzergrenadier Division Feldherrnhalle)
- Panzer Division Feldherrnhalle 2 (previously 13th Infantry Division, 13th Motorized Infantry Division, and 13th Panzer Division)
- Panzer Division Jüterbog
- Panzer Division Kempf (part *Heer*, part *Waffen-SS*)
- Panzer Division Kurmark
- Panzer-Lehr-Division (sometimes identified as 130th Panzer-Lehr Division)
- Panzer Division Müncheberg
- Panzer Division Tatra (later Panzer Training Division Tatra, 232nd Panzer Division)

throughout the war, its standard troop complement was about 14,000 soldiers. The 1940 divisional order of battle was altered further in the spring of 1942 with the organic rifle, or *schützen*, regiments redesignated as panzergrenadier regiments and the number of companies within each battalion reduced from five to four.

| PANZER REGIMENTS, 1939–45 | | |
|---|---|---|
| 1.Panzer-Regiment | 22.Panzer-Regiment | 102.Panzer-Regiment |
| 2.Panzer-Regiment | 23.Panzer-Regiment | 116.Panzer-Regiment |
| 3.Panzer-Regiment | 24.Panzer-Regiment | 117.Panzer-Regiment |
| 4.Panzer-Regiment | 25.Panzer-Regiment | 130.Panzer-Regiment |
| 5.Panzer-Regiment | 26.Panzer-Regiment | 201.Panzer-Regiment |
| 6.Panzer-Regiment | 27.Panzer-Regiment | 202.Panzer-Regiment |
| 7.Panzer-Regiment | 28.Panzer-Regiment | 203.Panzer-Regiment |
| 8.Panzer-Regiment | 29.Panzer-Regiment | 204.Panzer-Regiment |
| 9.Panzer-Regiment | 31.Panzer-Regiment | sch.Panzer-Regiment Bake |
| 10.Panzer-Regiment | 33.Panzer-Regiment | Panzer-Regiment Brandenburg |
| 11.Panzer-Regiment | 35.Panzer-Regiment | Panzer-Regiment Conze |
| 15.Panzer-Regiment | 36.Panzer-Regiment | Panzer-Regiment Feldherrnhalle 1 |
| 16.Panzer-Regiment | 39.Panzer-Regiment | Panzer-Regiment Feldherrnhalle 2 |
| 17.Panzer-Regiment | 69.Panzer-Regiment | Panzer-Regiment Grossdeutschland |
| 18.Panzer-Regiment | 100.Panzer-Regiment | Panzer-Regiment Kurmark |
| 21.Panzer-Regiment | 101.Panzer-Regiment | |

Machine-gun, flak and light-infantry-gun companies were added, and in early summer the *Heer* flak battalions which had been assigned to panzer divisions became collectively known as elements of the 4th Artillery Battalion for a brief period.

Through years of fighting, several panzer divisions were decimated or destroyed in combat, including the 10th, 14th, 15th, 16th, 21st, 24th and 27th. Only the 10th was not reconstituted, while the 15th was reincarnated as a panzergrenadier division. Although the composition of the panzer and panzergrenadier divisions changed regularly, the major revisions occurred in 1943 and 1944, particularly as those formations which had suffered heavy losses in men and equipment were withdrawn from combat, refitted and returned to service.

Some of these divisions were provided with a battalion of the PzKpfw V Panther medium tank, one of the finest fighting vehicles of its kind during World War II. However, these were in short supply and only one battalion was assigned to the common panzer division. Some of the Panthers and the bulk of the heavy PzKpfw VI Tiger and Tiger II (King Tiger) tanks were fielded by independent medium and heavy tank battalions of the *Waffen-SS* and the *Feldheer*.

On 24 September 1943, the reorganization of all panzer divisions, with the exception of the 21st and a single division in Norway, was ordered. In the Type 1943 panzer division the three panzergrenadier battalions were re-formed, each with three rifle companies, while each rifle company included 18 light and four

heavy machine guns. Within each battalion, the fourth company serviced heavy weapons, including three anti-tank guns, four machine guns, and four 81mm (3.2in) mortars. The infantry support gun company included six self-propelled assault guns, while the light flak company fielded a complement of a dozen 20mm (0.79in) self-propelled anti-aircraft guns.

The Type 1943 panzer division's infantry complement included only one motorized battalion which was transported in armoured halftracks, usually the Hanomag SdKfz 251, while the remainder travelled in trucks. These battalions consisted of three rifle companies with two 75mm (2.95in) guns, three 37mm (1.45in) anti-tank guns, 39 light machine guns and four heavy machine guns. A heavy weapons company fielded

## PANZER DIVISION ORGANIZATION, 1944

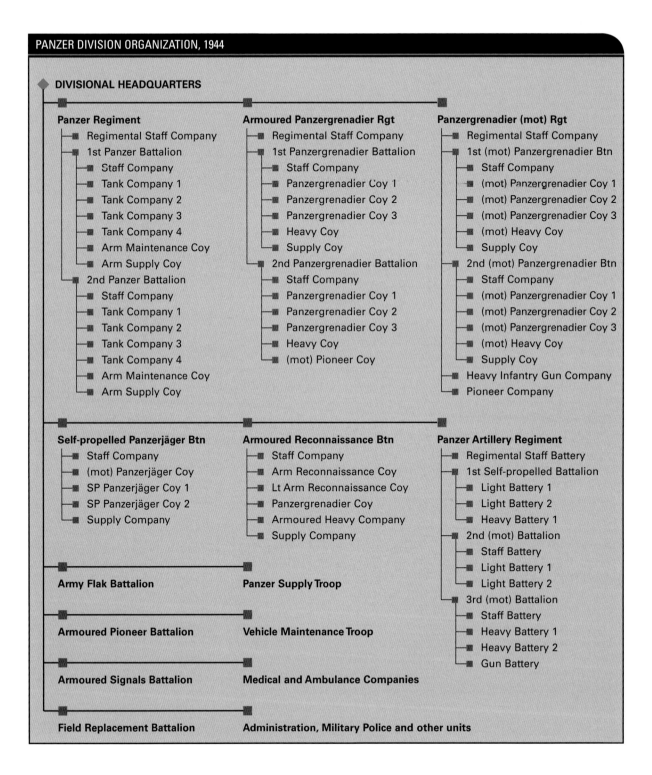

◆ **DIVISIONAL HEADQUARTERS**

**Panzer Regiment**
- Regimental Staff Company
- 1st Panzer Battalion
  - Staff Company
  - Tank Company 1
  - Tank Company 2
  - Tank Company 3
  - Tank Company 4
  - Arm Maintenance Coy
  - Arm Supply Coy
- 2nd Panzer Battalion
  - Staff Company
  - Tank Company 1
  - Tank Company 2
  - Tank Company 3
  - Tank Company 4
  - Arm Maintenance Coy
  - Arm Supply Coy

**Armoured Panzergrenadier Rgt**
- Regimental Staff Company
- 1st Panzergrenadier Battalion
  - Staff Company
  - Panzergrenadier Coy 1
  - Panzergrenadier Coy 2
  - Panzergrenadier Coy 3
  - Heavy Coy
  - Supply Coy
- 2nd Panzergrenadier Battalion
  - Staff Company
  - Panzergrenadier Coy 1
  - Panzergrenadier Coy 2
  - Panzergrenadier Coy 3
  - Heavy Coy
  - (mot) Pioneer Coy

**Panzergrenadier (mot) Rgt**
- Regimental Staff Company
- 1st (mot) Panzergrenadier Btn
  - Staff Company
  - (mot) Panzergrenadier Coy 1
  - (mot) Panzergrenadier Coy 2
  - (mot) Panzergrenadier Coy 3
  - (mot) Heavy Coy
  - Supply Coy
- 2nd (mot) Panzergrenadier Btn
  - Staff Company
  - (mot) Panzergrenadier Coy 1
  - (mot) Panzergrenadier Coy 2
  - (mot) Panzergrenadier Coy 3
  - (mot) Heavy Coy
  - Supply Coy
- Heavy Infantry Gun Company
- Pioneer Company

**Self-propelled Panzerjäger Btn**
- Staff Company
- (mot) Panzerjäger Coy
- SP Panzerjäger Coy 1
- SP Panzerjäger Coy 2
- Supply Company

**Armoured Reconnaissance Btn**
- Staff Company
- Arm Reconnaissance Coy
- Lt Arm Reconnaissance Coy
- Panzergrenadier Coy
- Armoured Heavy Company
- Supply Company

**Panzer Artillery Regiment**
- Regimental Staff Battery
- 1st Self-propelled Battalion
  - Light Battery 1
  - Light Battery 2
  - Heavy Battery 1
- 2nd (mot) Battalion
  - Staff Battery
  - Light Battery 1
  - Light Battery 2
- 3rd (mot) Battalion
  - Staff Battery
  - Heavy Battery 1
  - Heavy Battery 2
  - Gun Battery

**Army Flak Battalion**

**Panzer Supply Troop**

**Armoured Pioneer Battalion**

**Vehicle Maintenance Troop**

**Armoured Signals Battalion**

**Medical and Ambulance Companies**

**Field Replacement Battalion**

**Administration, Military Police and other units**

three 75mm (2.95in) PAK howitzers, two short-barrelled 75mm (2.95in) leIG infantry support guns, and six 75mm (2.95in) field guns. Later, an engineer platoon with six flamethrowers, a 37mm (1.45in) PAK 36 anti-tank gun, and 13 light machine guns was added for a short time.

## 1944 Establishment

Effective 1 August 1944, the panzer division order of battle was changed once again to include a panzer or self-propelled assault gun regiment with a complement of at least 48 armoured fighting vehicles, two panzergrenadier regiments, an armoured artillery regiment, flak, signals, reconnaissance, anti-tank and engineer battalions, and a service section which included supply, administrative, medical, maintenance, military police and postal personnel. The total equipment complement of the Type 1944 panzer division included an additional 136 armoured vehicles such as halftracks and armoured cars, nearly 2400 other motor vehicles, 469 motorcycles, more than 1000 light machine guns, 82 heavy machine guns, 52 81mm (3.2in) mortars, 24 120mm (4.7in) mortars, 54 field guns or howitzers of either 105mm (4.1in) or 150mm (5.9in) calibre, eight 88mm (3.5in) multipurpose guns, 74 75mm (2.95in) anti-tank guns, 38 20mm (0.79in) anti-tank guns, three 20mm (0.79in) quad flak guns, 63 20mm (0.79in) flak guns, and 26 flamethrowers.

The Type 1945 panzer division eliminated the distinction between the panzer and panzergrenadier divisions entirely. German industrial capacity had been stretched to its limit, and due to shortages of transportation and fuel many of the panzergrenadier formations were simply functioning as infantry.

At various times during World War II, new panzer divisions and brigades were formed while others were merged or disbanded. In 1941, the 21st Panzer Division was formed in North Africa, while the 22nd, 23rd, and 24th were constituted from conscripts in Germany. After both were shattered in the fighting in the Ukraine in 1943 and 1944, the 18th Panzer Division was disbanded and the 25th was reconstituted. Three reserve panzer divisions were formed in 1944, as was the elite *Panzer-Lehr-Division*. A dozen panzer brigades were formed in 1944 along similar lines to the Type 1945 panzer division and represented the melding of panzer and panzergrenadier formations into units which were actually of regimental strength. These brigades fielded a battalion of tanks and a battalion of panzergrenadiers in halftracks.

Also in 1944, three panzer corps were formed by combining panzer divisions and panzergrenadiers. The XXIV Panzer Corps included the 16th and 17th Panzer Divisions, the *Feldherrnhalle* Panzer Corps included the 1st and 2nd *Feldherrnhalle* Panzer Divisions, and the *Grossdeutschland* and *Brandenburg* Panzergrenadier Divisions combined to form the *Grossdeutschland* Panzer Corps.

# Panzergrenadier and Light Divisions

*The panzergrenadier divisions began their service lives as the motorized infantry or 'fast troops' of the* Heer. *Established officially in 1938, they included riflemen, motorized riflemen and even some personnel designated as motorized cavalrymen.*

By the summer of 1942, these soldiers were reclassified as armoured troops, and in 1943 their final designation as panzergrenadiers was adopted. Although they were theoretically considered armoured infantry, the majority of the panzergrenadiers were transported by trucks or marched on foot throughout the war. Often, only a single brigade was equipped with halftracks.

While personnel strength generally matched that of the panzer divisions with approximately 14,000 troops, the configuration of the panzergrenadier divisions was subject to change throughout World War II. At the outbreak of the war, only four *Heer* divisions were designated motorized. By the autumn of 1940, seven more had been organized. In September 1943, the panzergrenadier regiments of the *Heer* included three battalions with an artillery company of six 75mm (2.95in) and two 150mm (5.9in) infantry guns, a light flak company with a dozen 20mm (0.79in) self-propelled guns, and a pioneer company with 16 flamethrowers.

Three panzergrenadier divisions (at the time designated as motorized infantry divisions) were destroyed at Stalingrad. The 60th began to refit and rearm in the summer of 1943 but was later utilized as the basis of the *Feldherrnhalle* Panzergrenadier Division. The 3rd and 29th Divisions were reconstituted in France. During the course of the war, the typical panzergrenadier division included two regiments of infantry and their supporting units along with a battalion of tanks or self-propelled assault guns.

## Light divisions

The six light divisions of the *Heer* existed only during the transitional period from 1939 to 1940 as older cavalry units were absorbed into the modern armoured divisions of the German Army. The light divisions could be characterized as 'politically correct' in that they satisfied the desire of those old line officers who revered the cavalry as the elite of the *Heer*. Although they served their purpose, the light divisions were short-lived and became the nuclei of panzer divisions shortly after the Polish campaign. On 1 September 1939, the 1st Light Division included

the 4th Motorized Cavalry Regiment, a battalion of the 6th Reconnaissance Regiment, the 6th Motorcycle Battalion, 65th Panzer Battalion, 11th Panzer Regiment, 76th Artillery Regiment, 41st Anti-tank Battalion, 76th *Luftwaffe* Light Flak Battalion, 57th Pioneer Battalion, 82nd Signals Battalion, 57th Divisional Service Units, and administrative formations. Its complement of tanks totalled 65 PzKpfw II, 41 PzKpfw IV and 119 of the Czech-built Panzer 35(t) and Panzer 38(t) concentrated in the 1st and 2nd Battalions of the 11th Panzer Regiment and the 65th Panzer Battalion. Its personnel complement was nearly 10,000. A month after the conclusion of the Polish campaign, the 1st Light Division was absorbed into the 6th Panzer Division.

These early light divisions are not to be confused with the 90th Light Africa Division or the 5th Light Mechanized Division, which fought with distinction as part of General Erwin Rommel's *Afrika Korps*. A month after its arrival in North Africa, the 5th Light Mechanized Division

was composed of elements of the 3rd Panzer Division, two machine gun battalions, and other troops sent to aid the foundering Italian forces which had been roughly handled by the British in the early months of the desert war.

In March 1941, the 5th included its divisional headquarters, the 5th Panzer Regiment, 1st and 2nd

---

**LIGHT DIVISIONS, 1939–45**

- 1st Light Division (later 6th Panzer Division)
- 2nd Light Division (later 7th Panzer Division)
- 3rd Light Division (later 8th Panzer Division)
- 4th Light Division (later 9th Panzer Division)
- 5th Light Afrika Division (later 21st Panzer Division)

---

**ARMOURED INFANTRY BATTALION, JULY 1943**

| Unit | Equip | Total |
|---|---|---|
| Battalion HQ | Motorcycle | 3 |
| | Kettenrad | 2 |
| | Kubelwagen | 3 |
| | SdKfz 251/3 | 4 |
| | SdKfz 251/8 | 2 |
| | SdKfz 251/11 | 2 |
| Heavy Company | | |
| HQ | Motorcycle | 2 |
| | Kettenrad | 2 |
| | SdKfz 251/3 | 2 |
| | SdKfz 11 | 2 |
| Light Inf Gun Ptn | SdKfz 251/4 | 2 |
| | 75mm leIG (towed) | 2 |
| Infantry Gun Ptn | SdKfz 251/3 | 1 |
| | SdKfz 251/1 | 1 |
| | SdKfz 251/9 | 6 |
| Panzerjäger Ptn 1 | SdKfz 251/1 | 1 |
| | SdKfz 251/4 | 4 |
| | 75mm PAK 40 (towed) | 3 |
| Panzerjäger Ptn 2 | SdKfz 251/1 | 1 |
| | SdKfz 251/4/2.8cm sPzB41 | 3 |
| Company (x3) | | |
| HQ | Motorcycle | 2 |
| | Kubelwagen | 1 |
| | Kettenrad | 3 |
| | SdKfz 251/3 | 2 |
| Infantry Ptn (x3) | SdKfz 250/10 | 1 |
| | SdKfz 251/1 | 3 |
| Heavy Ptn | SdKfz 250/10 | 1 |
| HMG Scn | SdKfz 251/1 | 3 |
| Mortar Scn | SdKfz 251/2/80mm mortar | 2 |

Armoured Battalions, the headquarters of the 200th Infantry Regiment, the 2nd and 8th Motorized Machine Gun Battalions, 39th Motorized Anti-Tank Battalion, 3rd Armoured Reconnaissance Battalion, the 1st Battalion of the 75th Motorized Artillery Regiment, 605th Heavy Anti-Tank Battalion, 606th Light Anti-aircraft Battalion, and the 1st Motorized Battalion of the *Luftwaffe* 33rd Flak Regiment. Its armour consisted of 25 PzKpfw I, 45 PzKpfw II, 75 PzKpfw III and 20 PzKpfw IV tanks. In October 1941, the combat strength of the 5th was augmented to form the 21st Panzer Division.

The 90th Light Division was originally formed in August 1941 as *Afrika Division z.b.V.* (Africa Division for special purposes). The division was involved in heavy fighting at Tobruk in November of that year and reorganized at least three times during the war in North Africa. It was lost in Tunisia in the spring of 1943 with the surrender of the remnants of *Panzerarmee Afrika*.

In the spring of 1942, the 90th Light Division consisted of its headquarters complement, the 155th Motorized Infantry Regiment, the 1st Battalion of the 190th Motorized Artillery Regiment, 900th Motorized Pioneer Battalion, 580th Motorized Mixed Reconnaissance Company, 190th Motorized Anti-Tank Battalion, and the 2nd Company of the 190th Armoured Signal Battalion.

# Desert Discourse

*The harsh, unforgiving desert of North Africa provided ideal terrain for the war of rapid movement and armoured thrust which raised Rommel and the* Deutsches Afrika Korps *to mythical status, even in defeat.*

When the initial elements of the German military commitment on the continent arrived in Tripoli in mid-February 1941, their purpose was to reverse the deteriorating situation of the Italian forces, which had been mauled during a series of engagements with the British Western Desert Force. Although the Italians fought bravely, their equipment was inferior and their leadership often of questionable competence.

Axis forces in North Africa were never substantial enough to fully exploit the tactical victories achieved, much less gain control of the Mediterranean basin, sweep the British from Egypt, capture the Suez Canal and seize the vast oilfields of the Middle East. Rommel continually faced shortages in supplies, equipment and fuel as shipping was interdicted by air and naval attacks in the Mediterranean.

The *Deutsches Afrika Korps* was created on 19 February 1941, and by August included the 15th Panzer Division, 90th and 5th Light Divisions, and six Italian divisions, the *Savona*, *Brescia*, *Bologna*, *Pavia*, *Trieste* and *Ariete*. The German formations were then known as the *Afrika Korps*, while the entire command was officially known as *Panzerarmee Afrika*.

By early April, Rommel had launched an offensive and managed to besiege the port of Tobruk while forcing the British out of Libya to temporary safety in Egypt. During the ebb and flow of battle which ensued, the British relieved Tobruk but were again forced to retreat eastward by a renewed Axis offensive in the spring of 1942.

From the end of May until mid-July, the 15th and 21st Panzer Divisions reported destroying more than 1300 British tanks and armoured vehicles; however, these losses could be made good. In a costly war of attrition, Rommel was able to field only 36 operational *Afrika Korps* tanks during a temporary lull at the end of July. Those tanks, personnel and supplies which were received were precious, but the 'Desert Fox', as he came to be known, deployed them audaciously. At Alam Halfa in the first week of September 1942, one British armoured brigade lost 96 tanks in a day fighting the PzKpfw III and

| AXIS VERSUS ALLIED TANK STRENGTH, NORTH AFRICA | | | | | |
|---|---|---|---|---|---|
| | May 1941 Operation Battleaxe | Nov 1941 Operation Crusader | May 1942 Gazala | Oct 1942 El Alamein | Feb 1943 Kasserine |
| British | 200 | 700 | 849 | 1100 | – |
| American | – | – | – | – | 160 |
| Allied Total | 200 | 700 | 849 | 1100 | 160 |
| German | 170 | 249 | 332 | 210 | 150 |
| Italian | – | 150 | 228 | 280 | 20 |
| Axis Total | 170 | 399 | 560 (390 operational) | 490 | 170 |

PzKpfw IV tanks and anti-tank guns of 15th and 21st Panzer.

At Alam Halfa, Rommel commanded just over 500 tanks, about 230 of which were German but only 26 of these the powerful F2 variant of the PzKpfw IV, designated as 'Special' with its long-barrelled high velocity 75mm (2.95in) cannon. During the fighting, he lost more than 2200 dead and wounded, 49 tanks and 55 field and anti-tank guns, some of which were from his complement of 72 versatile 88mm (3.5in) guns.

By late summer, Axis forces were 97km (60 miles) from the great Egyptian port city of Alexandria. There, the British stopped Rommel's advance, their flanks anchored by the Mediterranean coast in the north and the impassable Qattara Depression in the south. The new commander of the British Eighth Army, General Bernard Law Montgomery, marshalled his forces for a decisive counter-attack.

### Decision at El Alamein

When Montgomery launched the counteroffensive against Rommel at El Alamein on 23 October 1942, his armoured force included 939 front-line tanks with more than 200 others

in various stages of repair, 892 artillery pieces and over 220,000 troops. Rommel had received welcome reinforcements of 18,000 troops, and his entire force totalled 108,000 men, about half of them German. Axis armoured strength amounted to just under 550 tanks with 249 of them German and about 1050 anti-tank guns.

On the eve of the Battle of El Alamein, Rommel commanded a combined Axis force designated as *Armeegruppe Afrika*, while General Wilhelm Ritter von Thoma nominally led *Panzerarmee Afrika* and General Georg Stumme, who died unexpectedly of a heart attack as the battle got underway, commanded the *Afrika Korps*. The entire army group consisted of the 15th and 21st Panzer Divisions, 90th and 164th Light Divisions, and the *Ramcke* Parachute Brigade, along with three Italian corps composed of two armoured divisions, two motorized infantry

divisions, three infantry divisions and a parachute division, plus two further independent Italian divisions.

The battle began with a tremendous British artillery barrage; however, little progress was made until sustained action had weakened the Axis forces substantially. The fighting at one geographic location known as 'Snipe' was indicative of the heavy losses sustained by Rommel. A battalion of British six-pounder (57mm/2.24in) anti-tank guns caught advancing German and Italian armour broadside and during several hours of fighting destroyed 33 tanks and five self-propelled guns with possibly another 20 German tanks damaged. At the same time, several British M4 Sherman tanks were destroyed. The fighting at 'Snipe' was

### ■ OPERATION 'SUPERCHARGE'
**Operation 'Supercharge' began on 2 November with an advance by more than 200 Allied armoured vehicles of the 1st Armoured Division toward Tel el Aqqaqir. The Allied 7th and 10th Armoured Divisions rapidly exploited the breakthrough. Sledgehammer attacks succeeded in clearing German positions between Kidney Ridge and the Mediterranean Sea.**

| TANK STRENGTH, EL ALAMEIN | |
|---|---|
| Unit | Strength |
| Panzerarmee Afrika | 548 |
| Eighth Army | 939 |

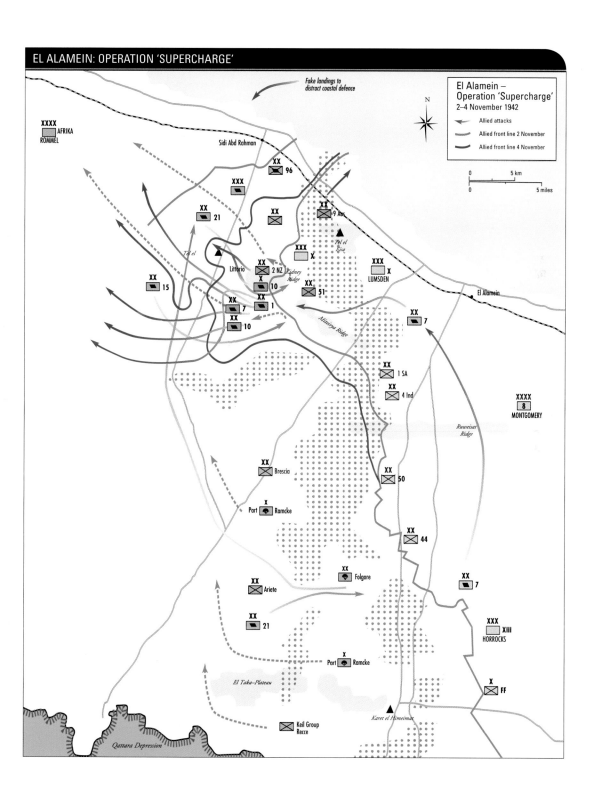

## EL ALAMEIN: OPERATION 'SUPERCHARGE'

Fake landings to
distract coastal defence

El Alamein –
Operation 'Supercharge'
2–4 November 1942

Allied attacks
Allied front line 2 November
Allied front line 4 November

0        5 km
0              5 miles

N

XXXX
AFRIKA
ROMMEL

Sidi Abd Rahman

XX
96

XXX

XX
21

XX

XX
9 Aus

Tel el Eisa

XXX
X

Tel el

Littorio

XX
X
2 NZ
10

Kidney
Ridge

XXX
X
LUMSDEN

XX
15

XX
7

XX
1

XX
10

XX
51

El Alamein

Mitieriya Ridge

XX
7

XX
1 SA

XX
4 Ind

XXXX
8
MONTGOMERY

Ruweisat
Ridge

XX
Brescia

XX
50

X
Part    Ramcke

XX
44

X
Folgore

XX
Ariete

XX
7

XX
21

XXX
XIII
HORROCKS

X
Part    Ramcke

X
FF

El Taka–Plateau

Keil Group
Recce

Karet el Himeimat

Qattara Depression

81

significant since Rommel could not replace the lost tanks. On 2 November, von Thoma reported that his German tank strength was down to 35 and that anti-tank and artillery units were only 33 per cent of their strength a week earlier.

On 4 November, Rommel realized that his situation was desperate and requested permission from Hitler to execute an orderly withdrawal. 'There were no reserves,' he later wrote, 'as every available man and gun had been put into the line. So

now it had come, the thing we had done everything in our power to avoid – our front broken and the mechanized enemy streaming into our rear … We had to save what we could.'

Losses during the El Alamein fighting and the subsequent withdrawal were catastrophic for the Axis, with at least 450 tanks and 1000 guns destroyed or captured and more than 50,000 dead and wounded. At El Alamein alone, British losses were 150 tanks destroyed and at least 350

damaged but recovered along with more than 13,000 casualties. On 8 November, Allied troops executed Operation 'Torch', landing at Oran, Algiers and Casablanca. While these troops pressed Axis forces from the west, Eighth Army pursued from the east. Seven months later, the remnants of *Armeegruppe Afrika*, under the command of General Hans-Jürgen von Arnim, surrendered in Tunisia. Rommel had previously been recalled to France to command the defences of Hitler's Atlantic Wall.

# The Führer's Brigades

*In the summer of 1944, Adolf Hitler introduced a more formalized battle-group structure to that which had been previously in use with* ad hoc Kampfgruppen, *those units formed during the heat of a campaign for a specific mission.*

In theory, the independent panzer brigades of the *Heer* would consist of up to 40 tanks, an anti-tank company including 37mm (1.45in) guns, along with flak batteries of 20mm (0.79in) and 37mm (1.45in) guns. The infantry component was to include a battalion transported by halftracks. The primary mission of these panzer brigades was to blunt the westward thrusts of Soviet armour, cut off large numbers of Red Army tanks and troops, and annihilate them in short order.

Originally, 12 of these brigades were to be raised; however, by mid-July the number had been reduced to 10, each with a panzer battalion consisting of three companies, two equipped with 11 of the formidable

## PANZER BRIGADES

- 1.Panzer-Brigade
- 2.Panzer-Brigade
- 3.Panzer-Brigade
- 4.Panzer-Brigade
- 5.Panzer-Brigade
- 6.Panzer-Brigade
- 8.Panzer-Brigade
- 10.Panzer-Brigade
- 18.Panzer-Brigade
- 21.Panzer-Brigade
- 100.Panzer-Brigade
- 101.Panzer-Brigade
- 102.Panzer-Brigade
- 103.Panzer-Brigade
- 104.Panzer-Brigade
- 105.Panzer-Brigade
- 106.Panzer-Brigade
- 107.Panzer-Brigade
- 108.Panzer-Brigade
- 109.Panzer-Brigade
- 110.Panzer-Brigade
- 111.Panzer-Brigade
- 112.Panzer-Brigade
- 113.Panzer-Brigade
- Panzer-Brigade Norwegen

PzKpfw V Panther medium tank mounting a long-barrelled 75mm (2.95in) cannon, which had entered service in late 1943, and an anti-tank company with 11 Jagdpanzer IV 70 (V) tank destroyers also mounting 75mm (2.95in) guns. Eventually, three more brigades were raised. These were equipped solely with the PzKpfw IV, 14 in each of three companies and three in the headquarters section.

One of these panzer brigades, the 105th, was formed on 31 August 1944, and included the 2105th Panzer Battalion, the five halftrack-borne companies of the 2105th Panzergrenadier Battalion, and support units. By September the brigade included 11 PzKpfw IV, 36 Panthers and 157 SdKfz 251 halftracks. Its short service life ended later that month as the bulk of the unit was reassigned to the 9th Panzer Division, a formation which had been devastated during the fighting in Normandy that summer.

# Independent Tank Battalions

*For Nazi Germany, the concept of superior weapons led to an emphasis on quality versus quantity, and it must also be acknowledged that German industrial capacity was strained by Allied air attacks and shortages of raw materials particularly during the later years of World War II.*

The development of superior armoured fighting vehicles had been undertaken in earnest during the 1930s, and a trio of fearsome tanks, the PzKpfw V Panther medium tank, the PzKpfw VI Tiger, and the King Tiger, or Tiger II, epitomized the finest in German engineering and weapons design. Although each of these tanks had its drawbacks, most notably in mechanical failures due to excessive weight or inadequate testing prior to their being deployed into combat, they were nevertheless respected for their heavy armour protection and survivability as well as their 75mm (2.95in) and 88mm (3.5in) heavy guns, which were capable of penetrating the armour of the heaviest Allied tanks at distances well beyond retaliatory range.

By war's end, nearly 6000 Panthers had been built, while only a relative handful of Tigers, 1354 Tiger I and 489

| TIGER BATTALION COMBAT PERFORMANCE, 1942–45 | | |
|---|---|---|
| *Battalion* | *Losses* | *Kills* |
| 501st Heavy Panzer Battalion | 120 | 450 |
| 502nd Heavy Panzer Battalion | 107 | 1400 |
| 503rd Heavy Panzer Battalion | 252 | 1700 |
| 504th Heavy Panzer Battalion | 109 | 250 |
| 505th Heavy Panzer Battalion | 126 | 900 |
| 506th Heavy Panzer Battalion | 179 | 400 |
| 507th Heavy Panzer Battalion | 104 | 600 |
| 508th Heavy Panzer Battalion | 78 | 100 |
| 509th Heavy Panzer Battalion | 120 | 500 |
| 510th Heavy Panzer Battalion | 65 | 200 |
| 13th Coy, Panzer Regt *Grossdeutschland* | 6 | 100 |
| 3rd Bn, Panzer Regt *Grossdeutschland* | 98 | 500 |
| 13th (Heavy) Coy, 1st SS Panzer Regt | 42 | 400 |
| 8th (Heavy) Coy, 2nd SS Panzer Regt | 31 | 250 |
| 9th (Heavy) Coy, 3rd SS Panzer Regt | 56 | 500 |
| 101st SS Heavy Panzer Battalion | 107 | 500 |
| 102nd SS Heavy Panzer Battalion | 76 | 600 |
| 103rd SS Heavy Panzer Battalion | 39 | 500 |
| **TOTAL** | **1715** | **9850** |

Tiger II models, had been manufactured.

While most of the Panthers were allocated to panzer divisions of the *Heer* and *Waffen-SS*, all of the Tigers were assigned to independent heavy tank battalions. The first heavy armoured formations in the *Heer* were the 501st and 502nd Heavy Panzer Companies, fielded in February 1942. These were combined to form the 501st Heavy Tank Battalion three weeks later. By the autumn of 1943, nine heavy panzer battalions were formed, each consisting of three Tiger companies of 14 tanks each and three additional Tigers in the headquarters section. Earlier battalion organizations included a mixed complement of 20 Tigers and 25 PzKpfw III tanks with 50mm (1.95in) cannon.

The 501st Heavy Tank Battalion entered combat in North Africa, and during a series of engagements in December 1942, a battle group which never consisted of more than four Tigers and a handful of PzKpfw IIIs at any given time knocked out dozens of Allied tanks. Following the Axis defeat in North Africa, the battalion was reconstituted and fought on the Eastern Front.

### Kill ratio

On 20 December 1943 the 501st destroyed 21 Red Army tanks and 28 guns for the loss of only two Tigers. In August 1944, the 501st was re-equipped with the new Tiger II and returned to service on the Eastern Front. On 12 January 1945, a single Tiger II with both its tracks blown off accounted for 20 Soviet tanks, while

as many as 60 were destroyed in all. Two independent Panther battalions, the 51st and 52nd, were formed in 1943 and reached a peak strength of 96 Panthers. Large numbers of tank destroyer and self-propelled assault gun formations were raised during the war; these vehicles, cheaper to produce because they did not have turrets, proved effective close-support weapons. *Jagdpanzer* and *Panzerjäger* brigades and battalions fielded the Marder, Hetzer, the tank destroyer variant of the PzKpfw IV, and later the Mark V Jagdpanther, Nashorn, and other vehicles. By far the most numerous self-propelled artillery pieces were the variants of the tracked *Sturmgeschütze* (assault guns), which were under the nominal control of the *Heer* Artillery Weapons Department.

## TIGER BATTALION KILL:LOSS RATIO, 1942–45

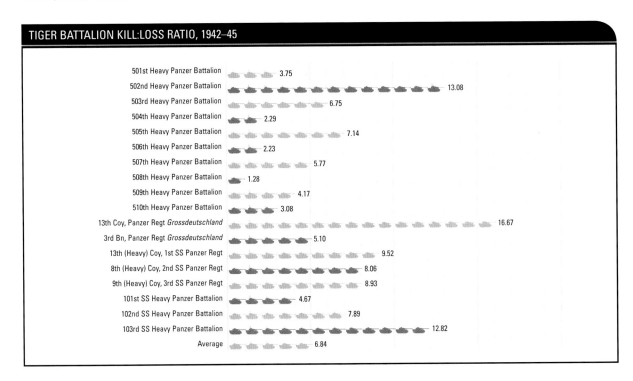

| Battalion | Ratio |
| --- | --- |
| 501st Heavy Panzer Battalion | 3.75 |
| 502nd Heavy Panzer Battalion | 13.08 |
| 503rd Heavy Panzer Battalion | 6.75 |
| 504th Heavy Panzer Battalion | 2.29 |
| 505th Heavy Panzer Battalion | 7.14 |
| 506th Heavy Panzer Battalion | 2.23 |
| 507th Heavy Panzer Battalion | 5.77 |
| 508th Heavy Panzer Battalion | 1.28 |
| 509th Heavy Panzer Battalion | 4.17 |
| 510th Heavy Panzer Battalion | 3.08 |
| 13th Coy, Panzer Regt *Grossdeutschland* | 16.67 |
| 3rd Bn, Panzer Regt *Grossdeutschland* | 5.10 |
| 13th (Heavy) Coy, 1st SS Panzer Regt | 9.52 |
| 8th (Heavy) Coy, 2nd SS Panzer Regt | 8.06 |
| 9th (Heavy) Coy, 3rd SS Panzer Regt | 8.93 |
| 101st SS Heavy Panzer Battalion | 4.67 |
| 102nd SS Heavy Panzer Battalion | 7.89 |
| 103rd SS Heavy Panzer Battalion | 12.82 |
| Average | 6.84 |

# The Panzer Army

*The largest armoured formations in the* Feldheer *were the panzer armies, six of which were constituted from 1939 to 1945.*

These consisted of multiple panzer corps and were sometimes placed under unified command with panzer divisions of the *Waffen-SS* or infantry divisions of the *Feldheer* to form army groups.

Typical of these largest armoured formations was the First Panzer Army, which was formed on 16 November 1940, originally as Panzer Group Kleist after its commander, Field Marshal Ewald von Kleist, and remained on the Eastern Front from October 1941 until it was disbanded at the end of the war. Following occupation duty in

France, the formation was transferred to the Balkans and participated in the invasion of Yugoslavia in April 1941. Elements of Panzer Group Kleist destroyed two Yugoslav field armies and entered the capital of Belgrade within days.

The following month, the formation was redesignated Panzer Group I and attached to Army Group South under Field Marshal Gerd von Rundstedt to participate in Operation 'Barbarossa'. When the invasion of the Soviet Union commenced on 22 June 1941, Panzer Group I consisted of the III, the XIV

and the XLVIII Motorized Army Corps, and was composed of nine panzer divisions, five of the *Feldheer* and four of the *Waffen-SS*. Fielding nearly 800 tanks, the formation was reinforced and renamed the First Panzer Army in October 1941, following the capture of Kiev, the capital city of the Ukraine. In November, Kleist led the First Panzer Army to victory at Rostov.

In early 1942, Kleist was elevated to command an army group which bore his name and included the battle-hardened First Panzer Army and the Seventeenth Army. After bitter fighting around the city of Kharkov, Kleist resumed command of the First Panzer Army, which was then attached to Army Group A under Field Marshal Wilhelm List. The First Panzer Army spearheaded the German thrust into the Caucasus, Operation 'Blue', in the summer of 1942, after which Kleist was again promoted to army group command, and Colonel-General Eberhard Mackensen took command of First Panzer Army.

Throughout 1943, the formation was engaged in the unsuccessful German efforts to stem the resurgent tide of the Soviet Red Army. The Sixth Army had been destroyed at Stalingrad, and the First Panzer Army withdrew west of the river Don in February to avoid encirclement. Several months later it had pulled out of the Ukraine and narrowly avoided annihilation in the

## FIRST PANZER ARMY STRENGTH, JUNE 1942

| Unit | Pz II | Pz III | Pz 38(t) | Pz IV | Pz Bef |
|------|-------|--------|----------|-------|--------|
| 3rd Pz Div, 6th Pz Rgt | 25 | 106 | 0 | 33 | 4 |
| 14th Pz Div, 36th Pz Rgt | 14 | 60 | 0 | 24 | 4 |
| 16th Pz Div, 2nd Pz Rgt | 13 | 58 | 0 | 27 | 3 |
| 22nd Pz Div, 204th Pz Rgt | 28 | 12 | 114 | 22 | 0 |
| 23rd Pz Div, 201st Pz Rgt | 27 | 84 | 0 | 17 | 10 |

## GERMAN PANZER ARMIES, 1940–45

| Panzer Army | Date Formed | Notes |
|-------------|-------------|-------|
| First Panzer Army | November 1940 | From Nov 1940 to Oct 1941 known as Panzer Group I |
| Second Panzer Army | November 1940 | From Nov 1940 to Oct 1941 known as Panzer Group II |
| Third Panzer Army | November 1940 | From Nov 1940 to Dec 1941 known as Panzer Group III |
| Fourth Panzer Army | February 1941 | From Feb 1941 to Dec 1941 known as Panzer Group IV |
| Fifth Panzer Army | December 1942 | Destroyed in May 1943, re-formed in July 1944 |
| Sixth Panzer Army | September 1944 | Created for the Ardennes offensive |
| Eleventh Panzer Army | January 1945 | Renamed Army Detachment *Steiner* in March 1945 |
| Panzer Army Afrika | August 1941 | Initially known as Panzer Group Afrika, becoming Army in Jan 1942 |

Kamenets-Podolsky Pocket. Breaking out of the Soviet trap, the First Panzer Army destroyed or captured 357 Soviet tanks, 42 assault guns and 280 artillery pieces.

By the spring of 1944, combat losses had significantly reduced the strength of the First Panzer Army. At peak strength it had four corps of *Heer* infantry and armour, *Waffen-SS*, mountain and motorized formations, and contingents of troops from other Axis nations. The war of attrition on the Eastern Front, however, left the First Panzer Army with three corps of three infantry, two panzer and one *Waffen-SS* division.

## Training ground to proving ground

Unique among the panzer divisions of the *Heer* in World War II was *Panzer-Lehr*, formed in December 1943 and equipped the next month in the Nancy-Verdun area of France. *Panzer-Lehr* came into being as an elite force composed of troops which had previously formed training and demonstration units of the German Army. Therefore, its status as an elite unit was understood from the beginning. As such, it was well equipped and capably led.

At its inception, *Panzer-Lehr* consisted of the 1st Battalion, 6th Panzer Regiment, composed of three companies of 22 PzKpfw V Panther medium tanks and a company of 22 Jagdpanther tank destroyers, the 2nd Battalion, *Panzer-Lehr* Regiment with four companies of 22 PzKpfw IV tanks, the 316th Panzer Company, four battalions of the 901st and 902nd *Panzergrenadier-Lehr* Regiments, the five companies of the 130th *Panzer-*

*Lehr* Reconnaissance Battalion, 130th *Panzer-Lehr* Anti-Tank Battalion, three battalions of the 130th Panzer Artillery Regiment, the 311th Flak Battalion, 130th Pioneer Battalion, signals, supply, support and headquarters units. In February 1944, the 316th Panzer Company was re-equipped with 14 King Tigers, and later it was renamed the 1st Battalion, 130th Panzer Regiment.

Following brief duty in Hungary, *Panzer-Lehr* was ordered back to France in anticipation of the Allied invasion of Western Europe, where it was reorganized to more closely resemble a Type 1944 panzer division. In April 1944, the *Panzer-Lehr* Reconnaissance Battalion, *Panzer-Lehr* Regiment, and Anti-Tank Battalion were each designated as the 130th, and the division was then sometimes referred to as 130th *Panzer-Lehr* Division.

In the days following the Allied landings in Normandy on 6 June 1944, *Panzer-Lehr* was heavily engaged in the defence of the vital town of Caen, suffering 2500 casualties and losing more than 100 tanks. By 21 June, its armoured strength had been reduced to nine assault guns, 101 PzKpfw IVs, 89 Panthers, three Tigers and 12 anti-aircraft Flakpanzer 38s. Further fighting in Normandy depleted the division to fewer than 30 operational tanks as the unit attempted to blunt the Allied breakout effort at St. Lo during Operation 'Cobra'. On 15 October 1944, *Panzer-Lehr* received 56 new tanks, including two battalions of Panthers and two battalions of PzKpfw IVs.

On 16 December 1944, Hitler launched the Ardennes offensive,

unleashing 30 divisions, a dozen of which were panzer and panzergrenadier, against the lightly defended American lines in the heavily forested region. With the objective of crossing the river Meuse, pressing on to capture the Belgian port of Antwerp and splitting the Allied armies in two, the offensive was initially successful, and about 90,000 American soldiers were killed, wounded or captured.

Elements of *Panzer-Lehr* attempted to seize the vital Belgian crossroads town of Bastogne but were thwarted by the US 101st Airborne Division. Other *Panzer-Lehr* units, spearheaded by the 902nd Panzergrenadier Regiment, attempted to seize the town of Dinant. A week before the offensive began, the division included the 2nd Battalion, 130th *Panzer-Lehr* Regiment, a panzer staff company, and an armoured battalion of four medium tank companies. Its armoured strength was composed of 27 PzKpfw IVs and 30 Panthers, with another 10 of each model yet to arrive, along with seven self-propelled flak vehicles.

As the offensive wore on, improving weather allowed Allied air strikes to resume, and German armour was decimated during daylight hours. The panzers were hampered by fuel shortages and stiffening resistance along the shoulders of the deep armoured penetration, and their momentum waned.

Within weeks, the Allies had regained the upper hand and restored the front to its original line. The Germans lost more than 600 tanks and assault guns during what became known as the Battle of the Bulge. *Panzer-Lehr* was virtually wiped out for a second time. After fighting in the Netherlands and an unsuccessful attempt to reduce the American bridgehead at Remagen, *Panzer-Lehr* ended the war a mere shadow of its original combat strength. In February 1945, it fielded 26 PzKpfw IVs, 32 Panthers, and 10 Flakpanzer IV anti-aircraft guns. *Panzer-Lehr* surrendered to US forces in the Ruhr Pocket on 16 April 1945.

# Tank Tactics

*As demonstrated in the* Blitzkrieg *offensive tactic, the land forces of the* Feldheer *engaged in combined-arms operations as often as possible. The tank commander often exerted overall command of an offensive operation due to his superior mobility and firepower compared to that of the infantry and other elements.*

Typically armour would lead an attack to breach the enemy defensive line, bypassing any strongly defended positions and advancing to rear areas as far as allowable. If anti-tank or artillery positions or enemy armour were located, the panzer commanders would assess the situation and respond accordingly, preferably while maintaining the momentum of the advance.

A second wave of attack followed, generally with motorized infantry or panzergrenadiers exiting their transport vehicles as close to the front line as possible and assaulting those positions which still resisted and had been bypassed by the armoured spearhead. A third wave reinforced the attack and secured the ground taken.

The tank unit in the vanguard of the attack, if regimental in size, generally deployed over an area of 700–1000m

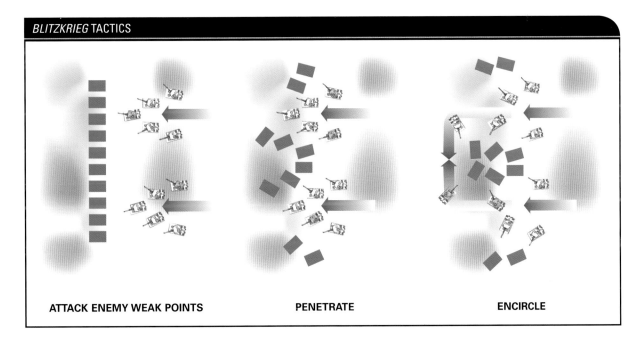

**BLITZKRIEG TACTICS**

**ATTACK ENEMY WEAK POINTS**          **PENETRATE**          **ENCIRCLE**

(765–1094 yards), with supporting panzergrenadiers close behind. The depth of the initial assault was up to 2000m (2200 yards). Flank protection was provided either by a panzergrenadier screen or self-propelled assault or anti-tank guns. The advance was often conducted with the flank protection leapfrogging forward as the main assault continued. If conditions were favourable, the attack would be pressed with the first and second waves advancing as the third wave moved forward to its rear.

### Wave tactics

According to the US War Department Technical Manual *TM-E 30-451: Handbook on German Military Forces* published in March 1945, a typical German divisional armoured attack might take place in the following manner: '… The first wave, on a frontage of about 2000 to 3000 yards, might consist of one tank battalion, two companies forward, supported on the flanks by elements of the assault gun battalion. Close to the rear of the first wave usually follow one or two Panzer Grenadier companies in armoured half-tracks.

About 150m (164 yards) to the rear of the first wave moves the second wave, formed of the second tank battalion in the same formation, closely followed by the remainder of the armoured Panzer Grenadiers, who are in turn followed at some distance by the motorized Panzer Grenadiers. The flanks are protected by anti-tank guns which normally operate by platoons, moving by bounds. The artillery forward observer travels in his armoured vehicles with the first wave, while the artillery commander of the supporting artillery units usually travels with the tank commander. Assault guns normally also accompany the second wave.'

Following the major defeats at El Alamein and Stalingrad in 1942–43, the *Feldheer* fought a primarily defensive war. With only a couple of notable exceptions, manpower and equipment were insufficient to sustain a major offensive for any length of time. Therefore, the development and refinement of defensive tactics became a requirement for the panzer forces.

However, even in a defensive role, German commanders considered the tank to be an offensive weapon. Supporting the concept of defence in depth, tanks were held in defensive reserve until needed to counter-attack an enemy breakthrough or engage in pursuit of a withdrawing force. Should enemy infantry and tanks penetrate the German lines, they would theoretically become trapped in the deep defences and present prime targets for the fast, hard-hitting tanks. One apparent drawback to this school of thought was that tanks were not expected to hold ground for extended periods without the support of infantry. On the actual battlefield, such was not always the case. Tanks might fire from concealed or hull-down positions for a while or possibly even advance; however, without infantry support they soon enough became vulnerable to mobile anti-tank guns or tank-killer teams of enemy infantry.

# Panzer Weapons

*From 1938 to 1945, German industry produced just under 30,000 tanks, including hundreds of variants of its main production models, each of these involving some combination of heavier armour protection, a higher performance powerplant, heavier weapons or other improvements.*

Both out of necessity due to limited production capacity and resources and due to the German penchant for precision workmanship, the quality of the tanks deployed by the *Feldheer* and *Waffen-SS* was stressed over the quantity available. The theory was simple. Superior weapons in fewer numbers would inevitably defeat a larger quantity of inferior tanks. In the end, the opposite proved to be true. German tanks were generally larger and heavier than Allied tanks. However, they were sometimes plagued by mechanical difficulties related to their great weight or due to problems which might have been identified and corrected prior to deployment absent the exigencies of wartime. By the end of the war, Germany had produced some of the most famous and ferocious armoured fighting vehicles of the twentieth century in its Tiger, Panther and workhorse PzKpfw IV tanks. Nevertheless, the ubiquitous American-built Sherman was produced in such large numbers that losses could be offset easily, while the Soviet T-34 was arguably the finest all-around tank to come out of the war, combining firepower, mobility and substantial numbers on the Eastern Front.

In contrast to the relatively low number of 6000 PzKpfw V Panthers produced in Germany, more than 49,000 Shermans were manufactured by the Allies from 1941 to 1945. During the course of the war, the Germans augmented their armoured formations by deploying an array of captured tanks, particularly the Czech-designed 38(t) and the French Char B1 bis.

A number of special-purpose armoured vehicles and trucks were in use with the *Feldheer* panzer and panzergrenadier divisions. Among these were several halftrack models, which were never available in sufficient numbers to serve as primary transport for mechanized infantry, so most panzergrenadiers were transported by truck throughout the war. Self-propelled assault guns and anti-aircraft vehicles were considered elements of the artillery.

**Panzer I**
The first notable tank produced for the burgeoning panzer formations of the *Feldheer* was the PzKpfw I Ausf. A. Weighing only slightly more than five tonnes (4.92 tons), the PzKpfw I entered service in 1934. Lightly armed, it mounted a pair of 7.92mm (0.31in) MG13 machine guns.

Nearly 1500 were produced, and for a time this was the heaviest tank in the German inventory, significantly outclassed by French and Soviet designs. An improved B variant weighed nearly 6.1 tonnes (six tons) and offered slightly better engine performance.

**Panzer II**
The PzKpfw II entered service in 1936 and mounted a 20mm (0.79in) cannon and armour protection of up to 35mm

(1.37in) for the three-man crew. Its six-cylinder engine was capable of a top speed of 54.1km/h (32mph) and its range was 180km (112 miles). Although it was a considerable advance in firepower and performance, the PzKpfw II remained best suited for reconnaissance. More than 1800 were built.

**Panzer III**
The PzKpfw III entered service in 1939, and no fewer than 11 variants of the original vehicle were produced.

### ARMOURED VEHICLE STRENGTHS ON EASTERN FRONT, 1941–45

| Date | German AFVs | Soviet AFVs |
|---|---|---|
| June 1941 | 3671 | 28,800 |
| March 1942 | 1503 | 4690 |
| May 1942 | 3981 | 6190 |
| Nov 1942 | 3133 | 4940 |
| March 1943 | 2374 | 7200 |
| August 1943 | 2555 | 6200 |
| June 1944 | 4470 | 11,600 |
| September 1944 | 4186 | 11,200 |
| October 1944 | 4917 | 11,900 |
| November 1944 | 5202 | 14,000 |
| December 1944 | 4785 | 15,000 |
| January 1945 | 4881 | 14,200 |

Source: John Ellis, The World War II Databook

### PANZER 38(T) & VARIANTS: PRODUCTION, 1939–45

| | 1939 | 1940 | 1941 | 1942 | 1943 | 1944 | 1945 | Total |
|---|---|---|---|---|---|---|---|---|
| Pz 38(t) | 153 | 367 | 678 | 198 | – | – | – | 1396 |
| Marder 138 | – | – | – | 110 | 783 | 323 | – | 1216 |
| Marder 139 | – | – | – | 344 | – | – | – | 344 |
| Grille | – | – | – | – | 225 | 346 | – | 571 |
| Hetzer | – | – | – | – | – | 1687 | 1335 | 3022 |
| Total | 153 | 367 | 678 | 652 | 1008 | 2356 | 1335 | 6549 |

Although the PzKpfw III was intended to engage enemy armoured units while the heavier PzKpfw IV was conceived as an infantry support tank, each vehicle performed similar tasks on the battlefield. Early versions of the PzKpfw III were equipped with a 37mm (1.45in) cannon, while later models mounted a 50mm (1.95in) or 75mm (2.95in) gun. In the summer of 1942, the Ausf. J was introduced on the Eastern Front in response to the appearance of the Soviet T-34 and equipped with a long-barrelled 50mm (1.95in) cannon to achieve greater

### PANZER II & VARIANTS: PRODUCTION, 1939–45

| | 1939 | 1940 | 1941 | 1942 | 1943 | 1944 | 1945 | Total |
|---|---|---|---|---|---|---|---|---|
| Pz II | 15 | 9 | 223 | 302 | 77 | 7 | – | 633 |
| Pz II (f) | – | 90 | 42 | 23 | – | – | – | 155 |
| Marder II | – | – | – | 511 | 212 | – | – | 723 |
| Wespe | – | – | – | – | 514 | 144 | – | 658 |
| Bison | – | – | – | 12 | – | – | – | 12 |
| Total | 15 | 99 | 265 | 848 | 803 | 151 | – | 2181 |

### PANZER III & VARIANTS: PRODUCTION, 1939–45

| | 1939 | 1940 | 1941 | 1942 | 1943 | 1944 | 1945 | Total |
|---|---|---|---|---|---|---|---|---|
| Pz III A-F | 157 | 396 | – | – | – | – | – | 553 |
| Pz III G-J | – | 466 | 1673 | 251 | – | – | – | 2390 |
| Pz III J/1-M | – | – | – | 1907 | 64 | – | – | 1971 |
| Pz III N | – | – | – | 449 | 213 | – | – | 662 |
| Pz III (f) | – | – | – | – | 100 | – | – | 100 |
| StuG III A-E | – | 192 | 540 | 93 | – | – | – | 825 |
| StuG III F-G | – | – | – | 695 | 3011 | 3849 | 1038 | 8593 |
| StuH 42 | – | – | – | 12 | 204 | 903 | 98 | 1217 |
| Total | 157 | 1054 | 2213 | 3407 | 3592 | 4752 | 1136 | 16,311 |

### PANZER IV & VARIANTS: PRODUCTION, 1939–45

| | 1939 | 1940 | 1941 | 1942 | 1943 | 1944 | 1945 | Total |
|---|---|---|---|---|---|---|---|---|
| Pz IV A-F1 | 45 | 268 | 467 | 124 | – | – | – | 904 |
| Pz IV F2-J | – | – | – | 870 | 3013 | 3126 | 385 | 7394 |
| StuG IV | – | – | – | – | 30 | 1006 | 105 | 1141 |
| Jagdpanzer IV | – | – | – | – | – | 769 | – | 769 |
| Jagdpanzer IV/70 | – | – | – | – | – | 767 | 441 | 1208 |
| Sturmpanzer IV | – | – | – | – | 66 | 215 | 17 | 298 |
| Hornisse | – | – | – | – | 345 | 133 | 16 | 494 |
| Hummel | – | – | – | – | 368 | 289 | 57 | 714 |
| Möbelwagen | – | – | – | – | – | 205 | 35 | 240 |
| Wirbelwind | – | – | – | – | – | 100 | 6 | 106 |
| Ostwind | – | – | – | – | – | 15 | 28 | 43 |
| Total | 45 | 268 | 467 | 994 | 3822 | 6625 | 1090 | 13,311 |

## MAIN PANZER TYPES, EARLY WAR

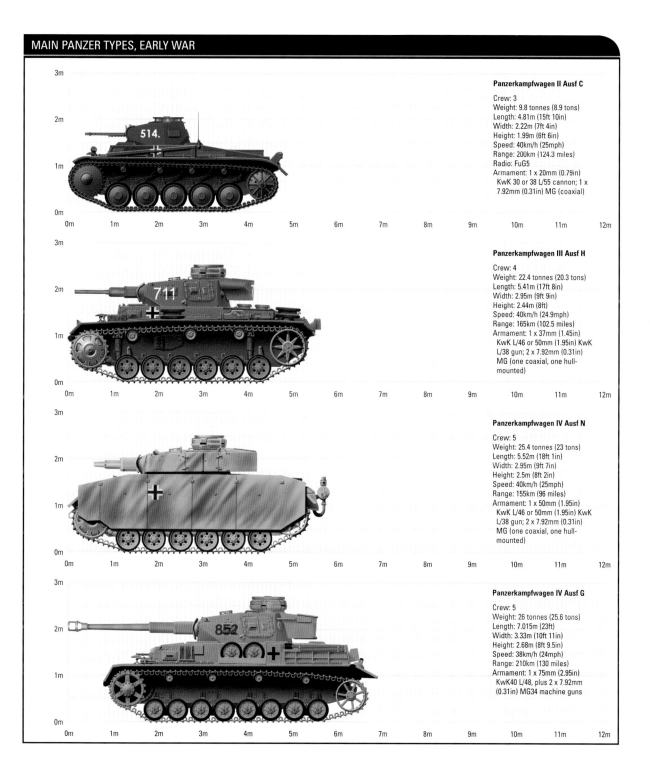

**Panzerkampfwagen II Ausf C**

Crew: 3
Weight: 9.8 tonnes (8.9 tons)
Length: 4.81m (15ft 10in)
Width: 2.22m (7ft 4in)
Height: 1.99m (6ft 6in)
Speed: 40km/h (25mph)
Range: 200km (124.3 miles)
Radio: FuG5
Armament: 1 x 20mm (0.79in)
KwK 30 or 38 L/55 cannon; 1 x
7.92mm (0.31in) MG (coaxial)

**Panzerkampfwagen III Ausf H**

Crew: 4
Weight: 22.4 tonnes (20.3 tons)
Length: 5.41m (17ft 8in)
Width: 2.95m (9ft 9in)
Height: 2.44m (8ft)
Speed: 40km/h (24.9mph)
Range: 165km (102.5 miles)
Armament: 1 x 37mm (1.45in)
KwK L/46 or 50mm (1.95in) KwK
L/38 gun; 2 x 7.92mm (0.31in)
MG (one coaxial, one hull-
mounted)

**Panzerkampfwagen IV Ausf N**

Crew: 5
Weight: 25.4 tonnes (23 tons)
Length: 5.52m (18ft 1in)
Width: 2.95m (9ft 7in)
Height: 2.5m (8ft 2in)
Speed: 40km/h (25mph)
Range: 155km (96 miles)
Armament: 1 x 50mm (1.95in)
KwK L/46 or 50mm (1.95in) KwK
L/38 gun; 2 x 7.92mm (0.31in)
MG (one coaxial, one hull-
mounted)

**Panzerkampfwagen IV Ausf G**

Crew: 5
Weight: 26 tonnes (25.6 tons)
Length: 7.015m (23ft)
Width: 3.33m (10ft 11in)
Height: 2.68m (8ft 9.5in)
Speed: 38km/h (24mph)
Range: 210km (130 miles)
Armament: 1 x 75mm (2.95in)
KwK40 L/48, plus 2 x 7.92mm
(0.31in) MG34 machine guns

## PANZER V (PANTHER): PRODUCTION, 1939–45

|  | 1943 | 1944 | 1945 | Total |
|---|---|---|---|---|
| Panther | 1848 | 3777 | 507 | 6132 |
| Jagdpanther | 1 | 226 | 198 | 425 |
| Total | 1849 | 4003 | 705 | 6557 |

## PANZER VI (TIGER): PRODUCTION, 1939–45

|  | 1942 | 1943 | 1944 | 1945 | Total |
|---|---|---|---|---|---|
| Tiger I | 78 | 649 | 623 | – | 1350 |
| Sturmtiger | – | – | 18 | – | 18 |
| Tiger II | – | 1 | 377 | 112 | 490 |
| Jagdtiger | – | – | 51 | 28 | 79 |
| Total | 78 | 650 | 1069 | 140 | 1937 |

high-velocity long-barrelled 75mm (2.95in) L/43 gun, which outranged contemporary Allied tanks considerably. The PzKpfw IV weighed approximately 24.3 tonnes (24 tons), and its five-man crew was protected by 60mm (2.36in) of frontal armour. Its versatile chassis served as the platform for numerous other self-propelled weapons.

### Panzer V Panther

The PzKpfw V Panther medium tank made its combat debut in the spring of 1943 and was seen in significant numbers for the first time at the pivotal Battle of Kursk in July of that year. The design of the Panther was based on that of a captured Soviet T-34, and its German engineering resulted in a formidable fighting machine. With a high-velocity 75mm (2.95in) KwK 42 L/70 main gun, the Panther was more than a match for most Allied tanks, while up to 80mm (3.15in) of frontal armour protected the crew of five, and the 510kW (690hp) Maybach V-12 engine was capable of a top speed of 48km/h (30mph). Variants of the Panther weighed up to 46.2 tonnes (45.5 tons),

muzzle velocity over the short-barrelled 50mm (1.95in) weapon. The PzKpfw III Ausf. N was delivered to combat units early in 1943 and equipped with the superb 75mm (2.95in) KwK L/24 gun. The average weight of the PzKpfw III was about 25.4 tonnes (25 tons), and production of all variants topped 5700.

### Panzer IV

The PzKpfw IV has the distinction of being the only German tank in

continuous production throughout World War II, and it served in every theatre in which the *Feldheer* was engaged. The workhorse of the panzer formations, more than 8500 were manufactured from 1936 to 1945. Specifications for the PzKpfw IV or 'Mark IV' were issued in January 1934, and early models were equipped with a short-barrelled 75mm (2.95in) cannon. The F2 variant introduced one of the tank's most significant modifications with the

## TOTAL PANZER PRODUCTION, 1939–45

|  | Pre-war | 1939 | 1940 | 1941 | 1942 | 1943 | 1944 | 1945 | Wartime | Total |
|---|---|---|---|---|---|---|---|---|---|---|
| Panzer I | 1893 | – | – | – | – | – | – | – | – | 1893 |
| Panzer II | 1223 | 15 | 99 | 265 | 848 | 803 | 151 | - | 2181 | 3404 |
| Panzer 38(t) | 78 | 153 | 367 | 678 | 652 | 1008 | 2356 | 1335 | 6549 | 6627 |
| Panzer III | 98 | 157 | 1054 | 2213 | 3407 | 3592 | 4752 | 1136 | 16,311 | 16,409 |
| Panzer IV | 211 | 45 | 268 | 467 | 994 | 3822 | 6625 | 1090 | 13,311 | 13,522 |
| Panzer V Panther | – | – | – | – | – | 1849 | 4003 | 705 | 6557 | 6557 |
| Panzer VI H Tiger I | – | – | – | – | 78 | 649 | 641 | – | 1368 | 1368 |
| Panzer VI B Tiger II | – | – | – | – | – | 1 | 428 | 140 | 569 | 569 |
| Elefant | – | – | – | – | – | 90 | – | – | 90 | 90 |
| Total | 3503 | 370 | 1788 | 3623 | 5979 | 11814 | 18,956 | 4406 | 46,936 | 50,439 |

## MAIN PANZER TYPES, LATE WAR

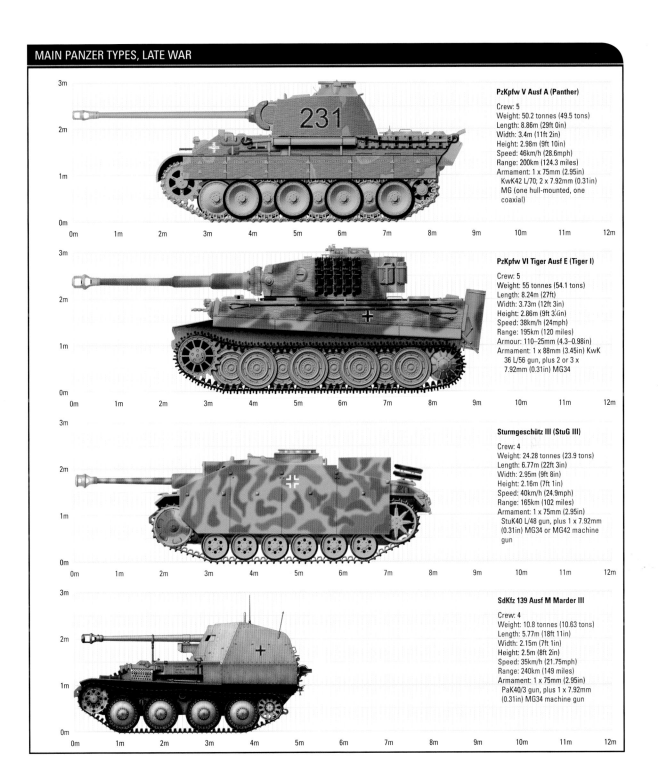

**PzKpfw V Ausf A (Panther)**
Crew: 5
Weight: 50.2 tonnes (49.5 tons)
Length: 8.86m (29ft 0in)
Width: 3.4m (11ft 2in)
Height: 2.98m (9ft 10in)
Speed: 46km/h (28.6mph)
Range: 200km (124.3 miles)
Armament: 1 x 75mm (2.95in)
    KwK42 L/70; 2 x 7.92mm (0.31in)
    MG (one hull-mounted, one
    coaxial)

**PzKpfw VI Tiger Ausf E (Tiger I)**
Crew: 5
Weight: 55 tonnes (54.1 tons)
Length: 8.24m (27ft)
Width: 3.73m (12ft 3in)
Height: 2.86m (9ft 3¼in)
Speed: 38km/h (24mph)
Range: 195km (120 miles)
Armour: 110–25mm (4.3–0.98in)
Armament: 1 x 88mm (3.45in) KwK
    36 L/56 gun, plus 2 or 3 x
    7.92mm (0.31in) MG34

**Sturmgeschütz III (StuG III)**
Crew: 4
Weight: 24.28 tonnes (23.9 tons)
Length: 6.77m (22ft 3in)
Width: 2.95m (9ft 8in)
Height: 2.16m (7ft 1in)
Speed: 40km/h (24.9mph)
Range: 165km (102 miles)
Armament: 1 x 75mm (2.95in)
    StuK40 L/48 gun, plus 1 x 7.92mm
    (0.31in) MG34 or MG42 machine
    gun

**SdKfz 139 Ausf M Marder III**
Crew: 4
Weight: 10.8 tonnes (10.63 tons)
Length: 5.77m (18ft 11in)
Width: 2.15m (7ft 1in)
Height: 2.5m (8ft 2in)
Speed: 35km/h (21.75mph)
Range: 240km (149 miles)
Armament: 1 x 75mm (2.95in)
    PaK40/3 gun, plus 1 x 7.92mm
    (0.31in) MG34 machine gun

## OTHER AFV TYPES

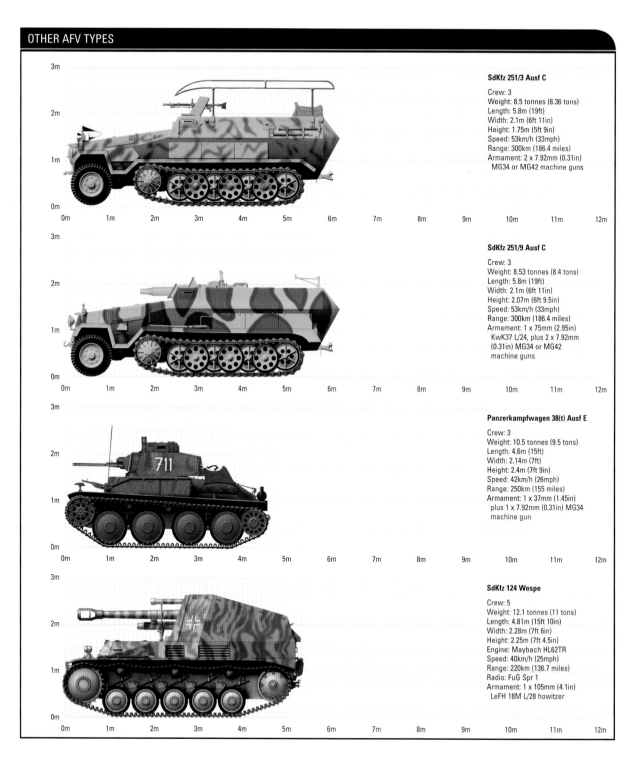

**SdKfz 251/3 Ausf C**

Crew: 3
Weight: 8.5 tonnes (8.36 tons)
Length: 5.8m (19ft)
Width: 2.1m (6ft 11in)
Height: 1.75m (5ft 9in)
Speed: 53km/h (33mph)
Range: 300km (186.4 miles)
Armament: 2 x 7.92mm (0.31in)
 MG34 or MG42 machine guns

**SdKfz 251/9 Ausf C**

Crew: 3
Weight: 8.53 tonnes (8.4 tons)
Length: 5.8m (19ft)
Width: 2.1m (6ft 11in)
Height: 2.07m (6ft 9.5in)
Speed: 53km/h (33mph)
Range: 300km (186.4 miles)
Armament: 1 x 75mm (2.95in)
 KwK37 L/24, plus 2 x 7.92mm
 (0.31in) MG34 or MG42
 machine guns

**Panzerkampfwagen 38(t) Ausf E**

Crew: 3
Weight: 10.5 tonnes (9.5 tons)
Length: 4.6m (15ft)
Width: 2.14m (7ft)
Height: 2.4m (7ft 9in)
Speed: 42km/h (26mph)
Range: 250km (155 miles)
Armament: 1 x 37mm (1.45in)
 plus 1 x 7.92mm (0.31in) MG34
 machine gun

**SdKfz 124 Wespe**

Crew: 5
Weight: 12.1 tonnes (11 tons)
Length: 4.81m (15ft 10in)
Width: 2.28m (7ft 6in)
Height: 2.25m (7ft 4.5in)
Engine: Maybach HL62TR
Speed: 40km/h (25mph)
Range: 220km (136.7 miles)
Radio: FuG Spr 1
Armament: 1 x 105mm (4.1in)
 LeFH 18M L/28 howitzer

and nearly half the number manufactured were of the G model, which included sloped armour on the upper hull, an improved exhaust system, and a rotating driver's periscope.

### Panzer VI Tiger

The mere presence of a PzKpfw VI Tiger tank could alter the course of a battle. At 57.9 tonnes (57 tons), the Henschel-designed Tiger was significantly larger than most Allied tanks, and its 88mm (3.5in) KwK 36 L/56 main gun was lethal against the frontal armour of most Allied tanks from a distance of more than 1.6km (one mile) with a muzzle velocity of more than 914m/sec (3000ft/sec). The Tiger was a demanding vehicle, however, and fewer than 1400 were produced from 1942 to 1944. Its high cost was more than twice that of a PzKpfw IV, and its engineering was complex. The Tiger was plagued by mechanical problems and was difficult to transport due to its considerable weight. Despite its drawbacks, the Tiger was capable of dominating the battlefield, and at least a dozen commanders of *Feldheer* and *Waffen-SS* Tigers claimed more than 100 enemy vehicles destroyed.

In 1944, production of the Tiger was halted in favour of the 69-tonne (68-ton) Tiger II of which only 490 were produced before the end of the war. Also known as the King Tiger, this behemoth mounted the 88mm (3.5in) KwK 43 L/71 cannon and was served by a crew of five. Its 12-cylinder Maybach engine could raise a sustained top speed of about 38km/h (24mph). The performance of the Tiger II was diminished primarily due

| ANNUAL ALLIED AND AXIS TANK PRODUCTION, 1939–45 | | | | | |
|---|---|---|---|---|---|
| *Date* | *USA* | *Soviet Union* | *UK* | *Germany* | *Italy* |
| 1939 | – | 2950 | 969 | 247 | 40 |
| 1940 | 331 | 2794 | 1399 | 1643 | 250 |
| 1941 | 4052 | 6590 | 4841 | 3790 | 595 |
| 1942 | 24,997 | 24,446 | 8611 | 6180 | 1252 |
| 1943 | 29,497 | 24,089 | 7476 | 12,063 | 336 |
| 1944 | 17,565 | 28,963 | 4600 | 19,002 | – |
| 1945 | 11,968 | 14,419 | ? | 3932 | – |
| Total | 88,410 | 104,251 | 27,896 | 46,857 | 2473 |

to leaking gaskets and an inadequate drive train for its considerable weight. The Tiger II served in combat in Normandy and on the Eastern Front.

### Halftracks and armoured cars

Among the combat vehicles which were in great demand by the *Feldheer* but in relatively short supply throughout World War II were the family of halftracks generally known as the Hanomag. Although more than 15,000 of the vehicles were built in more than 23 configurations, the primary function of the halftrack was to transport panzergrenadiers in combat zones.

The standard vehicle was designed during the 1930s with a capacity of six panzergrenadiers and armed with a pair of machine guns. The vehicle was powered by a six-cylinder Maybach gasoline engine and capable of a top speed of more than 52km/h (32mph). Other halftrack vehicles included the SdKfz Büssing-NAG, which carried up to 11 panzergrenadiers or five tonnes (five tons) of supplies while also serving as an artillery prime mover, and the heavy SdKfz 9, capable of transporting 18.2 tonnes (18 tons) of cargo and suitable for vehicle recovery.

Three principle armoured cars served with the *Feldheer*, including the light SdKfz 223, powered by a 3.5-litre V-8 engine. With a crew of three the SdKfz 223 mounted a machine gun for defence and served as a command and signals vehicle. Its 222 variant mounted a 20mm (0.79in) cannon. The Mercedes-Benz G3a/P was utilized for reconnaissance and was served by a three- or four-man crew. It mounted a 20mm (0.79in) cannon and a turret machine gun. The heavy Büssing-NAG SdKfz 231 and its variants were upgunned with 20mm (0.79in), 50mm (1.95in) or 75mm (2.95in) guns and a coaxial machine gun. Manned by a crew of four, the SdKfz 231 was a command and reconnaissance vehicle which was known as the Puma after 1944.

### Trucks

A variety of trucks operated with the *Feldheer*, including the light Büssing-NAG G31, designated the Kfz 76, which was capable of carrying a 2.03-tonne (two-ton) load, the Opel Blitz three-ton cargo truck, of which more than 140,000 were built, and the Mercedes-Benz L3000A/066 cargo truck, which could also transport up to 3.05 tonnes (three tons) of cargo.

# Tactical Insignia: Panzer Divisions

*In 1940 a new, simplified system of divisional markings was introduced. The new system used straight lines that were easy to apply, remember and recognize. A completely new set of temporary symbols was introduced in June 1943 for divisions taking part in the Battle of Kursk.*

**1st Panzer Division**
The 1st Panzer Division used an inverted 'Y' that was easily recognizable.

**2nd Panzer Division**
The division's symbol was the same as the 1st Division, with the addition of a short line next to the upright of the inverted 'Y'.

**3rd Panzer Division**
The division's symbol followed in sequence from the 1st and 2nd Divisions.

**4th Panzer Division**
The standard wartime insignia used by the division followed on from those used by the 1st, 2nd and 3rd Panzer Divisions.

**5th Panzer Division**
The standard tactical symbol used by the 5th Panzer Division in 1940 followed on from the first four panzer divisions.

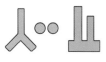

**6th Panzer Division**
Left: Standard tactical insignia. Right: New symbol introduced for the Battle of Kursk.

**7th Panzer Division**
Left: Standard tactical symbol introduced in the second half of 1940. Centre: New tactical symbol introduced in 1941, and used to the end of the war. Right: Tactical symbol adopted for the Battle of Kursk.

**8th Panzer Division**
Left: Standard tactical symbol used by the 8th Panzer Division in 1940. Right: Modified variant used by the division from 1941 to 1945.

**9th Panzer Division**
Left: Tactical symbol used after the French Campaign in 1940. Right: Modified tactical symbol used from 1941 to 1945.

**10th Panzer Division**
Left: Standard tactical symbol used in 1940. Right: Modified version used between 1941 and 1943.

**11th Panzer Division**
The standard tactical symbol used by the division from its foundation in 1940 to the end of the war.

**12th Panzer Division**
This tactical insignia was carried by the division's vehicles from its foundation in 1941 to the end of the war in 1945.

**13th Panzer Division**
Like the 12th Panzer Division, the division's vehicles carried the same tactical insignia from 1941 to the end of the war.

**14th Panzer Division**
The standard tactical symbol carried by the division from its foundation in August 1941. A similar, slightly elongated version was also used.

### 15th Panzer Division
The tactical insignia used in North Africa from 1941 to 1943. It was also seen in black, and in white on a solid red circle.

### 16th Panzer Division
Divisional tactical insignia used from 1941 to 1942. A similar symbol was used in Italy in 1943.

### 17th Panzer Division
The tactical insignia used from the formation's establishment in autumn 1940 until the end of the war.

### 18th Panzer Division
The standard tactical symbol was related to those of the 16th and 17th Divisions, with additional crossbars on the 'Y'.

### 19th Panzer Division
Left: The original tactical symbol was the ancient runic *Wolfsangel* (Wolf's Hook). Right: The new symbol used for the Battle of Kursk.

### 20th Panzer Division
From the middle of 1941, the division's vehicles bore a new symbol. Variants had curved and straight lines.

### 21st Panzer Division
After returning to Europe from North Africa in 1943, the division fought in Northwest Europe, using this new tactical symbol.

### 22nd Panzer Division
The division's tactical sign was related to the symbol used by the 21st Panzer Division, simply rotated anticlockwise through 45 degrees.

### 23rd Panzer Division
The tactical symbol followed on from the 21st and 22nd Panzer Divisions.

### 24th Panzer Division
Left: The division's insignia reflected its cavalry origins. Right: A simplified variant was also seen from 1943 onwards.

### 25th Panzer Division
Originally brightly coloured, a simplified version of the symbol was used in Russia.

### 26th Panzer Division
The tactical symbol of the division was a representation of a grenadier from the time of Frederick the Great.

### 116th Panzer Division
The division was known as the 'Greyhound Division'.

### (130th) Panzer-Lehr Division
The tactical symbol included the letter 'L' for *Lehr* (meaning 'demonstration'), inside the rhomboidal military map symbol for armour.

### 1st SS Panzer Division *LSSAH*
In honour of its commander, Sepp Dietrich, *LSSAH* used a skeleton key ('*Dietrich*' in German) as its divisional symbol.

### 2nd SS Panzer Division *Das Reich*
*Das Reich* was one of a number of divisions which used a runic 'Wolf's Hook' symbol.

### 3rd SS Panzer Division *Totenkopf*
The Death's Head symbolized the division's origins in pre-war *Totenkopf* units.

### 5th SS Panzer Division *Wiking*
*Wiking* Division carried a swastika variant of the ancient sun cross runic symbol.

### 9th SS Panzer Division *Hohenstaufen*
The insignia included a sword and the letter 'H', standing for the division's honour title.

### 10th SS Panzer Division *Frundsberg*
A Germanic letter 'F' for the unit's honour title was superimposed on to an oak leaf.

### 12th SS Panzer Division *Hitlerjugend*
The unit honoured its close association with the *LSSAH* by using a variant of the 'key' insignia.

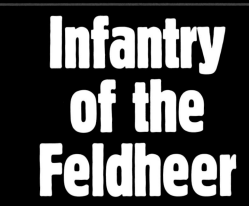

# CHAPTER 5

# Infantry of the Feldheer

*The infantry formations of the German Army were key elements in the combat capability of the Wehrmacht. With offensive-minded training and indoctrination, infantry assaulted and defeated the enemy on the ground, seizing, controlling and occupying territory.*

*The infantry's organization, firepower and equipment provided sufficient flexibility to perform a variety of operations while incorporating specialized and support troops as needed.*

*The configuration of the* Feldheer *infantry units evolved during the course of World War II, primarily due to manpower constraints and the demands of occupation, static defence, and eventually retreat.*

■ German infantry slog through the Greek town of Lamia, in mainland Greece, during the Balkans campaign, April 1941.

# 'Queen of Combat'

*The German Army formed at least 700 infantry divisions at various times throughout World War II and actually fielded more than 300 divisions of all types during the conflict. By far the largest number of these, more than 175, were designated as standard infantry divisions.*

In 1945, including the specialized mountain, light, motorized, coastal defence, security, and those *Volksgrenadier* (People's Infantry) divisions created late in the war, approximately 270 divisions of the *Feldheer* were variations on the basic theme of the infantry division.

At various times during the war, *Waffen-SS* divisions and *Luftwaffe* field divisions were under the direct command of the *Feldheer*. The former was particularly true on the Eastern Front, where SS formations were at times receiving orders from OKH. In both cases, the Army command structure coordinated such arrangements with the SS and *Luftwaffe* high commands.

Long recognized by the Army leadership and its career officer corps as the 'Queen of the Armed Forces', the infantry bore the brunt of the fighting and dying for Germany during more than six years of combat. As the war progressed, the infantry division reflected the changing character of the conflict from the German perspective. While casualties were extremely high and replacements of increasingly poor quality due to age and abbreviated training, the armed forces continued to stress the quality of arms and armaments above quantity, and it was hoped that superior technology

might indeed overcome the vast industrial capacity and seemingly limitless supply of manpower available to the Allies.

In the end, the *Feldheer* collapsed under the sheer weight of Allied military might and the exhaustion of resources available to continue waging war on the grand scale undertaken by Hitler from 1939 to 1941. Although the *Feldheer* was arguably the finest fighting force on land which the world had ever seen, its capability to endure and prevail in a sustained and protracted conflict was questionable from the outset. No doubt, the Allied leaders who opposed the Nazis were aware of this fact and exploited the Achilles heel of the *Wehrmacht* until victory was won.

## The infantry division

When German forces crossed the Polish frontier on 1 September 1939, unleashing a new form of offensive combat, the *Blitzkrieg*, on the defenders, the *Feldheer* infantry division was indeed a potent offensive weapon. Averaging a strength of 17,500 troops, including front-line combat soldiers, support and command personnel, the infantry division was commanded by a general officer and was composed of three regiments, each commanded by

a colonel and numbering slightly fewer than 3000 troops and 100 officers based upon a 1938 organizational alignment.

Within each regiment were three battalions, each commanded by a major and consisting of three infantry companies and including organic light and heavy machine gun and light mortar support. At the outbreak of the war, a standard infantry company included four officers and slightly fewer than 200 troops, while the combined strength of the battalion was generally 25 officers with about 800 men.

A separate heavy weapons company was subordinated to the battalion command and often consisted of as many as four 120mm (4.7in) and six 81mm (3.2in) mortars to augment the standard 50mm (1.97in) light infantry mortar, along with up to six heavy machine guns, usually on horse-drawn carriages or towed by trucks. With manpower virtually identical to the infantry company, the heavy weapons company could be deployed rapidly in support of an infantry advance, while the machine guns were often adequate to provide some measure of anti-aircraft defence. The horse was the primary source of transportation in the *Feldheer* throughout the war, and until 1942 a squadron of cavalry provided part of the reconnaissance support necessary for standard infantry operations.

The early German infantry division also contained an organic artillery component of six 75mm (2.95in) field guns and a pair of 150mm (5.9in) howitzers, typically horse-drawn, along with an anti-tank company with up to a dozen 37mm (1.45in) anti-tank guns. Essential to the mobility of the division were the pioneers, or combat engineers, usually in platoon strength and carrying explosives and demolition equipment, collapsible boats for crossing rivers and streams, and implements for clearing heavy vegetation which might hinder the progress of the division or prohibit the construction of defensive positions.

The signals battalion included soldiers trained to establish communications with forward elements and the command structure to the division's rear. These specialists were equipped with substantial cable for telephone connections, radios and other communications gear.

Altogether, the *Feldheer* infantry division of 1939 consisted of its headquarters, including the command, military police and other administrative personnel, three combat infantry regiments, a single artillery regiment, engineer, signals, reconnaissance and anti-tank battalions, and a service component

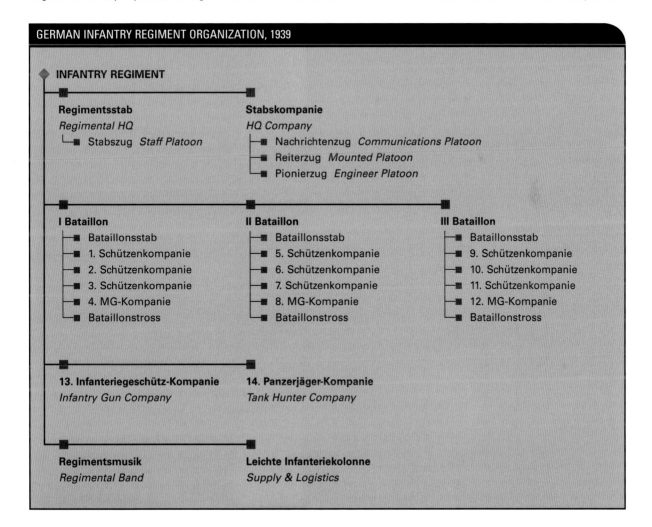

**GERMAN INFANTRY REGIMENT ORGANIZATION, 1939**

**INFANTRY REGIMENT**

**Regimentsstab**
*Regimental HQ*
  └─ Stabszug  *Staff Platoon*

**Stabskompanie**
*HQ Company*
  ├─ Nachrichtenzug  *Communications Platoon*
  ├─ Reiterzug  *Mounted Platoon*
  └─ Pionierzug  *Engineer Platoon*

**I Bataillon**
  ├─ Bataillonsstab
  ├─ 1. Schützenkompanie
  ├─ 2. Schützenkompanie
  ├─ 3. Schützenkompanie
  ├─ 4. MG-Kompanie
  └─ Bataillonstross

**II Bataillon**
  ├─ Bataillonsstab
  ├─ 5. Schützenkompanie
  ├─ 6. Schützenkompanie
  ├─ 7. Schützenkompanie
  ├─ 8. MG-Kompanie
  └─ Bataillonstross

**III Bataillon**
  ├─ Bataillonsstab
  ├─ 9. Schützenkompanie
  ├─ 10. Schützenkompanie
  ├─ 11. Schützenkompanie
  ├─ 12. MG-Kompanie
  └─ Bataillonstross

**13. Infanteriegeschütz-Kompanie**
*Infantry Gun Company*

**14. Panzerjäger-Kompanie**
*Tank Hunter Company*

**Regimentsmusik**
*Regimental Band*

**Leichte Infanteriekolonne**
*Supply & Logistics*

## NUMBERED INFANTRY DIVISIONS (1–159)

- 1st Infantry Division
- 2nd Motorized Infantry Division (later 12th Panzer Division)
- 3rd Motorized Infantry Division (later 3rd Panzergrenadier Division)
- 4th Infantry Division (later 14th Panzer Division)
- 5th Infantry Division (later 5th Light Infantry Division, 5th Jäger Division) Not related to the 5th Light Division.
- 6th Infantry Division (later 6th Grenadier Division, 6th Volksgrenadier Division)
- 7th Infantry Division
- 8th Infantry Division (later 8th Light Infantry Division, 8th Jäger Division)
- 9th Infantry Division (later 9th Volksgrenadier Division)
- 10th Infantry Division (later 10th Motorized Infantry Division, 10th Panzergrenadier Division)
- 11th Infantry Division
- 12th Infantry Division (later 12th Volksgrenadier Division)
- 13th Motorized Infantry Division (later 13th Panzer Division, Panzer Division Feldherrnhalle 2)
- 14th Infantry Division (later 14th Motorized Infantry Division, then 14th Infantry Division again)
- 14th Luftwaffe Infantry Division This unit was originally in the Luftwaffe as the 14th Luftwaffe Field Division.
- 15th Infantry Division
- 15th Panzergrenadier Division (previously 33rd Infantry Division, 15th Panzer Division) Not related to 15th Infantry Division.
- 16th Infantry Division (later split into: 16th Panzer Division, and 16th Motorized Infantry Division (later 16th Panzergrenadier Division, 116th Panzer Division)
- 16th Luftwaffe Infantry Division (later 16th Volksgrenadier Division) This unit was originally in the Luftwaffe as the 16th Luftwaffe Field Division.
- 17th Infantry Division
- 18th Infantry Division (later 18th Motorized Infantry Division, 18th Panzergrenadier Division)
- 18th Volksgrenadier Division Not related to the 18th Infantry Division.
- 19th Infantry Division (later 19th Panzer Division)
- 19th Grenadier Division (later 19th Volksgrenadier Division) This unit was originally in the Luftwaffe as the 19th Luftwaffe Field Division (later 19th Luftwaffe Sturm Division).
- 20th Motorized Infantry Division (later 20th Panzergrenadier Division)
- 21st Infantry Division
- 22nd Infantry Division (later 22nd Air Landing Division, 22nd Volksgrenadier Division)
- 23rd Infantry Division (later 26th Panzer Division) After being reorganized as the 26th Panzer Division, some of the 23rd Infantry Division's original components were used to create a new 23rd Infantry Division.
- 24th Infantry Division
- 25th Infantry Division (later 25th Motorized Infantry Division, 25th Panzergrenadier Division)
- 26th Infantry Division (later 26th Volksgrenadier Division)
- 27th Infantry Division (later 17th Panzer Division)
- 28th Light Infantry Division (later 28th Jäger Division)
- 29th Motorized Infantry Division (later 29th Panzergrenadier Division)
- 30th Infantry Division
- 31st Infantry Division (later 31st Grenadier Division, 31st Volksgrenadier Division)
- 32nd Infantry Division
- 33rd Infantry Division (later 15th Panzer Division, 15th Panzergrenadier Division)
- 34th Infantry Division
- 35th Infantry Division (later 35th Volksgrenadier Division)
- 36th Infantry Division (later 36th Motorized Infantry Division, then 36th Infantry Division again, 36th Grenadier Division, and finally 36th Volksgrenadier Division)
- 38th Infantry Division
- 39th Infantry Division (later 41st Fortress Division, 41st Infantry Division)
- 41st Infantry Division (previously 39th Infantry Division, 41st Fortress Division)
- 42nd Jäger Division (previously 187th Reserve Division)
- 44th Infantry Division (later 44th Reichsgrenadier Division Hoch und Deutschmeister)
- 45th Infantry Division (later 45th Grenadier Division, 45th Volksgrenadier Division)
- 46th Infantry Division

- 47th Infantry Division (previously Division Nr. 156, 156th Reserve Division; later 47th Volksgrenadier Division)
- 48th Infantry Division (later 48th Volksgrenadier Division)
- 49th Infantry Division
- 50th Infantry Division
- 52nd Infantry Division (later 52nd Field Training Division, 52nd Security Division)
- 56th Infantry Division
- 57th Infantry Division
- 58th Infantry Division
- 59th Infantry Division
- 60th Infantry Division (later 60th Motorized Infantry Division, Panzergrenadier Division Feldherrnhalle, and Panzer Division Feldherrnhalle 1)
- 61st Infantry Division (later 61st Volksgrenadier Division)
- 62nd Infantry Division (later 62nd Volksgrenadier Division)
- 64th Infantry Division
- 65th Infantry Division
- 68th Infantry Division
- 69th Infantry Division
- 70th Static Infantry Division
- 71st Infantry Division
- 72nd Infantry Division
- 73rd Infantry Division
- 75th Infantry Division
- 76th Infantry Division
- 77th Infantry Division
- 78th Infantry Division (later 78th Sturm Division, 78th Grenadier Division, 78th Volksgrenadier Division, and finally 78 Volkssturm Division)
- 79th Infantry Division (later 79th Volksgrenadier Division)
- 80th Infantry Division

- 81st Infantry Division
- 82nd Infantry Division
- 83rd Infantry Division
- 84th Infantry Division
- 85th Infantry Division
- 86th Infantry Division
- 87th Infantry Division
- 88th Infantry Division
- 89th Infantry Division
- 90th Light Infantry Division (previously the Division zbV Afrika; later 90th Light Afrika Division, 90th Panzergrenadier Division)
- 91st Infantry Division (later 91st Air Landing Division)
- 92nd Infantry Division
- 93rd Infantry Division
- 94th Infantry Division
- 95th Infantry Division (later 95th Volksgrenadier Division)
- 96th Infantry Division
- 97th Light Infantry Division (later 97th Jäger Division)
- 98th Infantry Division
- 99th Light Infantry Division (later 7th Mountain Division)
- 100th Light Infantry Division (later 100th Jäger Division)
- 101st Light Infantry Division (later 101st Jäger Division)
- 102nd Infantry Division
- 104th Jäger Division
- 106th Infantry Division
- 110th Infantry Division
- 114th Jäger Division
- 117th Jäger Division
- 118th Jäger Division
- 121st Infantry Division
- 122nd Infantry Division
- 126th Infantry Division

- 133rd Fortress Division
- Division zbV 140 (also 9th Mountain Division)
- 141st Reserve Division
- 143rd Reserve Division
- 147th Reserve Division
- 148th Reserve Division (redesignated 148th Infantry Division in September 1944)
- 149th Field Training Division
- 150th Field Training Division
- Division Nr. 151 (later 151st Reserve Division)
- Division Nr. 152
- Division Nr. 153 (later 153rd Reserve Division, 153rd Field Training Division, 153rd Grenadier Division)
- Division Nr. 154 (later 154th Reserve Division, 154th Field Training Division, 154th Infantry Division)
- Division Nr. 155 (later Division Nr. 155 (mot.), Panzer Division Nr. 155, 155th Reserve Panzer Division)
- 155th Field Training Division (later 155th Infantry Division) Not related to Division Nr. 155.
- Division Nr. 156 (later 156th Reserve Division, 47th Infantry Division, 47th Volksgrenadier Division)
- 156th Field Replacement Division (later 156th Infantry Division)
- Division Nr. 157 (later 157th Reserve Division, 157th Mountain Division, 8th Mountain Division)
- Division Nr. 158 (later 158th Reserve Division)
- Division Nr. 159 (later 159th Reserve Division, 159th Infantry Division)

## NUMBERED INFANTRY DIVISIONS (160–999)

- Division Nr. 160 (later 160th Reserve Division, 160th Infantry Division)
- 162nd Infantry Division (later 162nd Turkoman Division, with foreign troops)
- 163rd Infantry Division
- 164th Infantry Division (later Fortress Division Kreta, which split into: Fortress Brigade Kreta, and 164th Light Afrika Division)
- 165th Reserve Division
- 166th Reserve Division
- 167th Volksgrenadier Division
- 169th Infantry Division
- 170th Infantry Division
- 171st Reserve Division
- 172nd Reserve Division
- 173rd Reserve Division
- 174th Reserve Division
- 181st Infantry Division
- 182nd Reserve Division
- 183rd Volksgrenadier Division
- 187th Reserve Division (later 42nd Jäger Division)
- Division Nr. 188 (later 188th Reserve Mountain Division, 188th Mountain Division)
- 189th Reserve Division (later 189th Infantry Division)
- 191st Reserve Division
- 196th Infantry Division
- 197th Infantry Division
- 198th Infantry Division
- 199th Infantry Division
- 201st Security Division
- 203rd Security Division
- 205th Infantry Division (previously 14th Landwehr Division)
- 206th Infantry Division
- 207th Infantry Division (later 207th Security Division)
- 208th Infantry Division
- 210th Coastal Defence Division
- 211th Volksgrenadier Division
- 212th Infantry Division (later 578th Volksgrenadier Division, then renamed 212th Volksgrenadier Division)
- 213th Security Division
- 214th Infantry Division
- 216th Infantry Division
- 217th Infantry Division
- 218th Infantry Division
- 221st Security Division
- 227th Infantry Division
- 228th Infantry Division
- 230th Coastal Defence Division
- 232nd Infantry Division
- 233rd Panzergrenadier Division
- 237th Infantry Division
- 242nd Static Infantry Division
- 243rd Static Infantry Division
- 246th Volksgrenadier Division
- 250th Infantry Division (División Azul, the Spanish "Blue" Division in German service)
- 256th Infantry Division (Later 256th Volksgrenadier Division
- 257th Volksgrenadier Division
- 258th Infantry Division
- 264th Infantry Division
- 267th Infantry Division
- 268th Infantry Division
- 269th Infantry Division
- 270th Fortress Infantry Division
- 271st Volksgrenadier Division
- 272nd Volksgrenadier Division (previously 272nd Infantry Division)
- 274th Static Infantry Division
- 275th Infantry Division
- 276th Volksgrenadier Division
- 277th Infantry Division (later 277th Volksgrenadier Division)
- 278th Infantry Division
- 280th Fortress Infantry Division
- 281st Security Division (later 281st Infantry Division)
- 285th Security Division
- 286th Security Division
- 291st Infantry Division
- 295th Infantry Division (later 295th Fortress Infantry Division)
- 297th Infantry Division
- 300th Special Infantry Division
- 302nd Static Infantry Division (later 302nd Infantry Division)
- 305th Infantry Division
- 319th Infantry Division
- 320th Infantry Division (later 320th Volksgrenadier Division)
- 325th Security Division
- 326th Infantry Division (later 326th Volksgrenadier Division)
- 331st Infantry Division
- 332nd Static Infantry Division (later 332nd Infantry Division)
- 334th Infantry Division
- 337th Volksgrenadier Division
- 338th Infantry Division
- 340th Volksgrenadier Division
- 344th Static Infantry Division (later 344th Infantry Division)
- 345th Motorized Infantry Division
- 346th Infantry Division
- 347th Volksgrenadier Division
- 349th Volksgrenadier Division
- 352nd Infantry Division (later 352nd Volksgrenadier Division)
- 356th Infantry Division

- 361st Volksgrenadier Division
- 362nd Infantry Division
- 363rd Volksgrenadier Division
- 367th Infantry Division
- 369th Infantry Division
- 371st Infantry Division
- 373rd Infantry Division
- 376th Infantry Division
- 381st Field Training Division
- 382nd Field Training Division
- 384th Infantry Division
- 385th Infantry Division
- 386th Motorized Infantry Division
- 388th Field Training Division
- 389th Static Infantry Division
- 390th Security Division
- 390th Field Training Division
- 391st Security Division
- 391st Field Training Division
- 392nd Infantry Division
- 402nd Training Division
- 403rd Security Division
- 444th Security Division
- 454th Security Division
- 462nd Volksgrenadier Division
- 526th Reserve Division
- 541st Grenadier Division (later 541st Volksgrenadier Division)
- 542nd Grenadier Division (later 542nd Volksgrenadier Division)
- 543rd Grenadier Division
- 544th Grenadier Division (later 544th Volksgrenadier Division)
- 545th Grenadier Division (later 545th Volksgrenadier Division)
- 546th Grenadier Division
- 547th Grenadier Division (later 547th Volksgrenadier Division)
- 548th Grenadier Division (later 548th Volksgrenadier Division)

- 549th Grenadier Division (later 549th Volksgrenadier Division)
- 550th Grenadier Division
- 551st Grenadier Division (later 551st Volksgrenadier Division)
- 552nd Grenadier Division
- 553rd Grenadier Division (later 553rd Volksgrenadier Division)
- 558th Grenadier Division (later 558th Volksgrenadier Division)
- 559th Grenadier Division (later 559th Volksgrenadier Division)
- 560th Grenadier Division (later 560th Volksgrenadier Division)
- 561st Grenadier Division Ostpreußen 1 (later 561st Volksgrenadier Division)
- 562nd Grenadier Division Ostpreußen 2 (later 562nd Volksgrenadier Division)
- 563rd Grenadier Division (later 563rd Volksgrenadier Division)
- 564th Grenadier Division (later 564th Volksgrenadier Division)
- 565th Volksgrenadier Division
- 566th Volksgrenadier Division
- 567th Volksgrenadier Division
- 568th Volksgrenadier Division
- 569th Volksgrenadier Division
- 570th Volksgrenadier Division
- 571st Volksgrenadier Division
- 572nd Volksgrenadier Division
- 573rd Volksgrenadier Division
- 574th Volksgrenadier Division
- 575th Volksgrenadier Division (later 272nd Volksgrenadier Division)
- 576th Volksgrenadier Division
- 577th Volksgrenadier Division
- 578th Volksgrenadier Division (previously 212th Infantry Division; later 212th Volksgrenadier Division)

- 579th Volksgrenadier Division
- 580th Volksgrenadier Division
- 581st Volksgrenadier Division
- 582nd Volksgrenadier Division
- 583rd Volksgrenadier Division
- 584th Volksgrenadier Division
- 585th Volksgrenadier Division
- 586th Volksgrenadier Division
- 587th Volksgrenadier Division
- 588th Volksgrenadier Division
- 702nd Static Infantry Division
- 707th Security Division
- 708th Static Infantry Division (later 708th Coastal Defence Division, 708th Volksgrenadier Division)
- 709th Static Infantry Division
- 710th Static Infantry Division
- 715th Infantry Division
- 716th Static Infantry Division (later 716th Volksgrenadier Division)
- 719th Infantry Division
- Division Nr. 805
- 999th Light Afrika Division

of postal, supply, medical and veterinary troops. Its equipment included more than 640 light and heavy machine guns, 20 flamethrowers, nearly 100 7.92mm (0.31in) anti-tank rifles, up to 12 37mm (1.45in) anti-tank guns, approximately 150 50mm (1.97in), 81mm (3.2in) and later 120mm (4.7in) mortars, 75 75mm (2.95in), 105mm (4.1in) and 150mm (5.9in) artillery pieces, a small complement of armoured cars, nearly 1000 trucks, staff cars, and other vehicles, 450 motorcycles, over 1100 horse-drawn wagons or other transport, and 5400 horses.

By 1944, the composition of the *Feldheer* infantry division was markedly different. As early as 1941, several smaller divisions of two infantry regiments had been created, and the division of 1944, also referred to as 'Type 1944', had been reduced to an average complement of about 12,500 men. Although it retained the same basic structure, its equipment had been reduced as well, including fewer heavy machine guns and mortars. Most infantry divisions had also given up their complement of armoured cars by this time as well. Still, some modernization had occurred as firepower was

## GERMAN INFANTRY UNIT DESIGNATIONS

German infantry divisions had a variety of designations and specializations, though numbered in a single series. The major variations are as follows:

- **Fortress (*Festung*)**
  Divisions of non-standard organization used to garrison critical sites. The smaller ones might consist of only two or three battalions.

- **Grenadier**
  A morale-building honorific usually indicative of reduced strength when used alone.

- ***Jäger***
  Provided with partial horse or motor transport and usually lighter artillery, and reduced in size compared to an ordinary infantry division. Some of these were essentially identical to mountain divisions, and these were referred to as *Gebirgsjäger* (Mountain Light Infantry) divisions.

  This description does not apply to the light divisions in Africa (5th, 90th, 164th, 999th), nor to the five light mechanized divisions listed in their own subsection.

- **Motorized**
  Provided with full motor transport for all infantry and weapons systems. Usually reduced in size compared to an ordinary infantry division. Motorized infantry divisions were renamed Panzergrenadier (armoured infantry) divisions in 1943.

- ***Division Nummer***
  A sort of placeholder division, with a number (*Nummer*) and staff but few if any combat assets. These divisions started out without any type in their name (e.g., Division Nr. 179), though some acquired a type later on (e.g., Panzer Division Nr. 179).

- **Panzergrenadier**
  As motorized, but with more self-propelled weapons and an added battalion of tanks or fully armoured assault guns. What motorized divisions were referred to from 1943 forward.

- **Static (*bodenständige*)**
  Deficient in transport, even enough to move its own artillery. Many of these were divisions that had been mauled on the Eastern Front and were sent west to serve as coastal defence garrisons until sufficient resources were available to rehabilitate them.

- ***Volksgrenadier***
  A late-war reorganization with reduced size and increased short-range firepower. Many previously destroyed or badly mauled infantry divisions were reconstituted as *Volksgrenadier* divisions, and new ones were raised as well. Their fighting worth varied widely depending on unit experience and equipment. Not to be confused with *Volkssturm*, a national militia in which units were supposed to be organized by local Nazi Party leaders, trained by the SS, and come under *Wehrmacht* command in combat.

- **z.b.V.**
  ('z.b.V.' is an abbreviation meaning 'for special purposes') An *ad hoc* division created to meet a special requirement (e.g., Division z.b.V. *Afrika*).

augmented by the introduction of 120mm (4.7in) mortars, the 88mm (3.5in) shoulder-fired anti-tank *Panzerschreck*, which was patterned after the US Bazooka and rather cheaply produced, 75mm (2.95in) anti-tank and 150mm (5.9in) towed and self-propelled guns, and most notably the MP43 submachine gun and the Sturmgewehr 44 assault rifle, automatic weapons capable of substantially higher rates of fire than the standard bolt action Mauser K98k rifle. In due course, motor and horse transport were reduced in corresponding numbers to manpower and equipment. As always, the primary mode of transportation for the infantry of the *Heer* throughout World War II was the foot march.

By 1945, a number of infantry divisions had been so reduced in strength that they sometimes barely constituted more than a battalion or regiment in terms of combat personnel; however, these units generally maintained their divisional nomenclature which is sometimes

misleading to the casual observer. New divisions were created from the survivors of those which had been devastated in combat. Replacements sometimes were available to partially replenish the ranks.

In some cases, entirely new divisions were formed and given the same number as an earlier division which had been completely lost in action and possibly even removed from the active roll. Some infantry divisions were named for prominent individuals or locales, while most were numbered in a confusing linear process from 1 to 36 followed by 44, 45 and 46, then 50 to 100 and 200 to 300. Some of these divisions were later manned by old men or boys and renamed as *Volkssturm* divisions. Although the *Volksgrenadier* division also appeared later in the war, many of these were of good quality and acquitted themselves well in combat. As available manpower waned, conscripts from occupied territories, foreign volunteers, and even prisoners of war were pressed into

service, particularly in the static divisions which manned the Atlantic Wall defences or served as occupation troops.

The command structure of the German infantry division was divided into three primary groups, tactical, supply and personnel. Within the tactical group were operations and intelligence officers along with the commanders of the division artillery and engineers, a *Luftwaffe* liaison officer and others whose roles facilitated the coordination of air, armour and infantry assets during combat. In the supply group officers controlled the distribution of replacement weapons and ammunition, combat engineer deployment, food, payroll, medical, chaplaincy and other essential services. The personnel group primarily functioned as the division judge advocate corps, dealing with legal matters, while also processing personnel transfers, maintaining records and providing security for the division staff.

# Bitter Combat

*Among the* Feldheer *divisions typical of the early years of the war was the 216th, which was created just days before the invasion of Poland. Raised primarily from* Wehrkreis *XI, headquartered in the city of Hanover, the capital of the region of Lower Saxony, the 216th was a Wave Three division formed as the rearmament and expansion of the* Heer *were well underway.*

With a strength of 17,200 troops, the 216th Infantry Division occupied defensive positions along Germany's western frontier and did not take part

in the Polish campaign. By the spring of 1940, it consisted of Infantry Regiments 348, 396 and 398. Artillery Regiment 216 was also assigned,

along with the requisite pioneer, anti-tank, signals and services battalions, and a field replacement battalion. Following the fall of France, the division occupied the Channel Islands of Jersey and Guernsey.

In the wake of the Soviet winter counteroffensive on the Eastern Front during late 1941, the 216th Division was transferred to Russia and divided into several battle groups which fought with distinction, particularly an organization of the 348th Regiment, which was encircled in January 1942 by elements of the Soviet Tenth Army near the town of Sukhinitchi and managed to resist numerous attacks over an extended period before being relieved.

Later assigned to Army Group Centre, the 216th Division fought in numerous engagements on the

## INFANTRY REGIMENT ORGANIZATION, 1944

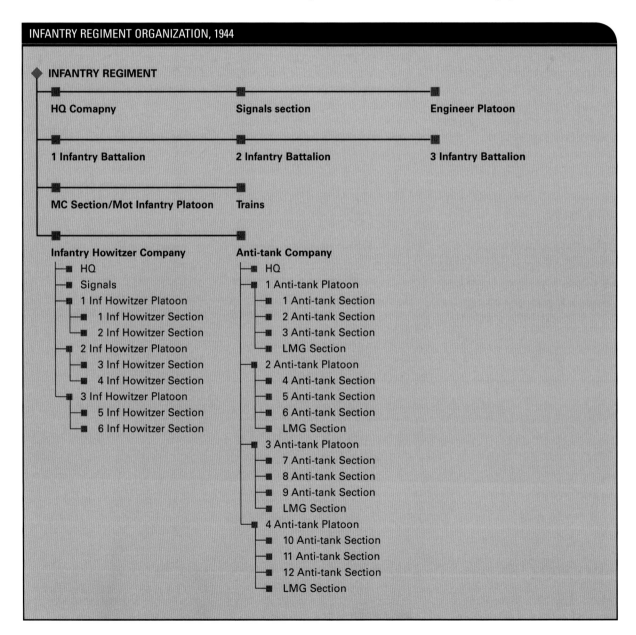

**INFANTRY REGIMENT**

- HQ Comapny
- Signals section
- Engineer Platoon
- 1 Infantry Battalion
- 2 Infantry Battalion
- 3 Infantry Battalion
- MC Section/Mot Infantry Platoon
- Trains

**Infantry Howitzer Company**
- HQ
- Signals
- 1 Inf Howitzer Platoon
  - 1 Inf Howitzer Section
  - 2 Inf Howitzer Section
- 2 Inf Howitzer Platoon
  - 3 Inf Howitzer Section
  - 4 Inf Howitzer Section
- 3 Inf Howitzer Platoon
  - 5 Inf Howitzer Section
  - 6 Inf Howitzer Section

**Anti-tank Company**
- HQ
- 1 Anti-tank Platoon
  - 1 Anti-tank Section
  - 2 Anti-tank Section
  - 3 Anti-tank Section
  - LMG Section
- 2 Anti-tank Platoon
  - 4 Anti-tank Section
  - 5 Anti-tank Section
  - 6 Anti-tank Section
  - LMG Section
- 3 Anti-tank Platoon
  - 7 Anti-tank Section
  - 8 Anti-tank Section
  - 9 Anti-tank Section
  - LMG Section
- 4 Anti-tank Platoon
  - 10 Anti-tank Section
  - 11 Anti-tank Section
  - 12 Anti-tank Section
  - LMG Section

Eastern Front, including Orel, Briansk and Rshev. During the Battle of Kursk in July 1943, the division was attached to Field Marshal Walter Model's Ninth Army and was involved in heavy action during German attacks along the north shoulder of the Kursk Salient, sustaining grievous losses. By the autumn of 1943, the division had been further depleted during the retreat to the defensive line along the Dnieper River. It was eventually disbanded, with elements including portions of its three infantry regiments, its organic artillery regiment, and its pioneer battalion transferring to Belgium to form the nucleus of the new 272nd Infantry Division, while other components remained on the Eastern Front and were absorbed by the 102nd Infantry Division.

The 272nd Infantry Division was officially formed in the vicinity of the

## INFANTRY BATTALION ORGANIZATION, 1944

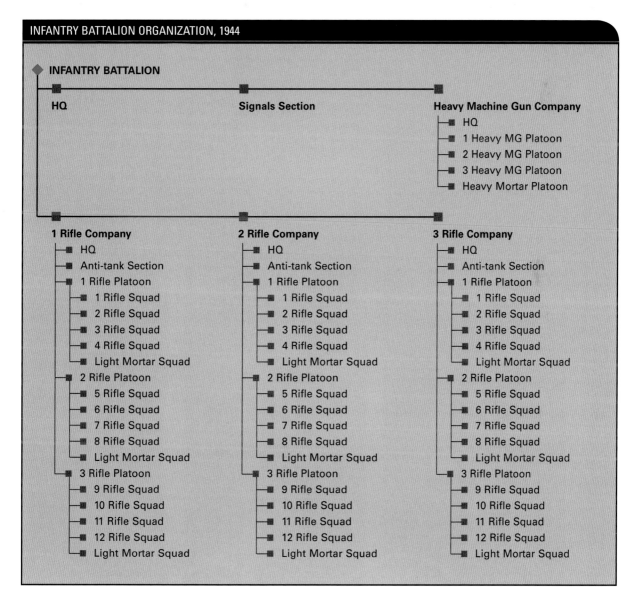

**INFANTRY BATTALION**

HQ

Signals Section

Heavy Machine Gun Company
- HQ
- 1 Heavy MG Platoon
- 2 Heavy MG Platoon
- 3 Heavy MG Platoon
- Heavy Mortar Platoon

**1 Rifle Company**
- HQ
- Anti-tank Section
- 1 Rifle Platoon
  - 1 Rifle Squad
  - 2 Rifle Squad
  - 3 Rifle Squad
  - 4 Rifle Squad
  - Light Mortar Squad
- 2 Rifle Platoon
  - 5 Rifle Squad
  - 6 Rifle Squad
  - 7 Rifle Squad
  - 8 Rifle Squad
  - Light Mortar Squad
- 3 Rifle Platoon
  - 9 Rifle Squad
  - 10 Rifle Squad
  - 11 Rifle Squad
  - 12 Rifle Squad
  - Light Mortar Squad

**2 Rifle Company**
- HQ
- Anti-tank Section
- 1 Rifle Platoon
  - 1 Rifle Squad
  - 2 Rifle Squad
  - 3 Rifle Squad
  - 4 Rifle Squad
  - Light Mortar Squad
- 2 Rifle Platoon
  - 5 Rifle Squad
  - 6 Rifle Squad
  - 7 Rifle Squad
  - 8 Rifle Squad
  - Light Mortar Squad
- 3 Rifle Platoon
  - 9 Rifle Squad
  - 10 Rifle Squad
  - 11 Rifle Squad
  - 12 Rifle Squad
  - Light Mortar Squad

**3 Rifle Company**
- HQ
- Anti-tank Section
- 1 Rifle Platoon
  - 1 Rifle Squad
  - 2 Rifle Squad
  - 3 Rifle Squad
  - 4 Rifle Squad
  - Light Mortar Squad
- 2 Rifle Platoon
  - 5 Rifle Squad
  - 6 Rifle Squad
  - 7 Rifle Squad
  - 8 Rifle Squad
  - Light Mortar Squad
- 3 Rifle Platoon
  - 9 Rifle Squad
  - 10 Rifle Squad
  - 11 Rifle Squad
  - 12 Rifle Squad
  - Light Mortar Squad

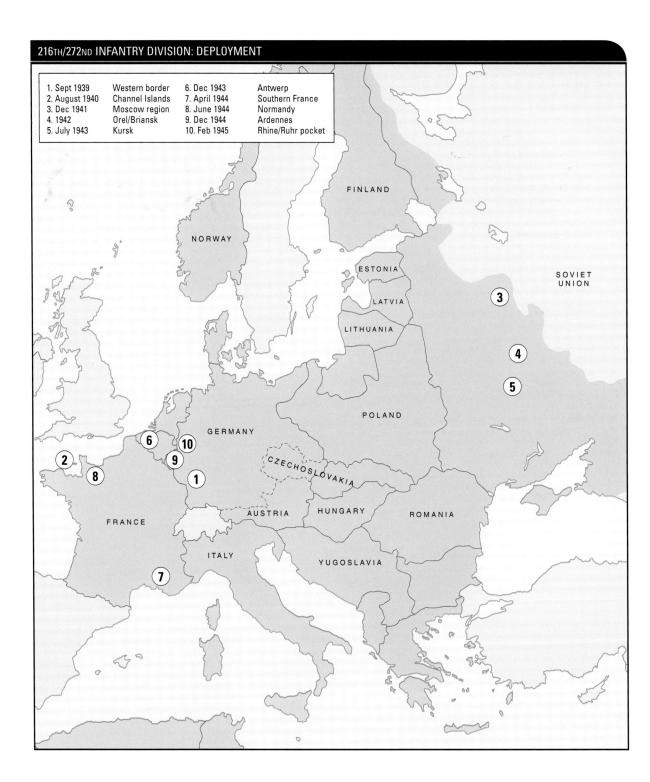

216TH/272ND INFANTRY DIVISION: DEPLOYMENT

| 1. Sept 1939 | Western border | 6. Dec 1943 | Antwerp |
| 2. August 1940 | Channel Islands | 7. April 1944 | Southern France |
| 3. Dec 1941 | Moscow region | 8. June 1944 | Normandy |
| 4. 1942 | Orel/Briansk | 9. Dec 1944 | Ardennes |
| 5. July 1943 | Kursk | 10. Feb 1945 | Rhine/Ruhr pocket |

Belgian port city of Antwerp on 12 December 1943, along the organizational template of the Type 1944 division. At inception, it consisted of the headquarters and other elements of the old 216th Division, which were simply renamed with the number of the new division. Infantry Regiments 396 and 398 were disbanded, with the exception of a single battalion of the 396th, which retained its commander from the Eastern Front and was renamed Fusilier Battalion 272.

Infantry Regiment 348 was redesignated Grenadier Regiment 980, while two additional grenadier regiments, 981 and 982, were composed of reservists and replacement troops drawn from the 182nd Reserve Division of the *Ersatzheer*. Other divisional units, including the anti-tank and pioneer battalions, were also formed from Replacement Army troops. Thus, the new 272nd Infantry Division was actually an amalgamation of veterans, reservists, and replacements. Its order of battle in early 1944 included the three grenadier regiments, 980, 981 and 982, Fusilier Battalion 272, and its artillery, pioneer, service and replacement battalions. Its total personnel numbered 12,725.

During nine months of service in the West, the 272nd Infantry Division trained in Belgium and transferred briefly to the coast of Southern France. In mid-June, its total strength included 1514 Russian prisoners who had reportedly volunteered for service with the *Feldheer* in order to escape the misery of life in a POW camp. Despite its patchwork composition, the division was instrumental in holding the strategically-important Norman town

■ **A rifle squad marches uphill in single file during the invasion of the Soviet Union, August 1941.**

## GERMAN DIVISIONS BY THEATRE, OCTOBER 1941

| Theatre | Divisions |
|---|---|
| Germany | 0 |
| East | 149 |
| West | 40 |
| Norway | 7 |
| Finland | 6 |
| South East | 9 |
| North Africa | 2 |

## EASTERN FRONT OPPOSING FORCES, MARCH 1945

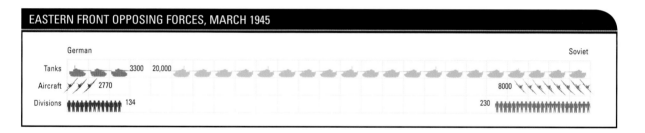

| | German | Soviet |
|---|---|---|
| Tanks | 3300 | 20,000 |
| Aircraft | 2770 | 8000 |
| Divisions | 134 | 230 |

of Caen against repeated Allied attacks following the D-Day landings of 6 June 1944. The division was twice recognized in German newspapers for its tenacity in battle. 'The 272nd Infantry Division, relying principally on the fierce resistance of its grenadiers, is thanked for its timely counter-attack against the enemy, preventing a breakthrough south of Caen,' read one account of the action. According to Allied planners, Caen was to have been captured on D-Day.

However, the Germans held the town for a month, disrupting the Allied timetable. The combat during 25–26 July was extraordinarily savage, with the 272nd defending Verrières Ridge against an offensive spearheaded by Canadian troops and preceded by a

heavy artillery bombardment. In early August, the division had sustained in excess of 60 per cent casualties and was withdrawn to the town of Troarn where it was reinforced by elements of the 16th *Luftwaffe* Field Division. Later, it executed a fighting retreat across the German frontier.

Shattered by the fighting in Normandy, the 272nd Infantry Division was redesignated the 272nd *Volksgrenadier* Division on 17 September 1944. With a strength of 10,000 troops, the division was then composed of the remnants of the old 272nd Division and the newly-formed 575th *Volksgrenadier* Division. The *Volksgrenadier* divisional organization included three infantry regiments of two battalions each, a fusilier company, an artillery regiment of four

battalions, anti-tank, pioneer and signals battalions, and support troops. Many of these troops were former members of the *Luftwaffe* or the *Kriegsmarine*, who had been pressed into service as infantrymen.

Following a six-week training period at Döberitz in Germany, the 272nd *Volksgrenadier* Division fought in the Hürtgen Forest and during the withdrawal across the Rhine River. At Kesternich, during savage fighting in mid-December 1944, the division participated in the Ardennes offensive and took more than 300 prisoners, virtually destroying the 310th Infantry Regiment of the US Army's 78th Infantry Division. In April 1945, the bulk of the division was trapped in the Ruhr Pocket and compelled to surrender to the Allies.

# Specialized Divisions

*As the fortunes of war turned against Germany, the need for manpower to defend conquered territory and then the homeland of the Reich increased substantially.*

Although they were divisions of the *Feldheer*, the *Volksgrenadier* divisions which emerged in late 1944 were created following the attempt on Hitler's life at the Wolf's Lair in East Prussia on 20 July of that year and were technically under the command of *Reichsführer-SS* Heinrich Himmler.

As with the 272nd *Volksgrenadier* Division, the concept of the people's infantry was established upon a battle-hardened foundation of combat veterans. Additional troops

were often of lower quality as training periods were compressed and personnel from other arms of the service were handed rifles. Although the projected strength of the *Volksgrenadier* division was similar to that of a Type 1944 division, the actual strength of these lower-quality formations was rarely greater than 10,000. As with other late-war infantry and armoured divisions of the *Feldheer*, it was expected that superior weapons technology might compensate for the

**LANDWEHR DIVISIONS**

- 14th Landwehr Division (later 205th Infantry Division)
- 97th Landwehr Division

deficiencies in numbers and training of the soldiers themselves.

The standard *Volksgrenadier* division included three infantry regiments, artillery and supply regiments, anti-tank, engineer and signals battalions, and a fusilier formation of either company or battalion size which was created to deploy the division's heaviest infantry weapons and to provide reconnaissance. Of particular interest is the fact that a consolidation of the organic units within the *Volksgrenadier* division as compared to the 1938 or 1944 infantry division tables of organization and equipment resulted in a requirement for fewer officers, non-commissioned officers and support personnel. Therefore, the theoretical combat capability of the *Volksgrenadier* division was not diminished.

The complement of weapons and equipment for a standard *Volksgrenadier* division included approximately 2000 submachine guns and assault rifles of the MP40 or Sturmgewehr 44 type and concentrated in the fusilier formation, nearly 450 heavy and light machine guns, 66 81mm (3.2in) and 120mm (4.7in) mortars, a dozen flamethrowers, more than 80 75mm (2.95in), 105mm (4.1in) and 150mm (5.9in) field guns and howitzers, a few 37mm (1.45in) anti-aircraft guns, more than 20 75mm (2.95in) anti-tank guns, over 200 anti-tank *Panzerschreck*,

## *VOLKSGRENADIER* DIVISIONS

| | | |
|---|---|---|
| ■ 6.Volksgrenadier-Division | ■ 277.Volksgrenadier-Division | ■ 564.Volksgrenadier-Division |
| ■ 9.Volksgrenadier-Division | ■ 320.Volksgrenadier-Division | ■ 565.Volksgrenadier-Division |
| ■ 12.Volksgrenadier-Division | ■ 326.Volksgrenadier-Division | ■ 566.Volksgrenadier-Division |
| ■ 16.Volksgrenadier-Division | ■ 337.Volksgrenadier-Division | ■ 567.Volksgrenadier-Division |
| ■ 18.Volksgrenadier-Division | ■ 340.Volksgrenadier-Division | ■ 568.Volksgrenadier-Division |
| ■ 19.Volksgrenadier-Division | ■ 347.Volksgrenadier-Division | ■ 569.Volksgrenadier-Division |
| ■ 22.Volksgrenadier-Division | ■ 349.Volksgrenadier-Division | ■ 570.Volksgrenadier-Division |
| ■ 26.Volksgrenadier-Division | ■ 352.Volksgrenadier-Division | ■ 571.Volksgrenadier-Division |
| ■ 31.Volksgrenadier-Division | ■ 361.Volksgrenadier-Division | ■ 572.Volksgrenadier-Division |
| ■ 36.Volksgrenadier-Division | ■ 363.Volksgrenadier-Division | ■ 573.Volksgrenadier-Division |
| ■ 45.Volksgrenadier-Division | ■ 462.Volksgrenadier-Division | ■ 574.Volksgrenadier-Division |
| ■ 47.Volksgrenadier-Division | ■ 541.Volksgrenadier-Division | ■ 575.Volksgrenadier-Division |
| ■ 61.Volksgrenadier-Division | ■ 542.Volksgrenadier-Division | ■ 576.Volksgrenadier-Division |
| ■ 62.Volksgrenadier-Division | ■ 544.Volksgrenadier-Division | ■ 577.Volksgrenadier-Division |
| ■ 78.Volksgrenadier-Division | ■ 545.Volksgrenadier-Division | ■ 578.Volksgrenadier-Division |
| ■ 79.Volksgrenadier-Division | ■ 547.Volksgrenadier-Division | ■ 579.Volksgrenadier-Division |
| ■ 167.Volksgrenadier-Division | ■ 548.Volksgrenadier-Division | ■ 580.Volksgrenadier-Division |
| ■ 183.Volksgrenadier-Division | ■ 549.Volksgrenadier-Division | ■ 581.Volksgrenadier-Division |
| ■ 211.Volksgrenadier-Division | ■ 551.Volksgrenadier-Division | ■ 582.Volksgrenadier-Division |
| ■ 212.Volksgrenadier-Division | ■ 553.Volksgrenadier-Division | ■ 583.Volksgrenadier-Division |
| ■ 246.Volksgrenadier-Division | ■ 558.Volksgrenadier-Division | ■ 584.Volksgrenadier-Division |
| ■ 256.Volksgrenadier-Division | ■ 559.Volksgrenadier-Division | ■ 585.Volksgrenadier-Division |
| ■ 257.Volksgrenadier-Division | ■ 560.Volksgrenadier-Division | ■ 586.Volksgrenadier-Division |
| ■ 271.Volksgrenadier-Division | ■ 561.Volksgrenadier-Division | ■ 587.Volksgrenadier-Division |
| ■ 272.Volksgrenadier-Division | ■ 562.Volksgrenadier-Division | ■ 588.Volksgrenadier-Division |
| ■ 276.Volksgrenadier-Division | ■ 563.Volksgrenadier-Division | ■ 708.Volksgrenadier-Division |

and a large quantity of the hollow-charge anti-tank *Panzerfaust* which was also fired from the shoulder. Transportation included more than 3000 horses, as the *Feldheer* continued to be heavily dependent on draught animals, 120 motorcycles, over 400 motorized vehicles, and about 1500 bicycles primarily in use with the pioneer battalion.

While the German airborne or parachute divisions were actually a component of the *Luftwaffe*, they were operationally under the control of OKH for the majority of the war. Created by General Kurt Student, the airborne, or *Fallschirmjäger*, were considered an elite corps within the German armed forces. These divisions were conceived during the

mid-1930s, and Student took command of the 7th *Fallschirmjäger* Division, the first of its kind, in September 1938.

German airborne divisions consisted initially of both parachute and glider-borne troops, and their combat prowess was demonstrated early in the war with the seizure of Fort Eben Emael in Belgium during the conquest of France and the Low Countries in the spring of 1940. In early 1941, however, the airborne troops were decimated during Operation 'Mercury', the invasion of the island of Crete in the Eastern Mediterranean, which was primarily conceived as an airborne operation.

As a result of these heavy losses, Hitler forbade further large-scale airborne operations for the remainder of the war.

Thus, as 10 airborne divisions were formed during the course of the war and an 11th was authorized but never fielded, the *Fallschirmjäger* fought primarily as infantry in World War II. These troops proved tenacious in the defensive role, particularly at Monte Cassino during the Italian campaign and in the hedgerows of Normandy in the summer of 1944. Intended as units with quick strike capability rather than formations which could function at high efficiency in combat zones for lengthy periods,

## NAMED DIVISIONS

- **Führer Begleit Division** Escort formation formed to protect Hitler's Eastern Front Headquarters.

- **Führer Grenadier Division**

- **Panzergrenadier Division Brandenburg**

- **Panzergrenadier Division Feldherrnhalle** (previously 60th Infantry Division, 60th Motorized Infantry Division; later Panzer Division Feldherrnhalle 1)

- **Panzergrenadier Division Grossdeutschland**

- **Grenadier Division Lehr** Not related to Panzer Lehr

- **Jäger Division Alpen**

- **Division von Broich/von Manteuffel** Tunisia Nov 1942 – May 1943

## *FALLSCHIRMJÄGER* DIVISIONS

The Hermann Göring formations grew from a single police detachment to an entire armoured corps over the course of the war. The later epithet *Fallschirm* ('Parachute') was purely honorific.

- Hermann Göring Division (later Panzer Division Hermann Göring, Parachute Panzer Division 1 Hermann Göring)

- Parachute Panzergrenadier Division 2 Hermann Göring

Airborne divisions
- 1st Parachute Division (April 1943 7th Flieger becomes 1st Fallschirmjäger)

- 2nd Parachute Division

- 3rd Parachute Division

- 4th Parachute Division

- 5th Parachute Division

- 6th Parachute Division

- 7th Parachute Division (previously Group Erdmann, an *ad hoc* collection of *Luftwaffe* assets on the Western Front)

- 8th Parachute Division

- 9th Parachute Division

- 10th Parachute Division

- 11th Parachute Division (started to be formed March 1945; fought as battle groups only)

- 20th Parachute Division (formation ordered 20 March 1945 in the Netherlands, from Parachute Training and Replacement Division; however, formation was not completed beyond cadre)

- 21st Parachute Division (formation ordered 5 April 1945 in the Netherlands, as a Field Training Division; however, formation was not completed beyond cadre)

*Fallschirmjäger* divisions were lightly armed. Actual troop strength was considerably lower than the originally planned complement of 16,000, which was never achieved.

The combat element of the division was grouped in three regiments, each containing three battalions of parachute infantrymen, headquarters, an anti-tank company, and a light gun or mortar company. In addition, the *Fallschirmjäger* division included an artillery regiment, anti-aircraft, pioneer, anti-tank, signals and heavy weapons battalions, a reconnaissance company and a services section.

The parachute infantryman with full combat load was distinguishable by his distinctive bowl-shaped steel helmet, thigh-length camouflage smock and baggy trousers. Organic weapons and support equipment fielded at the divisional level included more than 1000 light and heavy machine guns, up to 200 81mm (3.2in) and 120mm (4.7in) mortars, 20 flamethrowers, 250 anti-tank *Panzerschreck*, 2150 motor vehicles, 39 towed 20mm (0.79in) anti-aircraft guns, 12 heavier 88mm (3.5in) anti-aircraft guns, more than 50 75mm (2.95in) anti-tank and light artillery pieces, 36 105mm (4.1in) and 150mm (5.9in) howitzers, and nearly 400 motorcycles.

## 'Green Devils'

The hard-fighting *Fallschirmjäger* earned the nickname the 'Green Devils' from their adversaries, and among the best known of these divisions was the 2nd, formed in February 1943, in the province of Brittany in Western France. In the spring, the division was transferred to Italy, briefly occupying Rome. Its Company 1 participated in the rescue of the deposed Italian dictator Benito Mussolini from the Gran Sasso, high in the Italian Alps. Elements were later sent to the Eastern Front while others formed the nucleus of the 4th *Fallschirmjäger* Division and the remainder moved to the vicinity of Cologne in Western Germany for refitting.

Following the surrender of the bulk of the 2nd *Fallschirmjäger* Division at Brest in September 1944, it was reconstituted later in the same month as the scattered remnants of the original division were brought together in the Netherlands. After fighting through the winter of 1944–45, the division finally capitulated in the Ruhr Pocket.

In 1938, the *Feldheer* formed the first of nine lightly-equipped mountain divisions, each projected with a strength of slightly more than 13,000 troops. These *Gebirgsjäger* (mountain troops) were highly dependent upon horses and mules for transportation given the difficult terrain in which they were intended to operate. A division typically included more than 3000 pack animals which carried supplies, ammunition and artillery pieces broken down into a number of separate loads. The mountain divisions of the *Feldheer* fielded two *Gebirgsjäger* regiments, each consisting of three combat battalions, headquarters and anti-tank companies, and a service section. Other formations included reconnaissance, signals, and pioneer battalions, and an artillery regiment.

## PERSONAL FIREARMS OF THE GERMAN INFANTRYMAN

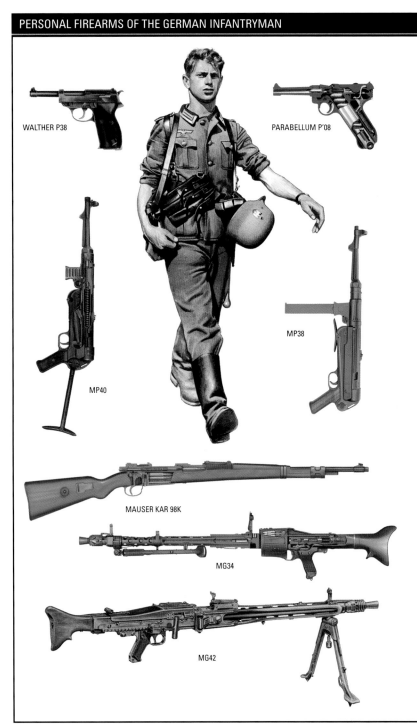

WALTHER P38

PARABELLUM P'08

MP38

MP40

MAUSER KAR 98K

MG34

MG42

**Walther P38**

CALIBRE: 9mm (0.354in) Parabellum
OPERATION: Short recoil
WEIGHT: 0.96kg (2.11lb)
LENGTH: 213mm (8.38in)
MUZZLE VELOCITY: 350m/sec (1150ft/sec)
RANGE: 30m (98ft)

**Parabellum P'08**

CALIBRE: 9mm (0.354in) Parabellum
OPERATION: Short recoil
WEIGHT: 0.87kg (1.92lb)
LENGTH: 233mm (8.75in)
MUZZLE VELOCITY: 380m/sec (1247ft/sec)
RANGE: 30m (98ft)

**MP38**

CALIBRE: 9mm (0.354in) Parabellum
OPERATION: Blowback
WEIGHT: 4.1kg (9.1lb)
LENGTH: 832mm (32.75in) stock extended
MUZZLE VELOCITY: 395m/sec (1300ft/sec)
RANGE: 70m (230ft)

**MP40**

CALIBRE: 9mm (0.354in) Parabellum
OPERATION: Blowback
WEIGHT: 3.97kg (8.75lb)
LENGTH: 832mm (32.75in) stock extended
MUZZLE VELOCITY: 395m/sec (1300ft/sec)
RANGE: 70m (230ft)

**Kar 98**

CALIBRE: 7.92mm (0.31in)
OPERATION: Bolt action
WEIGHT: 3.9kg (8.6lb)
LENGTH: 1110mm (43.7in)
MUZZLE VELOCITY: 745m/sec (2444ft/sec)
RANGE: 500m (547yd)

**MG34**

CALIBRE: 7.92mm (0.31in)
OPERATION: Recoil-operated, air-cooled
WEIGHT: 12.1kg (26.67lb)
LENGTH: 1219mm (48in)
MUZZLE VELOCITY: 762m/sec (2500ft/sec)
RANGE: 2000m (6600ft) plus

**MG42**

CALIBRE: 7.92mm (0.31in)
OPERATION: Short recoil, air-cooled
WEIGHT: 11.5kg (25.35lb)
LENGTH: 1220mm (48in)
MUZZLE VELOCITY: 800m/sec (2650ft/sec)
RANGE: 3000m (10,0000ft) plus

The *Gebirgs* division included special-purpose equipment for negotiating mountain peaks and passes, nearly 70 light 75mm (2.95in), 105mm (4.1in) and 150mm (5.9in) mountain howitzers, 24 75mm (2.95in) and three 37mm (1.45in) anti-tank guns, 72 *Panzerschreck*, a dozen 20mm (0.79in) anti-aircraft guns, 20 flamethrowers, 72 81mm (3.2in) and 120mm (4.7in) mortars, and nearly 500 light and heavy machine guns. During the war, an additional five mountain divisions were formed by the *Waffen-SS*.

The *Jäger* division, a type of light infantry formation, was roughly equivalent to the mountain division in terms of manpower. These highly-mobile divisions had motor vehicles and were less dependent on pack animals than the *Gebirgs* divisions. Their light armament was ideal for operations in difficult terrain, and they were used extensively in the war with the Soviet Union and in Greece and the Balkans.

# Polish Onslaught

*Fighting during the opening days of the war, the 1st* Gebirgs *Division spearheaded the advance of Army Group South toward the strategically-vital city of Lvov.*

Capturing and traversing the Dukla Pass in the Carpathian mountains of Southern Poland, elements of the division advanced more than 240km (150 miles) eastward toward their objective with a battle group of four *Gebirgsjäger* companies supported by anti-tank, artillery and pioneer units in the vanguard. Advancing rapidly and well ahead of any support, this battle group established a base for an anticipated assault against Lvov. However, this never materialized when troops of the Soviet Red Army, then allied with Germany during the early Polish campaign, invaded Poland from the east. Facing stiff Polish resistance around Lvov, the division lost 243 men killed in action and 400 wounded.

Following the Polish campaign, the 1st *Gebirgs* Division was moved to the West and participated in the invasion of France and the Low Countries, crossing difficult terrain and traversing three major rivers, the Aisne, the Maas and the Loire. Held in reserve for the anticipated invasion of Great Britain or an attempt to capture Gibraltar, neither of which took place, the division was then transferred to Yugoslavia and eventually to the Eastern Front.

During months of combat against the Red Army, the division was divided into a pair of smaller formations. One of these, in company with elements of the 4th *Gebirgs* Division, held Mount Elbrus in the Caucasus – at an elevation of more than 4700m (15,500ft), the tenth-highest peak in the world – against assaults by Red Army mountain troops. The 1st *Gebirgs* Division fought during the retreat from the Caucasus and in the Balkans and Hungary, before moving into Austria near the end of the war and surrendering to US forces.

### Other divisions
A variety of special-purpose divisions were formed under the auspices of the *Feldheer* during World War II. Among these were the seven fortress divisions, which were limited in combat capability and intended to garrison strategically-important cities or geographic areas and named for these. The fortress divisions were not formed along the lines of standard infantry divisions and included fewer troops and often inferior equipment.

| GEBIRGSJÄGER (MOUNTAIN TROOPS) DIVISION EQUIPMENT, 1938 | |
|---|---|
| Equipment | Total |
| Troops | 13,000 |
| Pack animals | 3000 |
| Mountain howtzers | 70 |
| 37mm (1.45in) anti-tank guns | 3 |
| Panzerschreck | 72 |
| 20mm (0.79in) anti-aircraft guns | 12 |
| Flamethrowers | 20 |
| Mortars | 72 |
| Machine guns | 500 |

## THE BRANDENBURGERS

German special forces and elite units earned reputations for skill, daring and combat prowess during World War II. While the SS commandos led by Major Otto Skorzeny are perhaps the best known, the Brandenburg Regiment, which originated during the inter-war years, was under the operational control of OKH rather than a subordinate command of the Heer until 1944 when it was transferred to the Grossdeutschland Panzer Corps. The Brandenburg Regiment began the war as Bataillon Ebbinghaus and participated in the Polish campaign. The unit included Polish-speaking Germans who achieved great success in the opening days of the campaign, operating behind Polish lines to disrupt communications, seize bridges and crossroads, and gather intelligence.

Although its combat debut was a resounding success, Bataillon Ebbinghaus was disbanded following the Polish campaign. Within a month, Admiral Wilhelm Canaris, chief of the Abwehr, authorized the formation of a regiment under its nominal control with the euphemistic name of Lehr und Bau Kompanie z.b.V. 800, or Training and Construction Company No. 800. Canaris received support from OKW to raise the company under the auspices of the Abwehr; however, the unit remained under the operational command of OKH. Originally, the regiment included four companies of multi-lingual special-forces soldiers along with parachute and motorcycle platoons.

■ Brandenburgers prepare for covert operations during the invasion of Poland, September 1939.

During the German invasion of the Low Countries, commandos dressed as Dutch civilians and soldiers escorting German prisoners successfully seized a key bridge across the Meuse River. While training for the expected invasion of Great Britain and a possible move to capture Gibraltar, the unit increased in size and was designated the Brandenburg Regiment. Its troops operated in small detachments consisting of as few as 12 men or in formations as large as a 250-man group. Skilled in demolition, the use of enemy weapons, the customs and mannerisms of non-Germans, and escape and evasion, the Brandenburgers operated almost exclusively behind enemy lines. Their units deployed in the Balkans, North Africa, the Eastern Front, and in the Mediterranean.

By 1944, the mistrust of the Abwehr was growing among top-ranking Nazis, and following the 20 July attempt to assassinate Hitler, the last vestiges of control of the Brandenburg Regiment were stripped from Canaris and passed briefly to the intelligence arm of the SS. Shortly thereafter, it was attached to the Grossdeutschland Panzer Corps, the descendant of one of the elite divisions of the Feldheer. It was renamed the Infantry Division Brandenburg (Motorized), and the majority of the troops were transferred to the Eastern Front, although about 1800 Brandenburgers were allowed to join Skorzeny's elite SS commandos. In the autumn of 1944, a panzer regiment was acquired, and the unit was designated Panzergrenadier Division Brandenburg.

During its later incarnations, the Brandenburg Division of 1943–44 included four light infantry regiments, an artillery regiment, coastal raider and parachute battalions, specialized tropical and desert units, an independent parachute company, and a signals company. The Panzergrenadier Division Brandenburg, which operated in 1944–45, consisted of two regiments of motorized light infantry, an artillery regiment, anti-tank, flak, reconnaissance, pioneer and signals battalions, and a panzer regiment.

These divisions were named Fortress Division Danzig, Warsaw, Swinemünde, Stettin, Frankfurt-Oder, Kreta and Gotenhafen.

Some of those divisions which were decimated in combat on the Eastern Front and transferred to other areas for garrison duty were designated as static divisions. These divisions were deficient in transport and often unable to move their organic units or equipment. At times, this transportation capability and some heavy equipment had been stripped from depleted divisions for use elsewhere. A number of static divisions remained in coastal defence roles through to the end of the war, while others were reconstituted, re-equipped and returned to the front lines.

In order to provide troops for the land army, both *Luftwaffe* and *Kriegsmarine* divisions were formed during the war. Among the six naval infantry divisions organized, the 1st Naval Division was formed in Stettin in February 1945 from naval

replacement troops and the Marine *Schützen* Brigade Nord, which had been constituted in the autumn of 1944 for the defence of the Baltic coast of Germany. The division included three infantry regiments, an artillery regiment, a fusilier company, and anti-tank, pioneer and logistics battalions.

The *Luftwaffe* field divisions were authorized in 1942, when it was originally suggested that other branches of the service could augment the ground divisions of the *Heer*. Rather than place command of these divisions directly within the *Heer*, *Luftwaffe* chief Hermann Göring intended to maintain control of the units, which were raised from a pool of more than 200,000 *Luftwaffe* ground staff and administrative personnel who were serving in non-essential roles. Göring maintained a strong suspicion of the Army high command throughout the war and was reluctant to relinquish authority over any *Luftwaffe* personnel.

The *Luftwaffe* divisions initially included two infantry regiments of three battalions, along with complementary artillery and administrative units. They were considerably smaller than the divisions of the *Heer*. Originally, they were intended to garrison quiet occupied sectors, freeing *Heer* troops for combat; however, several of the divisions were transferred to the Eastern Front and participated in numerous battles. By 1943, some of the *Luftwaffe* field divisions had

■ **Göring (right) was determined to maintain control of all *Luftwaffe* ground troops.**

| MOUNTAIN DIVISIONS |
| --- |
| ■ 1st Mountain Division (later 1st Volksgebirgs Division) |
| ■ 2nd Mountain Division |
| ■ 3rd Mountain Division |
| ■ 4th Mountain Division |
| ■ 5th Mountain Division |
| ■ 6th Mountain Division |
| ■ 7th Mountain Division (previously 99th Light Infantry Division) |
| ■ 8th Mountain Division (previously Division Nr. 157, 157th Reserve Division, 157th Mountain Division) |
| ■ 9th Mountain Division (previously Shadow Division Steiermark and Division zbV 140) |
| ■ 188th Mountain Division (previously Division Nr. 188, 188th Reserve Mountain Division) |
| Ski division |
| ■ 1st Ski Division |

already been disbanded, and those which remained intact were released to the *Heer*. They were re-formed along the lines of standard Army divisions but retained their numbering and the designation as *Luftwaffe* units in order to avoid confusion with original *Heer* divisions bearing the same numbers. At least 22 *Luftwaffe* field divisions were formed during World War II. In addition, several training divisions, reservist *Landwehr* divisions, a single ski division, and up to four cavalry divisions were formed by the *Heer* before and during the war.

# Infantry Platoon: Combat Workhorse

*The infantry platoon was considered by most officers to be the decisive element in winning the war on the ground.*

In 1939, the infantry platoon consisted of typically 46 personnel, including three squads of 13 riflemen, a three-man 50mm (1.97in) light mortar section, and a headquarters consisting of at least one officer and three other ranks, usually designated as couriers and carrying rifles. The platoon commander, usually a lieutenant or captain, was armed with a pistol, while a non-commissioned officer, typically in command of the mortar section, carried a rifle.

Each of the three squads consisted of a pair of non-commissioned officers, who served as squad leader and assistant squad leader, seven riflemen, and four soldiers who served an MG34 machine gun. Of these, three soldiers carried pistols while one was usually armed with a rifle.

By 1943, the infantry platoon had been reduced in size to include three squads of 10 soldiers, a three-man 50mm (1.97in) mortar section, and a headquarters of a single officer and five men. The reduction in squad size had developed largely as a result of the infantry experience in Poland, where the 13-man squad proved unwieldy and difficult to control in combat. Soldiers whose primary duties were as riflemen were often further designated as stretcher-bearers or snipers, carrying rifles with improved optics. The 50mm (1.97in) mortar was considered by

many veterans to be of limited value and was rarely deployed on the Eastern Front. Later in the war, the 81mm (3.2in) and 120mm (4.7in) mortars became prevalent throughout the ranks.

The *Volksgrenadier* combat formations fielded late in the war compensated for lower numbers with the increased firepower of automatic weapons. The *Volksgrenadier* rifle platoon included three squads of nine soldiers, two armed with MP40 submachine guns or Sturmgewehr 44 assault rifles, two serving a heavier MG42 machine gun, and five riflemen.

Completing the *Volksgrenadier* table of organization and equipment were the headquarters section, with two machine gunners and two riflemen, and a pair of automatic weapons platoons, each with three squads. Two of these squads consisted of nine soldiers armed with automatic weapons, while the third included two machine gunners, five soldiers armed with automatic weapons, and a pair of riflemen.

## Offensive manoeuvres

The primary doctrine of the *Feldheer* was that of the offensive. German field commanders learned quickly that indecision or failure to seize the initiative were considered potentially greater failures than aggressive tactics which resulted in heavy casualties. According to *German

Infantry In Action: Minor Tactics*, published in 1941, the German infantry platoon advanced in an arrowhead formation with a single section, consisting of 12 to 14 soldiers in two squads, forward, another on either flank and slightly behind with about 91m (100 yards) of separation. Other infantry sections followed in a linear arrangement with one mortar section toward the front and the second bringing up the rear. Two or three riflemen acted as scouts and deployed up to 411m (450 yards) ahead of the advancing platoon.

The infantry platoon commander determined the objective of the advance and the specific assignments for the various elements of his command. When the platoon encountered enemy fire, a rapid response with direct return fire fixed the enemy positions while the formation deployed into a staggered line with the soldiers several paces apart as the commander determined the prospects for a successful assault, assessing the locations of weak points in the enemy defences and devising methods to exploit them. The German platoon commander was empowered with the ability to make tactical decisions in a rapidly-changing combat environment and typically displayed great skill and personal courage.

The platoon commander defined the area of operations for his troops

## INFANTRY PLATOON, 1939

*The* Feldheer *infantry platoon which went to war in Poland in 1939 was responsible for the taking and holding of territory, as well as the destruction of enemy ground forces. To accomplish this task, the 13-man infantry squad could be deployed in a variety of formations for mutual support or for individual squad-level operations.*

Headquarters

50mm (1.97in) Light Mortar Section

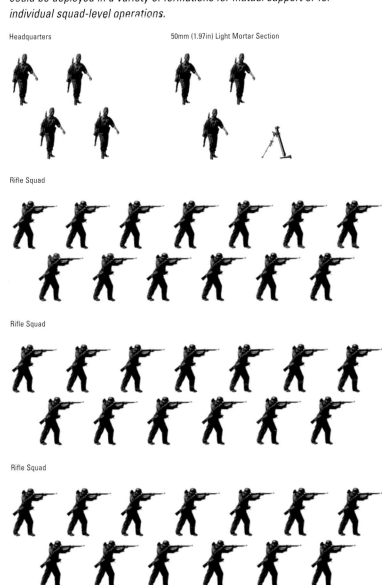

Rifle Squad

Rifle Squad

Rifle Squad

and was authorized to act promptly to bring about decisive results. In a successful attack 'even if penetration is made only on a narrow front,' instructed *German Infantry In Action: Minor Tactics*, 'the attack must be pressed forward into the depth of the enemy position. At this moment, the personal example of the platoon commander, who must concentrate on maintaining the momentum of the attack, is of tremendous importance. Immediate pursuit at places where the enemy resistance weakens is, therefore, required. Premature movement to a flank before the enemy position has been completely penetrated is incorrect. The flanks of attacking sections must be protected by troops in the rear. It is the duty of reserves following up the attack to destroy any centres of resistance which remain.'

### At squad level
The infantry squad, usually led by a veteran non-commissioned officer, was taught aggressive tactics as well. Infantrymen understood that their primary purpose was to prevail in the inevitable firefight with the enemy. Concentrated, heavy and sustained fire against the enemy, which included the coordinated effort of the riflemen and the machine gun section, would commence with the greatest effectiveness at a distance of 366m (400 yards) and an extreme range of 549m (600 yards). When not in combat, the infantry squad endeavoured to remain in camouflage or concealment. Unnecessary movement which might present a tempting target to the enemy was strongly discouraged.

Infantry squads often advanced in a loose linear formation with the squad leader and machine gunners to the front while the riflemen followed and the assistant squad leader brought up the rear. When resistance was encountered, deployment was rapid and a base of fire could be quickly established as the squad moved into a frontal formation – often to the left and right of the machine-gun position. Squads typically moved from sight point to sight point, and when engaged with the enemy, fire and manoeuvre tactics were employed. Actual firing, particularly that of the machine gun, was to begin as late as was practical in order to prevent the squad's heaviest weapon from becoming exposed early.

Standard procedures for squad-level offensive operations, according to *German Infantry In Action: Minor Tactics*, consisted of four elements once the unit had closed with the enemy, the firefight, the advance, the assault, and occupation of a position.

## INFANTRY PLATOON, 1943

*By 1943, the basic infantry squad had been reduced from 13 soldiers to 10; therefore, the platoon was downsized accordingly to an approximate strength of up to 40 men. The larger squad had proven difficult to deploy effectively in the early campaigns of the war in the East. Further, the platoon's firepower was later augmented with a new generation of automatic weapons. The role of the platoon leader in combat was critical to success on a tactical level. It was he who determined the best course of action on the battlefield.*

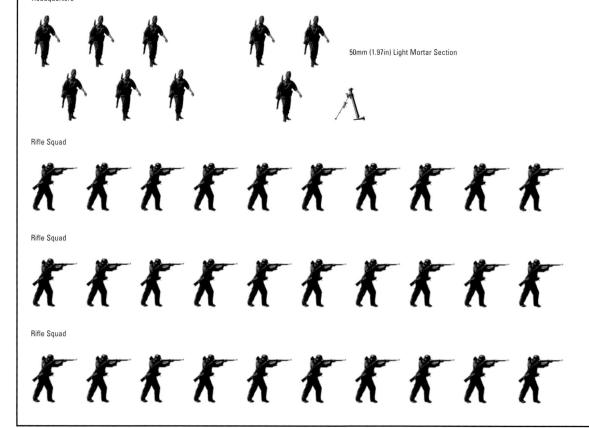

Headquarters

50mm (1.97in) Light Mortar Section

Rifle Squad

Rifle Squad

Rifle Squad

## GERMAN INFANTRY TACTICS

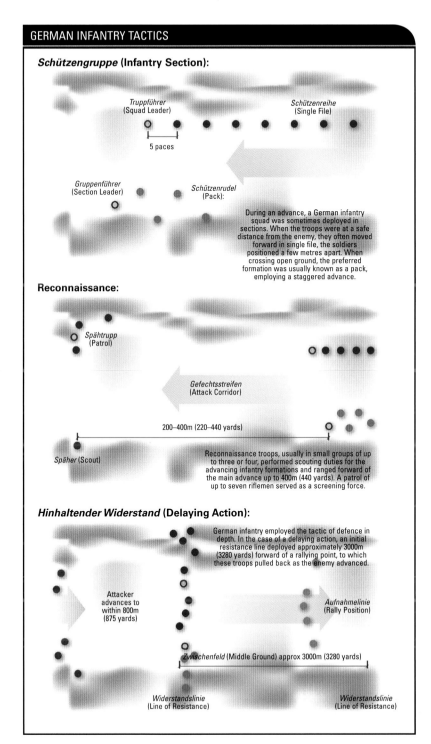

**Schützengruppe (Infantry Section):**

Truppführer
(Squad Leader)

Schützenreihe
(Single File)

5 paces

Gruppenführer
(Section Leader)

Schützenrudel
(Pack):

During an advance, a German infantry squad was sometimes deployed in sections. When the troops were at a safe distance from the enemy, they often moved forward in single file, the soldiers positioned a few metres apart. When crossing open ground, the preferred formation was usually known as a pack, employing a staggered advance.

**Reconnaissance:**

Spähtrupp
(Patrol)

Gefechtsstreifen
(Attack Corridor)

200–400m (220–440 yards)

Späher (Scout)

Reconnaissance troops, usually in small groups of up to three or four, performed scouting duties for the advancing infantry formations and ranged forward of the main advance up to 400m (440 yards). A patrol of up to seven riflemen served as a screening force.

**Hinhaltender Widerstand (Delaying Action):**

German infantry employed the tactic of defence in depth. In the case of a delaying action, an initial resistance line deployed approximately 3000m (3280 yards) forward of a rallying point, to which these troops pulled back as the enemy advanced.

Attacker advances to within 800m (875 yards)

Aufnahmelinie
(Rally Position)

Zwischenfeld (Middle Ground) approx 3000m (3280 yards)

Widerstandslinie
(Line of Resistance)

Widerstandslinie
(Line of Resistance)

## TACTICAL TERMINOLOGY

| German | Translation |
|---|---|
| Anschluss | The Lead |
| Schwerpunkt | Main Point of Attack |
| Gefechtsstreifen | Attack Corridor |
| Abschnitt | Defence Sector |
| Hauptkampflinie | Main Line of Battle |
| Entfaltung | Operational Deployment |
| Entwicklung | Tactical Deployment |
| Ausdehnung | Dispersal |
| Schützenreihe | Single File |
| Schützenrudel | Pack/Swarm |

Therefore, it instructed the following:

**'The Firefight:** The section is the fire unit. When fire has to be opened, the section commander usually opens with the light machine gun only. He directs its fire. When good fire effect is possible and plenty of cover exists, the riflemen take part early in the firefight. The majority of riflemen should be in the front line and taking part in the firefight at the latest when the assault is about to be made. They usually fire independently unless the section commander decides to concentrate all of their fire on a single target.

**The Advance:** The section works its way forward in a loose formation. Within the section, the light machine gun usually forms the spearhead of the attack. The longer the riflemen follow the light machine gun in narrow, deep formation, the longer will the machine guns in the rear be able to shoot past the section.

**The Assault:** The section commander takes any opportunity that presents itself to carry out an assault and does not wait for orders to do so. He rushes the whole section forward into the assault, leading the way himself. Before and during the assault the enemy must be engaged by all weapons at the maximum rate of fire. The light machine gun number one takes part in the assault, firing on the move. With a cheer, the section attempts to break the enemy's resistance, using hand grenades, machine pistols, rifles, pistols, and entrenching tools. After the assault, the section must reorganize quickly.

**Occupation of a Position:** When occupying a position, the riflemen group themselves in twos and threes around the light machine gun in such a way that they are within voice control of the section commander.'

The individual German soldier was expected to act decisively and with considerable élan. His squad leader, each non-commissioned officer and every officer in the chain of command was expected to exhibit personal bravery. Therefore, cowardice was not tolerated, and a significant number of field and junior officers lost their lives in World War II while leading from the front during offensive operations.

# The Defensive Fight

*German defensive tactics at the lowest levels stressed the concept of defence in depth and mutual support of prepared positions. A squad typically was responsible for covering a front line of up to 41m (45 yards).*

The machine gun was a key element in the defence, and numerous positions for supporting machine-gun fire, as well as positions for potential relocation, were sited approximately 46m (50 yards) apart. The machine gun was intended to take an advancing enemy under fire first, while supporting riflemen were responsible for repelling the enemy at closer range.

Digging of foxholes, trenches or pits for cover was accomplished with a pair of soldiers performing the work and alternately serving as a sentry to prevent surprise attack. Neighbouring positions were within a few metres of one another to facilitate communications. Often, such positions were staggered or dug in echelon to minimize the effectiveness of enemy fire. If time permitted, a trench or shallow ditch was dug to the immediate rear of the infantry positions to allow the bulk of a squad to take safer shelter until called upon.

When an enemy assault was detected, the machine gun opened fire, while rifles remained silent until necessary and within effective range. Defence against tanks was accomplished with an emphasis on shoulder-fired weapons such as the *Panzerfaust* or *Panzerschreck* late in the war. Squads with at least one anti-tank weapon were routinely sent on patrol to intercept enemy armour before it contacted the main line of defence. Resistance to an armoured attack was also somewhat dependent on the choice of a defensive position which was favourable for defence, possibly requiring an enemy tank to expose its vulnerable underside or rear armour to an anti-tank weapon.

Hand grenades were often lethal, and the German infantryman was taught to seek cover quickly or seize the grenade and throw it back. Artillery support was often critical to the ability of the infantry to hold its position, and forward observers were typically assigned to any substantial defensive position to direct such heavy fire.

Some German infantry squads were detailed in forward positions, usually within range of covering mortar, artillery or machine-gun positions, to observe enemy movement and alert the main line to a potential attack. Such advanced squads were instructed to withdraw to the main defence line along predetermined routes.

The typical rifle position was slightly more than 1.4m (4.5ft) deep with a sump pit for drainage. The infantrymen often took advantage of a slope or hillside to improve concealment. Machine-gun positions

were usually about four times as large as rifle pits and sometimes covered with brush or camouflage netting. Deep and narrow positions afforded the best protection against enemy small-arms fire, aerial attack or artillery bombardment.

### Fit for fighting

The typical German infantryman carried no fewer than 30 items of clothing and equipment along with enough food and ammunition to sustain him in the field. A standard black leather belt was the foundation of the soldier's combat load, usually with leather or canvas ammunition pouches attached and a stamped buckle with the motto '*Gott mit Uns*' ('God is with Us') plainly legible. The

standard *Feldheer* rucksack, the *Tornister*, was designed to provide ample space to carry rations, socks, shoes, overcoat, personal hygiene items, shelter-half and tent pieces, and cooking utensils.

The gas mask was contained in an aluminium canister and slung over the shoulder, while a small canvas bread bag might contain food within easy reach while on the march along with the soldier's soft headgear. The bag, a one-litre (1.8-pint) drinking bottle, and a short entrenching tool were attached to the belt. The entire kit often weighed in excess of 22kg (50lbs). On extended field deployments, infantrymen sometimes placed their *Tornister* with their platoon baggage train.

■ **INFANTRY SERGEANT, 1944**
**This *Feldwebel* (sergeant) carries the typical equipment of the German infantry soldier of 1944, including a Mauser Kar 98 rifle, cylindrical gas mask case, *Zeltbahn* 31 poncho/tent-quarter, water bottle and forage bag.**

# Weapons of War

*The* Feldheer *provided a variety of weapons for its soldiers during World War II, including those held over from World War I and others developed during the course of the war.*

Since wartime offers the ultimate proving ground, significant advances in infantry weapons were achieved as the war progressed. In most cases, however, these entered service too late and in too small numbers to affect the outcome of the war significantly. Innovative weapons such as the anti-tank

*Panzerfaust*, which was effective against armour with a hollow charge, and the *Sturmgewehr* assault rifle were significant advances in battlefield technology.

One of the world's most famous shoulder arms, the Mauser Gewehr 98 was the standard rifle of the *Feldheer* during World War II. The

original design for the Mauser 98 dated back to 1898, and during the war the weapon was shortened to a carbine version for easier carry. This new version was designated the Karabiner 98b and later the 98k. The original rifle weighed slightly more than 4kg (9lbs), and the 98k about 3.5kg (8.5lbs). Each was operated by bolt action and fed by a five-round clip. The weapon was modified in numerous ways, such as with high-powered optics for sniper use and a folding stock for airborne operations.

The *Feldheer* was one of the world's first land forces to deploy automatic weapons in significant numbers, including the landmark Sturmgewehr 43 and 44 assault rifles, which were capable of semi-automatic and fully automatic fire. These weapons were distinguishable for their sleek look and long magazines which held up to 30 rounds of 7.92mm (0.31in) ammunition. The MP43 was truly the first weapon which could be classified as an assault rifle, and its development was held up by Hitler for a time. The Sturmgewehr 44 was

## INFANTRY WEAPONS

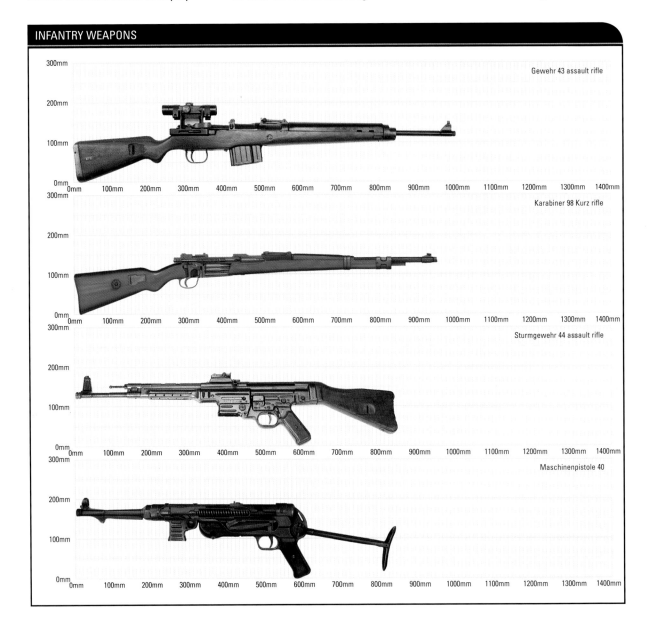

Gewehr 43 assault rifle

Karabiner 98 Kurz rifle

Sturmgewehr 44 assault rifle

Maschinenpistole 40

actually the production version of the MP43 and was capable of firing at a cyclic rate of 500 rounds per minute with a range of up to 300m (330 yards). When priority was given to the manufacture of the Sturmgewehr 44, most of these weapons were sent to the Eastern Front or distributed among elite troops of the *Heer* and the *Waffen-SS*.

The most famous of German pistols utilized by the *Heer* was the Pistole Parabellum 1908 (P'08), commonly known as the Luger. A 9mm (0.354in) pistol, the Luger was named for its designer and introduced to the Army in 1908. It remained standard issue until replaced by the 9mm (0.354in) Walther P38 three decades later. The P38 proved a capable weapon in the hands of *Heer* officers and was also issued to some lower ranks. The Luger was produced until 1942;

however, it was costly to manufacture and difficult to maintain in the field, requiring too many matching parts to function well. Another notable pistol was the 7.65mm (0.3in) Walther PPK, produced originally as a police weapon and issued to military police as well. All three pistols were issued to *Heer* officers or *Luftwaffe* officer corps personnel.

The arms designer Hugo Schmeisser was largely responsible for the early versions of the submachine gun which entered service with the Imperial German Army in the waning months of World War I. The MP18 remained in service until 1943, and a succession of variants was introduced through the 1920s and 1930s. These weapons generally fired 32-round clips of 9mm (0.354in) Parabellum ammunition

identical in most cases to pistol cartridges. They were capable of single shot and automatic modes of fire. Designed by Hugo Vollmer, the MP38 was notable because of its ease of manufacture. Metal stamping and die-cast parts replaced finely-honed production methods, and wood fittings were a thing of the past. The MP38 utilized a folding stock which eased carry. Improvements, which included the elimination of a hazard which caused the weapon to discharge inadvertently, were made, and even further mass production efforts were employed in the improved MP40. Thousands of examples of the MP40 were produced, and the weapon was prized by Allied soldiers who captured it and often pressed it into service.

At the beginning of World War II, the dominant machine gun on the

## INFANTRY HEAVY MACHINE GUNS

Maschinengewehr 34

Maschinengewehr 42

battlefield was the German MG34, which appeared during the wave of rearmament under the Nazis during the mid-1930s. It replaced many of the holdover machine guns which had been in use with the Army since World War I.

The Treaty of Versailles had prohibited the development in Germany of any sustained fire weapon; however, Rheinmetall Borsig began the development of the MG34 in a subsidiary company located in Switzerland.

### MG support

The MG34 has been acclaimed as one of the finest machine guns ever in service. It was carried by a squad of infantrymen and could be fired from a stabilized tripod or a bipod mount. The barrel was easily changed for cooling purposes, and the weapon was capable of a cyclic rate of fire of up to 900 rounds per minute. The most significant drawback of the MG34 was its complex manufacturing process, which drained the resources of German industry and resulted in a necessary transition.

Designers from Mauser tackled the problems associated with the MG34 and applied similar mass-production techniques which had proven successful with the MP38 submachine gun. The result was the MG42, one of the best known machine guns of World War II. The MG42 was highly effective, and Allied veterans remember to this day the distinctive 'ripping' sound of its report, signifying a high rate of fire which reached an astounding maximum of 1550 rounds per minute.

Like the MG34, the MG42 was served by an infantry team. Its 7.92mm (0.31in) ammunition was fed from a 50-round belt, and the weapon was fired from a tripod or a bipod. The weapon debuted on the Eastern Front and in North Africa in 1942. Subsequently, it was widely distributed and became one of the most recognized weapons of the _Heer_ in World War II.

### Infantry support

On the battlefield, the timely introduction of support weapons frequently means the difference between victory and defeat. During World War II, the _Feldheer_ introduced a number of such weapons, continually striving to improve their quality.

The standard light mortar, a 50mm (1.97in) design by Rheinmetall Borsig, was introduced in 1936. Heavy at 14kg (31lbs), it was nevertheless carried by a single soldier. In combat, the weapon proved a disappointment with a range of only 520m (569 yards) and a projectile with a paltry overall weight of just under 900g (2lbs). The weapon was also difficult to operate. The 81mm (3.2in) mortar was just the opposite, remaining in service with the _Feldheer_ throughout World War II and undergoing two major revisions. Its rate of fire was substantial at 10 to 12 rounds per minute, and it required a crew of six to operate. Other mortars included the heavier 100mm (3.94in) Nebelwerfer NbW 35 and NbW 40 and the 120mm (4.7in) heavy mortar, which was mounted on a two-wheel carriage.

At the beginning of the war, 75mm (2.95in) and 150mm (5.9in) artillery pieces were organic to _Feldheer_ infantry battalions. The 75mm (2.95in) light infantry gun was developed during the clandestine period of German rearmament in the late 1920s and entered service in 1932. The weapon proved a welcome addition to infantry units but had a range of only 3550m (3882 yards), although later upgrades increased this by about one-third. Mountain and airborne variants of the gun were also produced.

The 150mm (5.9in) heavy infantry gun Model 1933 was effective at a range of 4700m (5140 yards) and was towed by either a vehicle or draught horses. Although a howitzer, it was designated as a gun, and its substantial weight of 1750kg (3858lbs) made transporting it an arduous task for infantry units. This problem was not solved until a self-propelled version was introduced in 1940.

### Grenades

One of the most recognizable German infantry weapons of the war was the ubiquitous Type 24 or 43 hand grenade along with its Type 39 and 39B variants. Popularly known as the 'Potato Masher', thousands of these were manufactured during World War II with fuse delay options of four to seven seconds and a range of about 50m (55 yards) depending on the skill of the soldier throwing it. Other hand grenades were produced for anti-tank and anti-personnel use; however, none were supplied to the German soldier in such quantity as the 'Potato Masher'.

The flamethrower had been utilized by German troops in World War I and remained a terrifying weapon from

## INFANTRY ANTI-TANK WEAPONS

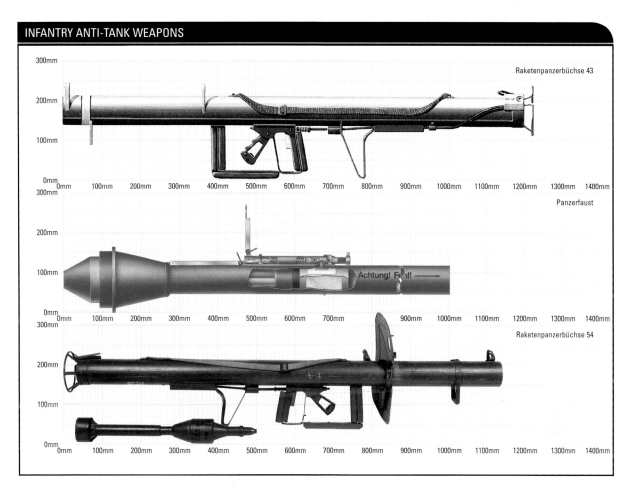

Raketenpanzerbüchse 43

Panzerfaust

Raketenpanzerbüchse 54

1939 to 1945. Usually operated in combat by pioneers, at least five variants of the weapon were introduced, each with a range of about 40m (44 yards). The Type 35 was capable of discharging flame in a 10- to 12-second stream with bursts of two to three seconds. The medium flamethrower could discharge a 25-second stream of fire.

German soldiers were issued several light anti-tank weapons in addition to 37mm (1.45in) and 75mm (2.95in) guns. Among the most successful of these were the RP43

*Panzerschreck* and the variants of the hollow-charge *Panzerfaust*. When the Germans captured examples of the American bazooka during the fighting in North Africa, they quickly adapted the firing tube to accommodate the 88mm (3.5in) rocket of the *Panzerschreck* with a range of up to 150m (164 yards) and a rate of fire of four to five rounds per minute. The *Panzerfaust* was inexpensive to produce and appeared in quantity on the battlefield in 1943. A simple firing tube with primitive sights, the weapon could be operated

with minimal training. Its range was nearly 60m (66 yards); therefore, it was a close-range weapon, but it was capable of penetrating nearly 203mm (8in) of armour.

Other infantry anti-tank weapons included the 7.92mm (0.31in) Panzerbüchse 38 and 39 rifles and the *Panzerwurfmine*, a hand-held grenade utilized by armour-killing squads and designed to be thrown by a soldier who had to close within 27m (30 yards) of an enemy tank. The weapon proved difficult to operate and unpopular with the troops.

# CHAPTER 6

# Artillery

*The wars of the nineteenth and early twentieth centuries had proven to the high command of the German Army that powerful artillery could indeed influence the outcome of a battle.*

*Although the restrictions of the Treaty of Versailles limited the types and numbers of artillery the Reichswehr was allowed to field and banned heavy artillery altogether, the covert and overt rearmament of the German armed forces during the inter-war years included an array of such weapons, which were either integral to the organization of the Feldheer infantry divisions during World War II or controlled by higher echelons of the command structure and assigned as needed.*

■ *Wehrmacht* horse-drawn artillery pieces parade down the *Avenue des Champs-Élysées* following the occupation of Paris, August 1940.

# Storm of Steel

*When the combined-arms might of the* Wehrmacht *was unleashed against the Soviet Union in the predawn hours of 22 June 1941, more than 45,000 guns of the* Feldheer *thundered across a front of 1609km (1000 miles). German artillery pounded Red Army frontier posts, command and communication centres, railway lines and troop concentrations previously identified by* Luftwaffe *reconnaissance aircraft.*

Each infantry and armoured division which rolled forward included an organic artillery regiment, while the bulk of the artillery units were held in a reserve or pool administered by the general headquarters of the *Feldheer*. The three infantry regiments comprising a division each were assigned a company of two heavy 150mm (5.9in) and six light 75mm (2.95in) howitzers, while the panzer artillery typically included six batteries of light howitzers grouped

into two battalions. During the opening months of World War II, the 48 guns of the standard infantry division's artillery regiment included three horse-drawn batteries of four 75mm (2.95in) howitzers in each of three battalions, along with one heavy battalion of 150mm (5.9in) howitzers divided into three batteries of four guns.

By 1943, the artillery regiment was reorganized into a heavy battalion of two 150mm (5.9in) batteries, each

with three guns, and three light artillery battalions, each with a single battery of 75mm (2.95in) guns and two 105mm (4.1in) batteries with four guns each.

**Foreign guns**
As the need arose, the *Feldheer* pressed a number of foreign-made guns into service, particularly after the occupation of Czechoslovakia and the seizure of its Skoda munitions factories and the early

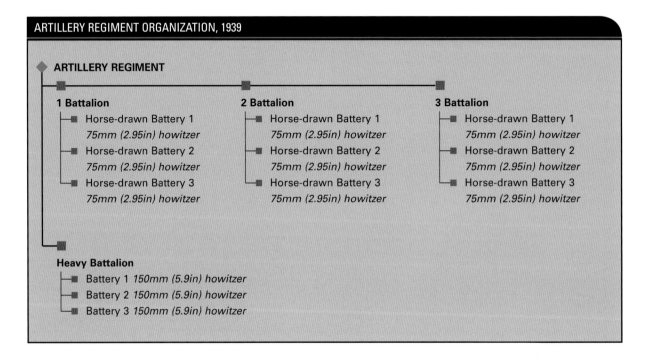

**ARTILLERY REGIMENT ORGANIZATION, 1939**

◆ **ARTILLERY REGIMENT**

**1 Battalion**
- Horse-drawn Battery 1
  *75mm (2.95in) howitzer*
- Horse-drawn Battery 2
  *75mm (2.95in) howitzer*
- Horse-drawn Battery 3
  *75mm (2.95in) howitzer*

**2 Battalion**
- Horse-drawn Battery 1
  *75mm (2.95in) howitzer*
- Horse-drawn Battery 2
  *75mm (2.95in) howitzer*
- Horse-drawn Battery 3
  *75mm (2.95in) howitzer*

**3 Battalion**
- Horse-drawn Battery 1
  *75mm (2.95in) howitzer*
- Horse-drawn Battery 2
  *75mm (2.95in) howitzer*
- Horse-drawn Battery 3
  *75mm (2.95in) howitzer*

**Heavy Battalion**
- Battery 1 *150mm (5.9in) howitzer*
- Battery 2 *150mm (5.9in) howitzer*
- Battery 3 *150mm (5.9in) howitzer*

successes on the Eastern Front, which resulted in the capture of large quantities of Red Army field artillery. Among the most prominent of the Soviet guns pressed into service with the *Feldheer* was the modified 76mm (3in) M1936 F-22. The *Feldheer* captured nearly 1300 of these weapons during the opening phase of Operation 'Barbarossa', and approximately 560 were rechambered to accept more powerful ammunition along with other modifications, designated the Pak 36(r) – Panzeabwehrkanone 36 Russisch –

## ARTILLERY WEAPON PRODUCTION: *LUFTWAFFE* FLAK GUNS, 1939–45

| Equipment | 1939 | 1940 | 1941 | 1942 | 1943 | 1944 | 1945 | Equipment | 1939 | 1940 | 1941 | 1942 | 1943 | 1944 | 1945 |
|---|---|---|---|---|---|---|---|---|---|---|---|---|---|---|---|
| 20mm Flak 30 and 38 | 1160 | 6609 | 11,006 | 22,372 | 31,503 | 42,688 | 6339 | 88mm Flak 18, 36 and 38 | 183 | 1130 | 1872 | 2876 | 4416 | 1933 | 715 |
| 37mm Flak 18 and 36 | 180 | 675 | 1188 | 2136 | 4077 | 3620 | 158 | 105mm Flak 38 and 39 | 38 | 290 | 509 | 701 | 1220 | 1131 | 92 |
| 37mm Flak 43 | – | – | – | – | 54 | 4684 | 1180 | 128mm Flak 40 | 4 | – | – | 65 | 298 | 664 | 98 |

## ARTILLERY WEAPON PRODUCTION: INFANTRY GUNS, 1939–45

| Equipment | 1939 | 1940 | 1941 | 1942 | 1943 | 1944 | 1945 | Equipment | 1939 | 1940 | 1941 | 1942 | 1943 | 1944 | 1945 |
|---|---|---|---|---|---|---|---|---|---|---|---|---|---|---|---|
| 75mm leIG 18 | 290 | 850 | 1115 | 1188 | 1965 | 2309 | 549 | 75mm IG 42 | – | – | – | – | 258 | 269 | – |
| 75mm IG 37 | – | – | – | – | 2279 | – | – | 150mm sIG 33 | 48 | 310 | 492 | 420 | 862 | 1613 | 410 |

## ARTILLERY WEAPON PRODUCTION: ARMY FLAK GUNS, 1939–45

| Equipment | 1939 | 1940 | 1941 | 1942 | 1943 | 1944 | 1945 | Equipment | 1939 | 1940 | 1941 | 1942 | 1943 | 1944 | 1945 |
|---|---|---|---|---|---|---|---|---|---|---|---|---|---|---|---|
| 20mm Flak 30 and 38 | 95 | 863 | 873 | 2502 | 3732 | 5041 | 739 | 30mm MK. 303 | – | – | – | – | – | 32 | 190 |
| 20mm Flakvierling 38 | | 42 | 320 | 599 | 483 | 573 | 123 | 37mm Flak 18 and 36 | – | – | – | – | 27 | 592 | 559 | – |
| 20mm Flak Scotti and Breda | – | – | – | – | 361 | – | | 37mm Flak 43 | – | – | – | – | – | 776 | 152 |
| 20mm MG 151/20 Drilling | – | – | – | – | – | 3141 | 973 | 37mm Flakzwilling 43 | – | – | – | – | – | 142 | 43 |
| 30mm Flak 103/38 Jaboschreck | – | – | – | – | – | 149 | | 88mm Flak 18 and 36 | – | – | 126 | 176 | 296 | 549 | 23 |

## ARTILLERY WEAPON PRODUCTION: FIELD AND SIEGE ARTILLERY, 1939–45

| Equipment | 1939 | 1940 | 1941 | 1942 | 1943 | 1944 | 1945 | Equipment | 1939 | 1940 | 1941 | 1942 | 1943 | 1944 | 1945 |
|---|---|---|---|---|---|---|---|---|---|---|---|---|---|---|---|
| 75mm leFK 18 | 8 | 96 | – | – | – | – | – | 150mm K. 39 | 15 | 11 | 25 | 13 | – | – | – |
| 75mm leFK 38 | – | – | – | 80 | – | – | – | 150mm in Mrs.-Laf. | – | 8 | – | – | – | – | – |
| 75mm FK 7M 59 | – | – | – | – | – | – | 10 | 170mm in Mrs.-Laf. | – | – | 91 | 126 | 78 | 40 | 3 |
| 75mm FK 7M 85 | – | – | – | – | – | 10 | – | 210mm Mörser 18 | 58 | 275 | 167 | – | 100 | 103 | 8 |
| 105mm K. 18 | 8 | 35 | 108 | 135 | 454 | 701 | 74 | 210mm K. 38 | – | – | 1 | 6 | 7 | 1 | – |
| 105mm leFH 18 | 483 | 1380 | 1160 | 1237 | 1661 | 1009 | 56 | 210mm K. 39/40/41 | – | 12 | 22 | 3 | 11 | 11 | – |
| 105mm leFH 18/40 | – | – | – | – | 1872 | 7827 | 566 | 210mm K. 52 | – | – | – | – | – | 6 | 6 |
| 105mm leFH Sfl. | – | – | – | 12 | 570 | 197 | 402 | 240mm K. 3 | – | 3 | 1 | 4 | – | 2 | – |
| 150mm sFH 18 | 190 | 580 | 516 | 636 | 785 | 2295 | 401 | 240mm H. 39/40 | 1 | 9 | – | 8 | – | – | – |
| 150mm sFH Sfl. | – | – | – | – | 436 | 724 | 55 | 355mm M 1 | 1 | – | – | 5 | 1 | 1 | – |
| 150mm K. 18 | – | 21 | 45 | 25 | 10 | – | – | 420mm Gamma | – | 1 | – | – | – | – | – |

## ARTILLERY WEAPON PRODUCTION: RAILROAD GUNS, 1939–45

| Equipment | 1939 | 1940 | 1941 | 1942 | 1943 | 1944 | 1945 | Equipment | 1939 | 1940 | 1941 | 1942 | 1943 | 1944 | 1945 |
|---|---|---|---|---|---|---|---|---|---|---|---|---|---|---|---|
| 203mm K.(E) | – | – | 4 | 4 | – | – | – | 310mm K.5 Glatt(E) | – | – | – | – | – | 2 | – |
| 210mm K. 12N.(E) | – | 1 | – | – | – | – | – | 380mm Siegfried(E) | – | – | – | 2 | 1 | – | – |
| 280mm Kz.Br.K.(E) | – | – | 2 | – | – | – | – | 800mm Dora(E) | – | – | 1 | 1 | – | – | – |
| 280mm Br.KN.(E) | – | – | 3 | – | – | – | – | | | | | | | | |

## ARTILLERY WEAPON PRODUCTION: ROCKET LAUNCHERS, 1939–45

| Equipment | 1939 | 1940 | 1941 | 1942 | 1943 | 1944 | 1945 | Equipment | 1939 | 1940 | 1941 | 1942 | 1943 | 1944 | 1945 |
|---|---|---|---|---|---|---|---|---|---|---|---|---|---|---|---|
| 150mm Nb.W. 41 | – | 282 | 652 | 969 | 1188 | 2336 | 342 | 30mm R.Wfr. 56 | – | – | – | – | – | 544 | 150 |
| 150mm Pz.W. 42 | – | – | – | 188 | 52 | – | | sW.G. 40 | – | 9552 | – | – | – | – | – |
| 210mm Nb.W. 42 | – | – | – | 407 | 100 | 835 | 145 | sW.G. 41 | – | – | – | 2510 | 1493 | – | – |
| 280/320mm Nb.W. 41 | – | – | 34 | 311 | – | – | | sWu.R. 40 | – | 1980 | – | – | – | – | – |
| 300mm Nb.W. 42 | – | – | – | – | 380 | – | | | | | | | | | |

## ARTILLERY WEAPON PRODUCTION: MOUNTAIN GUNS, 1939–45

| Equipment | 1939 | 1940 | 1941 | 1942 | 1943 | 1944 | 1945 | Equipment | 1939 | 1940 | 1941 | 1942 | 1943 | 1944 | 1945 |
|---|---|---|---|---|---|---|---|---|---|---|---|---|---|---|---|
| 75mm Geb.Gesch. 36 | 59 | 70 | 84 | 216 | 242 | 456 | 66 | 105mm Geb.H. 40 | – | – | – | 30 | 104 | 223 | 63 |

## ARTILLERY WEAPON PRODUCTION: RECOILLESS RIFLES, 1939–45

| Equipment | 1939 | 1940 | 1941 | 1942 | 1943 | 1944 | 1945 | Equipment | 1939 | 1940 | 1941 | 1942 | 1943 | 1944 | 1945 |
|---|---|---|---|---|---|---|---|---|---|---|---|---|---|---|---|
| 75mm L.G. | – | 184 | 9 | 91 | 132 | 237 | – | 105mm L.G. | – | – | 184 | 82 | 104 | 158 | – |

## ARTILLERY WEAPON PRODUCTION: ANTI-TANK GUNS, 1939–45

| Equipment | 1939 | 1940 | 1941 | 1942 | 1943 | 1944 | 1945 | Equipment | 1939 | 1940 | 1941 | 1942 | 1943 | 1944 | 1945 |
|---|---|---|---|---|---|---|---|---|---|---|---|---|---|---|---|
| 37mm Pak 35/36 | 1229 | 2713 | 1365 | 32 | – | – | – | 75mm Pak 40 | – | – | – | 2114 | 8740 | 11,728 | 721 |
| 37mm Pak M 37(t) | 277 | 236 | – | – | – | – | – | 75mm Pak 41 | – | – | – | 150 | – | – | – |
| 37mm Pak 39/40 | – | – | – | 34 | – | – | – | 75mm Pak 42 | – | – | – | 253 | – | 863 | 346 |
| 42mm Pak 41 | – | – | 27 | 286 | – | – | – | 76.2mm Pak 36(r) | – | – | – | 358 | 169 | 33 | – |
| 47mm Pak 46(t) | 200 | 73 | – | – | – | – | – | 88mm Pak 43/41 | – | – | – | – | 1152 | 251 | – |
| 47mm Pak (t) | – | 95 | 51 | 68 | – | – | – | 88mm Pak 434 | – | – | – | – | 6 | 1766 | 326 |
| 47mm Pak 35/36 (ö) | – | 150 | – | – | – | – | – | 128mm Pak 80 | – | – | – | – | 2 | 118 | 30 |
| 50mm Pak 38 | 2 | 388 | 2072 | 4480 | 2626 | – | – | 7.5mm Rf.K 43 | – | – | – | – | 798 | 124 | – |
| 75mm Pak 37 | – | – | – | – | – | 358 | – | 88mm R.Wfr. 43 | – | – | – | – | 2862 | 288 | – |
| 75mm Pak 97/38 | – | – | – | 2854 | 858 | – | – | PWK 8 H 63 | – | – | – | – | – | 40 | 220 |
| 75mm Pak 39 | – | – | – | – | 15 | 2599 | 552 | | | | | | | | |

and deployed with German units from 1943 until the end of the war.

Although Allied bombing and combat losses taxed German industrial capacity, the production of artillery peaked in 1944 with nearly 10,000 105mm (4.1in) guns produced in that year alone. The production of the standard 75mm (2.95in) and 150mm (5.9in) infantry guns topped 6600 in 1944, while nearly 12,000 of the 75mm (2.95in) Pak 40 anti-tank gun rolled off the assembly lines. From 1939 to 1945, the number of barrels produced, including field and siege artillery, mountain guns, anti-tank guns, infantry guns, rocket launchers, recoilless rifles, flak guns and massive railway guns, exceeded 150,000. In the autumn of 1939, the *Feldheer* fielded 35 artillery battalions. However, after the outbreak of war the number expanded rapidly and reached at

least 117 by the eve of the invasion of France and the Low Countries in the spring of 1940.

### Organized firepower

Throughout World War II the *Feldheer* artillery which had not been allocated to divisional tables of organization and equipment remained under the rigid control of the general headquarters and was allocated to the army group, army, corps or division level corresponding to the tactical need in the execution of offensive or defensive operations. The officer with overall responsibility for the artillery was a member of the general headquarters staff and held a rank equivalent to that of a modern lieutenant-general (*General der Artillerie*). He also commanded a staff of officers which engaged in planning, supply and other administrative functions. Army or

army group reserve artillery command structures were identified with the beginning number of 301, while corps and division reserve formations were originally designated from 44 to 101 and later from 401 to 500.

Artillery units which were organic to the infantry or panzer divisions were placed under the direction of the artillery regiment's commanding officer. In the course of normal operations, the regimental artillery officer functioned essentially as the artillery officer for the entire division and advised the divisional commander on the deployment, logistical support, fire support missions and movements of the artillery of the organic regiment. When artillery formations from the general headquarters reserve were attached to divisions, a complete cadre of staff officers accompanied the combat troops and their

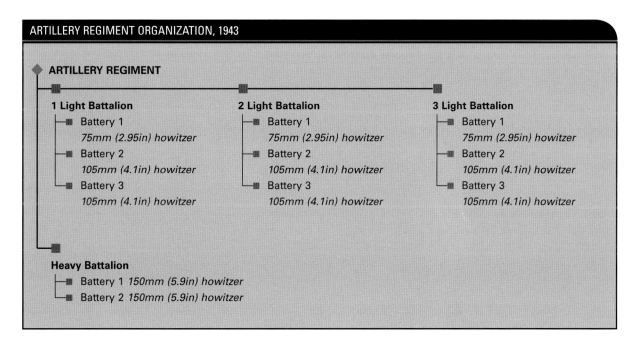

**ARTILLERY REGIMENT ORGANIZATION, 1943**

◆ **ARTILLERY REGIMENT**

**1 Light Battalion**
- Battery 1
  *75mm (2.95in) howitzer*
- Battery 2
  *105mm (4.1in) howitzer*
- Battery 3
  *105mm (4.1in) howitzer*

**2 Light Battalion**
- Battery 1
  *75mm (2.95in) howitzer*
- Battery 2
  *105mm (4.1in) howitzer*
- Battery 3
  *105mm (4.1in) howitzer*

**3 Light Battalion**
- Battery 1
  *75mm (2.95in) howitzer*
- Battery 2
  *105mm (4.1in) howitzer*
- Battery 3
  *105mm (4.1in) howitzer*

**Heavy Battalion**
- Battery 1 *150mm (5.9in) howitzer*
- Battery 2 *150mm (5.9in) howitzer*

equipment. The commander of this assigned unit typically took control of all artillery within the division, including the organic regiment, whose commander assumed a subordinate role. Such an arrangement was indicative of the failed effort to standardize each division within the *Feldheer* with a divisional-level artillery officer to direct combined operations.

Specialized or independent formations of the artillery included those responsible for coastal defence, railway guns, *Sturmgeschütze* self-propelled assault guns and anti-aircraft weapons, although for the duration of the war much of the responsibility for anti-aircraft defence rested with flak batteries under the command of the *Luftwaffe*.

# Varied Responsibilities

*Numerous functions and formations fell within the purview of the* Feldheer *general headquarters artillery staff during World War II. These supported the missions of the weapons themselves and were sometimes specific to a type of gun.*

The command of the artillery training regiments served not only to train new recruits but also to field test new weapons systems and provide demonstrations, while the Army Coast Artillery was responsible for those units which occupied sections of defended coastline, often in cooperation with the *Kriegsmarine* and routinely under its direct command.

The Artillery Regimental Staff of the general headquarters was in charge of the assignment of staff units which accompanied artillery allocated to a specific unit from the general headquarters artillery pool. Army flak detachments included those anti-aircraft units not under the command of the *Luftwaffe*, while many of the assault guns, or *Sturmgeschütze*, were organized in independent battalions under the control of the general headquarters rather than organic to infantry divisions.

Artillery park formations maintained weapons and associated equipment which were not deployed, while observation detachments performed intelligence-related work and were assigned to units as a component of the fire-control system, using flash- and sound-ranging equipment. Velocity-measuring platoons were numbered from 701 and made certain that weapons were calibrated properly, as did the astronomical calibration platoons, which utilized stars as fixed points for the purpose.

Survey and mapping detachments assisted in the siting of guns and requisitioned their maps from the Army map depots, numbered in sequence from 501 to 600, which housed and catalogued these for the artillery, and the meteorological section included units also numbered from 501 to 600, which provided weather-related data to the artillery units deployed from the general headquarters pool.

The smallest operational artillery formation was the battery, and its composition varied as to the type of gun and the reorganizations of the general headquarters pool artillery which took place on several occasions during the course of the war as units were allocated to combat formations. The general headquarters pool was substantially reorganized at least four times, in mid-May 1941, October 1942, the summer of 1943 and January 1944.

An artillery detachment or battalion was sometimes detailed for combined-arms operations and consisted of two or three batteries as needed. Throughout the war, individual artillery pieces were routinely horse-drawn; however, some medium and heavy weapons were also towed by truck or halftrack.

## Artillery divisions
Only in isolated cases were *Feldheer* artillery units grouped together and classified as divisions during the war. In each situation, the circumstances were somewhat unusual. The 18th

Panzer Division had served on the Eastern Front and sustained heavy losses during fighting at Orel in 1942 and at Kursk in the summer of 1943. The division was officially disbanded; however, its core artillery units served as the nucleus for the 18th Artillery Division.

In November 1943, the 310th, 311th and 312th Artillery Divisions were formed on the Eastern Front and included a number of independent artillery battalions. These were short-lived formations, which were broken up on 20 July 1944, and reassigned to units of the *Waffen-SS*. Concurrent with the Eastern Front divisions, the 309th was formed in the West.

When it was fully organized, the 18th Artillery Division was composed of the 88th, 288th, and 388th Artillery Regiments, the 741st *Sturmgeschütz* Battery, 280th Flak Battalion, 88th *Schützen* Battalion, 18th Fire Control Battery, 88th Division Signals Battalion, 88th Supply Troop, and medical, military police, postal and administrative detachments. The artillery regiments were equipped with towed 105mm (4.1in) and 150mm (5.9in) guns, the 105mm (4.1in) leFH-Sfl Wespe self-propelled howitzer,

100mm (3.94in) field guns, 210mm (8.3in) mortars, and 20mm (0.79in) flak guns. Scarcely two months after it was formed, the 18th Artillery Division was reorganized to include 150mm (5.9in) self-propelled guns, 170mm (6.7in) guns, and heavy 88mm (3.5in) flak guns. It was disbanded by the end of August 1944.

The divisional staff organization of the 309th Artillery Division was indicative of the structure of the four artillery divisions formed in the autumn of 1943. It included the 309th Artillery Brigade staff, two motorized maintenance battalions, two

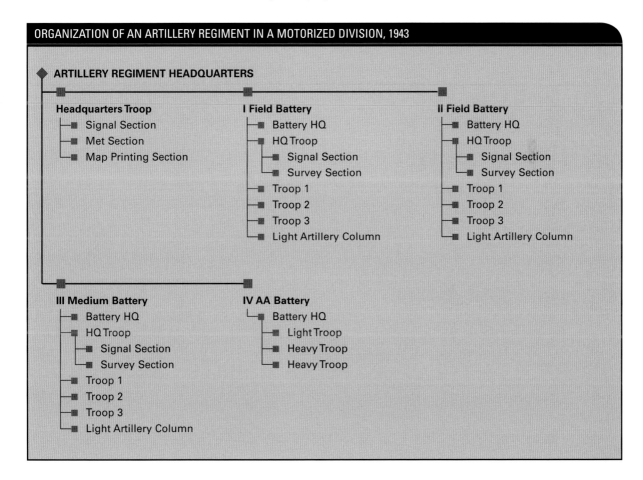

## ORGANIZATION OF AN ARTILLERY REGIMENT IN A MOTORIZED DIVISION, 1943

◆ **ARTILLERY REGIMENT HEADQUARTERS**

**Headquarters Troop**
- Signal Section
- Met Section
- Map Printing Section

**I Field Battery**
- Battery HQ
- HQ Troop
  - Signal Section
  - Survey Section
- Troop 1
- Troop 2
- Troop 3
- Light Artillery Column

**II Field Battery**
- Battery HQ
- HQ Troop
  - Signal Section
  - Survey Section
- Troop 1
- Troop 2
- Troop 3
- Light Artillery Column

**III Medium Battery**
- Battery HQ
- HQ Troop
  - Signal Section
  - Survey Section
- Troop 1
- Troop 2
- Troop 3
- Light Artillery Column

**IV AA Battery**
- Battery HQ
  - Light Troop
  - Heavy Troop
  - Heavy Troop

motorized transportation battalions, a motorized signals company with a semi-motorized signals supply column, a semi-motorized telephone company, and a motorized mapping detachment.

## Artillery action

In both offensive and defensive action, the German armed forces stressed cooperation, employing combined-arms tactics whenever possible. The principle of the *Schwerpunkt* was both an offensive and defensive concept as well, identifying the area of the enemy front where a penetration was most likely to be achieved, or conversely the area of the German front at which an enemy attack was most likely to be launched, and concentrating resources as appropriate.

---

**18TH ARTILLERY DIVISION: ORDER OF BATTLE**

- Stab
- Artillerie-Regiment 88 (mot)
- Artillerie-Regiment 288 (mot)
- Artillerie-Regiment 388 (mot)
- Sturmgeschütz-Batterie 741
- Heeres-Flakartillerie-Abteilung 280
- Beobachtungs-Abteilung 4
- Divisions-Nachrichten-Abteilung 88
- Artillerie-Feldersatz-Abteilung 88
- Schützen-Abteilung (mot) 88
- Kommandeur der Div.Nachschubtruppen 88
- Verwaltungseinheiten 88
- Sanitätseinheiten 88

---

During offensive operations, the artillery commander accompanied the overall commander of the attacking force. In the instance of combined-arms action, this was most often the panzer commander. The attack was prosecuted in waves, with the artillery forward observers moving ahead with the first wave, either in light armoured transportation of their own, aboard advancing tanks or on foot. Self-propelled artillery often protected the flanks of the attacking formation, while anti-tank weapons were deployed forward in the event that enemy armour should be encountered. Heavier guns were well behind the attacking troops, and those assigned as infantry guns were often difficult to relocate without motorized transportation due to their significant weight.

According to the US War Department Technical Manual *TM-E 30-451: Handbook on German Military Forces* published in March 1945, the *Feldheer* perspective on artillery had been influenced by the proliferation of the panzers. 'Great emphasis in German offensive theory is laid on the role of the artillery, but in practice the artillery-support role has devolved to an ever-increasing

---

**18TH ARTILLERY DIVISION: COMMANDERS**

- Generalleutnant Karl Thoholte (20 Oct 1943 – 28 Feb 1944)
- Generalmajor Gerhard Müller (28 Feb 1944 – Apr 1944)
- Generalleutnant Karl Thoholte (Apr 1944 – Jul 1944)

---

degree on the tanks and assault guns,' it reads. 'Nevertheless, the principle that the supporting fire should be concentrated on a narrow frontage where the tanks and infantry are most likely to achieve a breakthrough has been retained.

'The fact that a part of the enemy resistance is likely to remain undisclosed until the attack has already begun has caused the Germans permanently to decentralize a portion of the field artillery. This tendency has led to the emergence and continual development of the assault guns, whose main function is the close support of infantry and tanks in the attack. Their armour and mobility allow them to operate much farther forward than the field artillery.

'The tendency to detach field artillery battalions from their field artillery regiment remains strong. In fact, this tendency is so prevalent that a concentration of massed artillery preceding an attack seldom is achieved, necessitating, as it does, a great degree of centralized control. The Germans, however, replace the massed artillery fire to a large extent with the fire of multi-barrelled mortars and rocket projectors, though these latter have not the accuracy of the former.'

In support of an armoured assault, the artillery was responsible for several aspects of a successful operation, including maintaining counter-battery fire against enemy artillery positions which could fire on the advancing panzers, concentration on any assembly areas utilized by enemy tanks, harassing fire against areas where enemy anti-tank units could assemble and with a particular concentration on terrain in which panzers could not operate effectively but from which enemy fire might emanate, and adjusting appropriate fire against enemy observation posts to destroy or blind them as the attack commenced. During the attack, artillery assets screened the flanks of the attack and continued to impede the deployment of enemy armour while firing well ahead of the advancing panzers.

**Defensive artillery**

On the defensive, artillery and mortar positions were located to provide the maximum coverage of the anticipated fire zone, each responsible for a section which would not only protect the fixed defensive positions such as machine-gun emplacements and bunkers but also cover any gaps between fortifications. Secondary positions were laid out in order to provide options for relocation during combat. Typically, one gun of a battery would remain mobile as far as possible, relocating with greater ease than the others which had been placed in prepared positions. Observation posts were constructed near the front line to direct artillery fire on the attacking enemy.

For both attack and defence, the artillery was recognized in the *Feldheer* as a decisive weapon on the battlefield. The Germans were known to have manufactured and deployed outstanding and versatile artillery pieces such as the 88mm (3.5in) flak gun, which proved lethal in the anti-tank role as well, and became a legendary weapon of World War II – so much so that Allied soldiers

typically referred to any German artillery shell which landed near them as an '88'. In fact, the standard 75mm (2.95in), 105mm (4.1in) and 150mm (5.9in) guns were most often those which shelled with consistency.

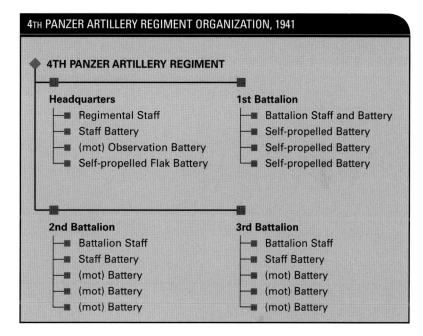

### 4TH PANZER ARTILLERY REGIMENT ORGANIZATION, 1941

**4TH PANZER ARTILLERY REGIMENT**

**Headquarters**
- Regimental Staff
- Staff Battery
- (mot) Observation Battery
- Self-propelled Flak Battery

**1st Battalion**
- Battalion Staff and Battery
- Self-propelled Battery
- Self-propelled Battery
- Self-propelled Battery

**2nd Battalion**
- Battalion Staff
- Staff Battery
- (mot) Battery
- (mot) Battery
- (mot) Battery

**3rd Battalion**
- Battalion Staff
- Staff Battery
- (mot) Battery
- (mot) Battery
- (mot) Battery

### 4TH PANZER ARTILLERY REGIMENT, 1941

| Unit | Equipment | Strength |
|---|---|---|
| Regimental Staff Battery | LMG | 6 |
| (mot) Observation Battery | LMG | 12 |
| Self-propelled Flak Battery | quad 20mm guns | 4 |
| 1st Battalion Staff Battery | LMG | 6 |
| Self-propelled Battery 1 | 105mm leFH SdKfz 124 Wespe | 6 |
| | LMG | 4 |
| Self-propelled Battery 2 | 105mm leFH SdKfz 124 Wespe | 6 |
| | LMG | 4 |
| Self-propelled Battery 3 | 105mm sFH SdKfz 165 Hummel | 6 |
| | LMG | 4 |
| 2nd Battalion Staff Battery | LMG | 6 |
| (mot) Battery 1 | 150mm sFH | 3 |
| | LMG | 2 |
| (mot) Battery 2 | 150mm sFH | 3 |
| | LMG | 2 |
| (mot) Battery 3 | 100mm K. 18 guns | 3 |
| | LMG | 2 |

# Flak Artillery

*In violation of the terms of the Treaty of Versailles, the* Reichswehr *formed seven flak batteries in 1928.*

Clever aliases were coined for these units in the early 1930s, including 'transport detachments' for the early flak formations and a number of anti-aircraft machine-gun companies which followed, and they were designated as a part of the 'German Air Sports Union'. These remained secret until Hitler openly repudiated the Treaty in 1935.

In 1934, the covert flak units were removed from the control of the German Army and placed under the euphemistic Reich Ministry of Air Travel. Technically, the administrative realignment placed all flak units within the control of the *Luftwaffe*. During the next seven years, the number of flak units increased steadily, growing from 18 in 1935 to 115 in 1939 and eventually 841 by 1941.

Although *Luftwaffe* flak capabilities were substantial, the leadership of the *Heer* clamoured for authorization to form its own anti-aircraft units. Early in 1941, although the *Luftwaffe* maintained control of guns, ammunition supplies and equipment necessary to operate the weapons, the Army was granted permission to form flak battalions for both infantry and artillery air defence. These were initially numbered in sequence from 22nd to 66th; however, this was changed in the spring of 1941 to primarily include battalions numbered 601st to 620th. As the number of *Heer* flak units increased, their

designations became somewhat haphazard, while a few were deployed without numerical recognition at all.

By early 1944, as the role of the flak units became increasingly defensive, the battalion formation was substantially discarded in favour of independent platoons. Those battalions which continued were primarily static formations. While larger *Feldheer* formations maintained their own organic flak platoons, the result was a reduced number of independent flak units.

During World War II, flak units

included towed and self-propelled weapons of single or multiple barrels, and some units operated by rail. The composition of flak battalions varied, most having three or four companies of 20mm (0.79in) guns.

In early 1941, the 601st Flak Battalion consisted of four self-propelled companies, each with a dozen 20mm (0.79in) cannon. The 273rd Flak Battalion included a motorized staff company, a pair of motorized batteries composed of four 88mm (3.5in) and three 20mm (0.79in) guns each, and a single motorized battery of 12 20mm (0.79in) guns.

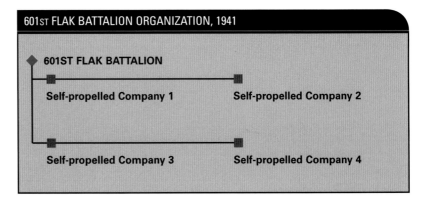

**601ST FLAK BATTALION ORGANIZATION, 1941**

◆ **601ST FLAK BATTALION**

**Self-propelled Company 1**

**Self-propelled Company 2**

**Self-propelled Company 3**

**Self-propelled Company 4**

**601ST FLAK BATTALION, 1941**

| Unit | Equipment | Strength |
| --- | --- | --- |
| Self-propelled Company 1 | 20mm (0.79in) cannon | 12 |
| Self-propelled Company 2 | 20mm (0.79in) cannon | 12 |
| Self-propelled Company 3 | 20mm (0.79in) cannon | 12 |
| Self-propelled Company 4 | 20mm (0.79in) cannon | 12 |

## 273RD FLAK BATTALION, 1941

| Unit | Equipment | Strength |
|------|-----------|----------|
| (mot) Staff Company | – | – |
| (mot) Battery 1 | 88mm (3.5in) gun | 4 |
|  | 20mm (0.79in) gun | 3 |
| (mot) Battery 2 | 88mm (3.5in) gun | 4 |
|  | 20mm (0.79in) gun | 3 |
| (mot) Battery 3 | 20mm (0.79in) gun | 12 |

## 273RD FLAK BATTALION ORGANIZATION, 1941

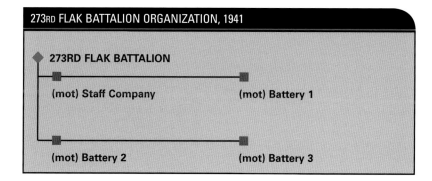

**273RD FLAK BATTALION**

(mot) Staff Company

(mot) Battery 1

(mot) Battery 2

(mot) Battery 3

### Fortress flak and artillery

The *Wehrmacht* recognized two types of fixed artillery positions, the coastal artillery which was primarily administered by the *Kriegsmarine* much in the same manner as the *Luftwaffe* asserted primary control of at least 30 flak divisions and brigade formations, and the fortress artillery which remained under the control of the *Heer*. In the wake of World War I, the German fortress artillery consisted of only one prominent concentration, at Königsberg on the Baltic coast of East Prussia where about 25 guns, the largest being 170mm (6.7in), were located. As German rearmament was by

definition offensive-minded, the fortified positions of the Siegfried Line were defended by a relative few guns; however, this number was augmented by captured weapons and

ammunition thanks to the early conquests of the *Feldheer* during World War II.

As early as the spring of 1941, it became apparent to the OKW that an invasion of the European continent might indeed occur and that coastal defences should be enhanced. During the following two years, the coasts of occupied France, Denmark and Norway were allocated increased numbers of artillery pieces. Coastal defence artillery battalions included a variety of weapons. For example, the 828th Battalion, stationed along the coast of Greece in the summer of 1941, served three batteries of six 150mm (5.9in) guns of French manufacture and two batteries of four 100mm (3.94in) guns. Defending the German coastline along the Baltic in January 1944, the 1230th Coast Artillery Battalion included six batteries of 105mm (4.1in), 170mm (6.7in) and 152mm (6in) guns manufactured in Germany, the Soviet Union, France, Czechoslovakia and Poland.

■ **A heavy coastal gun protrudes from a bunker forming part of the Atlantic Wall defences, Pas de Calais, 1944.**

## GERMAN FORTRESSES

1. Alderney
2. Boulogne
3. Breslau
4. Brest
5. Calais
6. Dieppe
7. Dunkirk
8. Kolberg
9. Königsberg
10. Küstrin
11. Le Havre
12. Posen
13. St Malo
14. Warsaw

# Atlantic Wall

*With the fall of France in June 1940, the Germans took over existing French fortifications along the coast of the occupied country.*

Subsequently, with the reversal of fortune encountered during the Battle of Britain, Operation 'Sealion', an amphibious invasion of England, was shelved and the construction of more formidable defences along the English Channel coast continued. At the end of 1941, construction of numerous concrete bunkers to house railway guns and heavy artillery had been completed in France, the Netherlands and Norway.

Among the most prominent of these were seven emplacements along the French coastline. These

## ■ GERMAN FORTRESSES

**The coastal batteries of the Atlantic Wall were considered vital to the German defensive plans against the anticipated Allied invasion, which occurred in Normandy on 6 June 1944. These heavy guns, typically of 105mm (4.1in) or greater, were positioned in thick concrete casemates and sited to bring fire on invasion beaches or port areas and disrupt infantry landings or to engage Allied landing craft. Pre-invasion Allied bombing was generally ineffective in reducing the volume of fire these guns were capable of generating. Other German fortresses included those cities designated by Hitler as 'fortress cities', such as Warsaw, Boulogne, or Königsberg, where German troops were ordered to fight to the last man.**

included the four 280mm (11in) guns of Battery Graf Spee at the port city of Brest, Battery Grosser Kurfürst and Battery Prince Heinrich with a total of six 280mm (11in) guns at Framzelle, Battery Oldenburg with two 240mm (9.4in) guns at Calais, the three 406mm (16in) guns of Battery Schleswig-Holstein (later renamed Battery Lindemann after the captain of the battleship *Bismarck*) at Sangatte, and the four 150mm (5.9in) guns of Battery Brommy and four 240mm (9.4in) guns of Battery Hamburg at Cherbourg.

By the spring of 1942, the construction of Atlantic Wall fortifications was being undertaken with greater urgency as labourers of

the Todt Organization and slave workers procured from concentration camps set about making an impregnable line of fortifications stretching from the Arctic to the Atlantic. In August 1942, Hitler issued his Directive Number 40, ordering the construction of fortified positions for anti-tank guns and machine guns which could provide protection for 30 to 70 men. Each of these was to provide interlocking fields of fire to cover sections of the anticipated landing beaches, particularly at the Pas de Calais, which was the shortest distance to the Continent from England. Hitler had initially mandated the construction of 15,000 concrete

## ATLANTIC WALL FORTRESSES

| Location | Commander | Garrison |
|---|---|---|
| Cherbourg | General von Schlieben | 47,000 men in whole Cotentin Peninsula |
| Saint-Malo/Dinard | Colonel von Aulock | 12,000+ men including paratroopers and SS |
| Alderney | – | – |
| Brest | General Ramcke | 38,000+ men including the 2nd Parachute Division |
| Lorient | General Junck | 15,000 |
| Quiberon Bay and Belle Île | General Fahrmbacher | 25,000 |
| St. Nazaire | General Junck | 35,000 |
| La Rochelle/La Pallice | Admiral Schirlitz | Naval Units, 158th Reserve Infantry Division |
| Le Havre | Colonel Wildermuth | 14,000 |
| Boulogne | General Heim | 10,000 |
| Calais/Cap Gris-Nez | Lt-Colonel Schroeder | 9000 |
| Dunkirk | Admiral Friedrich Frisius | 12,000 from the 18th Luftwaffe Ground Division |
| Ostend | – | – |
| Zeebrugge | General Eberding | 14,000 |
| Scheldt Fortress | General Daser | 8000 |

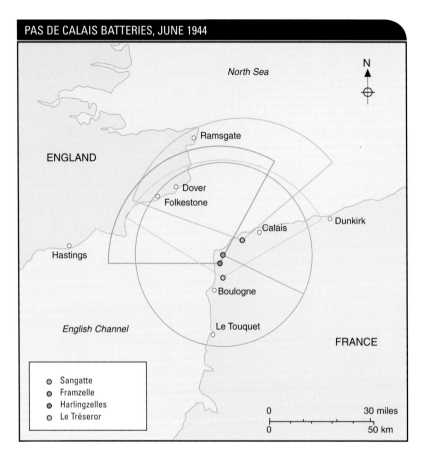

**PAS DE CALAIS BATTERIES, JUNE 1944**

North Sea

ENGLAND

Ramsgate

Dover
Folkestone

Calais

Dunkirk

Hastings

Boulogne

English Channel

Le Touquet

FRANCE

N

○ Sangatte
○ Framzelle
○ Harlingzelles
○ Le Tréseror

0        30 miles
0        50 km

■ **PAS DE CALAIS BATTERIES (left)**
The defensive guns of the batteries located in the Pas de Calais were of heavy calibre – 240mm (9.4in) and 280mm (11in). Their concrete casemates were built to withstand the heavy bombardment of Allied warships and aerial bombing. The batteries in the area were particularly situated to contest a landing where the Germans considered an invasion most likely. The Pas de Calais was the shortest distance from England to the continent of Europe, and Allied deception efforts, codenamed Operation 'Fortitude', convinced the Germans that this was the location of the invasion. For weeks after the 6 June 1944 landings in Normandy, Hitler refused to believe that the real invasion had occurred.

■ **POINTE DU HOC BATTERIES (right)**
One of the most heroic efforts on D-Day was the storming of the 30-metre (96ft) cliffs at Pointe du Hoc by 225th US Army Rangers utilizing ropes with grappling hooks and ladders. The Rangers were tasked with silencing a battery of heavy guns which Allied Intelligence had detected through aerial reconnaissance. The guns were believed to be 155mm (6.1in) and menaced the intended landing areas of both Utah and Omaha beaches. The Rangers took heavy casualties but drove the defending German infantry from the cliffs, only to discover that the guns had been removed some time earlier. Some enterprising Rangers set off to follow some vehicle tracks, and discovered the guns camouflaged in an orchard, where they disabled them with thermite grenades.

bunkers and gun positions to be garrisoned by up to 300,000 troops.

Although such scale was never achieved, the project did produce a major obstacle to the Allied landings in Normandy on 6 June 1944. At its peak in April 1943, the construction of the Atlantic Wall consumed 760,000 cubic metres (26.8 million cubic feet) of concrete with heavy activity taking place from mid-1943 until the D-Day landings. Portions of the Atlantic Wall were designated as 'Defensive Areas' which consisted of guns of 150mm (5.9in) or greater surrounded by concrete casemates, barbed wire, minefields, supporting

machine-gun nests, trenches and anti-tank ditches. These were also supported by smaller positions which included quarters for soldiers, generators, ammunition stores and communications centres. Other positions could accommodate up to a platoon of defending infantrymen. At Boulogne, which had been designated a fortress city, the defences included more than 40 fortified positions, half of these along the nearby beaches. Boulogne's batteries were armed with 155mm (6.1in), 138mm (5.4in), 105mm (4.1in), 94mm (3.7in), 88mm (3.5in) and 75mm (2.95in) guns.

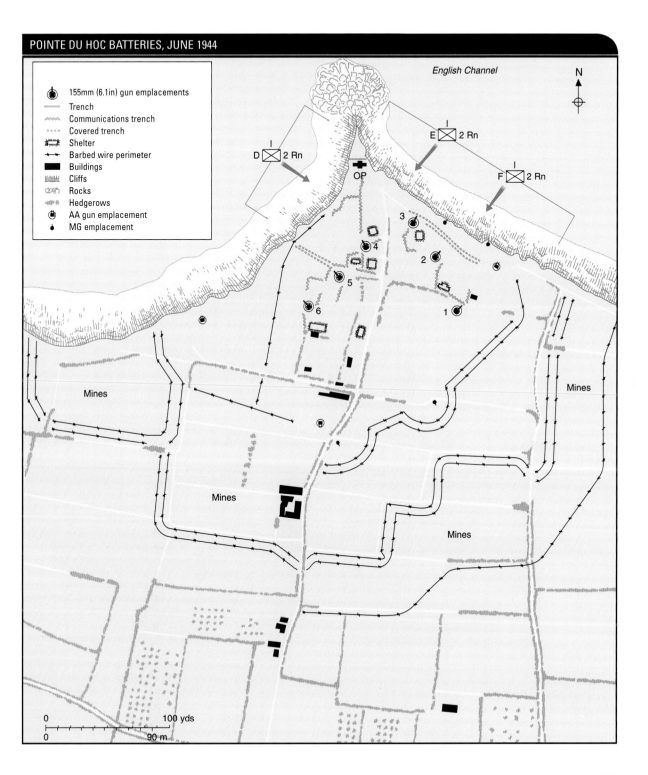

POINTE DU HOC BATTERIES, JUNE 1944

*English Channel*

N

**Legend:**
- 155mm (6.1in) gun emplacements
- Trench
- Communications trench
- Covered trench
- Shelter
- Barbed wire perimeter
- Buildings
- Cliffs
- Rocks
- Hedgerows
- AA gun emplacement
- MG emplacement

D ⊠ 2 Rn

E ⊠ 2 Rn

F ⊠ 2 Rn

OP

3
4
2
5
1
6

Mines

Mines

Mines

Mines

0      100 yds

0      90 m

# Railway Artillery

*The railway artillery of the* Feldheer *included light flak weapons and heavy-calibre guns, particularly those which were so ponderous that their weight prevented transportation by other means.*

Standard rail flak guns were of 20mm (0.79in) or 37mm (1.45in), and these were often deployed in company with the heavier guns to ward off enemy air attacks.

Heavier weapons generally required greater numbers of crewmen to serve them and were well-known to have low rates of fire. However, it was readily apparent that both the physical and psychological damage which could be inflicted on the enemy by powerful railway guns was significant. Since the *Feldheer* depended on horse transportation for the majority of its artillery mobility, it was obvious that above

210mm (8.3in) it was by far more efficient to mount many of these weapons on rail cars. These heavy guns or batteries often included flak detachments, teams of signals and rangefinding troops, a baggage

train, and a gun crew which might exceed 200 men.

Heavy guns also had an extended range, with the 283mm (11.1in) Kanone 5 capable of sending a shell an astounding 61km (38 miles). Nine

■ SUPERGUNS

The presence of the heaviest German artillery pieces on the battlefield had more than simply a psychological effect on Allied troops. The mammoth 283mm (11.1in) K5 and 800mm (31.5in) weapons produced by Krupp delivered shells distances of 61km (38 miles) and 47km (29 miles) respectively. The K5 was particularly effective at Anzio, where Allied troops were often restricted to movement during nocturnal hours for fear of attracting the attention of German gunners. The story of the gigantic 800mm (31.5in) guns, two of which were said to have been produced, is shrouded in conjecture. One of them, nicknamed Dora, was reported in action during the siege of Sevastopol; however, the ultimate fate of the weapons has never been determined.

## 800MM (31.5IN) GUSTAV GERÄT 'DORA'

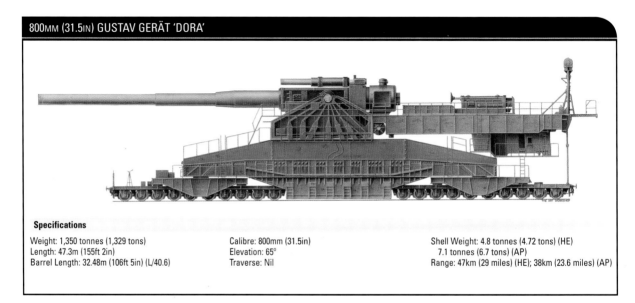

**Specifications**

Weight: 1,350 tonnes (1,329 tons)
Length: 47.3m (155ft 2in)
Barrel Length: 32.48m (106ft 5in) (L/40.6)

Calibre: 800mm (31.5in)
Elevation: 65°
Traverse: Nil

Shell Weight: 4.8 tonnes (4.72 tons) (HE)
7.1 tonnes (6.7 tons) (AP)
Range: 47km (29 miles) (HE); 38km (23.6 miles) (AP)

## K5 RAILWAY GUN

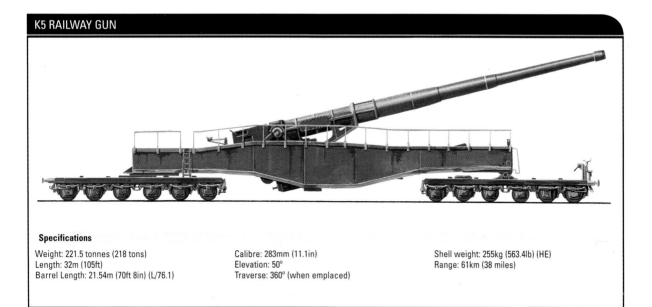

**Specifications**

Weight: 221.5 tonnes (218 tons)
Length: 32m (105ft)
Barrel Length: 21.54m (70ft 8in) (L/76.1)

Calibre: 283mm (11.1in)
Elevation: 50°
Traverse: 360° (when emplaced)

Shell weight: 255kg (563.4lb) (HE)
Range: 61km (38 miles)

Kanone 5 batteries were known to have operated during 1941 and 1942, particularly during the siege of Sevastopol in the Crimea and later at the siege of Leningrad and the investment of the Anzio beachhead in Italy. Due either to attrition or lack of servicing capability, only the 686th Railway Battery is known to have continued operating the Kanone 5 from 1943. At Anzio, the Germans were reported to have brought forward a pair of the K5 guns, which they had nicknamed 'Robert' and 'Leopold'. Despite a rate of fire of only one round every three to five minutes, the guns were nevertheless fearsome. The collective Allied nickname for the pair was 'Anzio Annie'.

### Size matters
The heavy railway guns generally ranged in size from 210mm (8.3in) to a monstrous 800mm (31.5in),

although some smaller weapons, including captured Soviet 152mm (6in) guns, were also mounted on railway cars. The smaller weapons utilized outrigger systems for stabilization and could fire in a 360-degree arc. The largest of these guns required at least two railway cars for transportation, with the barrel suspended between them, while aiming was a complex operation involving turntable systems or a combination of tracks which allowed the railway cars to be moved in multiple directions as the weapon was brought to bear on a selected target.

Some conjecture surrounds the service life of the massive 800mm (31.5in) cannon produced by Krupp. While historians argue as to whether one or two of the behemoths were actually constructed, it is known that the weapon weighed 1,350 tonnes (1329 tons) and was so large that it

required two parallel railway tracks to move. It fired a shell weighing 4.8 tonnes (4.72 tons) a distance of up to 47km (29 miles).

### Mystery guns
It has been suggested that Krupp produced a pair of the 800mm (31.5in) guns. The two were reportedly named 'Gustav' and 'Dora' for the head of the Krupp firm and the wife of the system's chief project engineer respectively. At least one of the weapons operated during the siege of Sevastopol and was reported to have fired up to 55 rounds in combat. The largest rifled weapon in history, its fate is unknown.

The Soviets denied capturing such a weapon, and it may have been broken up for scrap. One of the guns is known to have been operating with the 672nd Railway Battery in the summer of 1943.

Other heavy weapons of note were the 520mm (20.5in) *Langer Gustav*, which was intended to fire a rocket-propelled shell weighing 680kg (1499lb) a distance of 190km (118 miles), and the mysterious V-3 cannon, about which little is known other than it was intended as one of Hitler's vengeance weapons and was potentially capable of hitting London from underground chambers in the French countryside.

## RAILWAY GUN BATTERIES: DEPLOYMENT

| Battery | Type of Gun | Number of Guns | Posting |
|---|---|---|---|
| Battery 717 | 17cm (6.7in) KE | 3 | Artillery regiment 676, Aug 1944 |
| Battery 718 | 17cm (6.7in) KE | 3 | Artillery regiment 676, Aug 1944 |
| Battery 701 | 21cm (8.3in) K12 V | 1 | (Qty 1 in 1941, Qty 2 in 1943–44) Artillery regiment 655, Aug 1944 |
| Battery 686 | 28cm (11in) K5 + 40cm (15.8in) 752 (f) | 2 + 4 | Artillery regiment 679, Aug 1944 |
| Battery 688 | 28cm (11in) K5 | 2 | |
| Battery 689 | 28cm (11in) *Schwere Bruno* L/42 | 2 | |
| Battery 710 | 28cm (11in) K5 | 2 | Artillery regiment 655, Aug 1944 |
| Battery 711 | 37cm (14.6in) (f) MIS | 2 | Captured gun (no longer a unit in 1941 forward) |
| Battery 712 | 28cm (11in) K5 | 2 | Artillery regiment 646, Aug 1944 |
| Battery 697 | 28cm (11in) K5 | 2 | Velocity measuring troop |
| Battery 713 | 28cm (11in) K5 | 2 | |
| Batteries 765 and 617 | 28cm (11in) K5 | 2 | Velocity measuring troop |
| Detachment 100 | 28cm (11in) K5 | 2 | Training and replacement |
| Battery 690 | 28cm (11in) *Kurze Bruno* | 2 | (Qty 2 in 1941, Qty 4 in Jan 1944) Coastal Artillery regiment 676, Aug 1944 |
| Battery 694 | 28cm (11in) *Kurze Bruno* | 2 | 1941, no longer a unit in 1943–44 |
| Battery 695 | 28cm (11in) *Kurze Bruno* | 2 | (Qty 1 in 1941, +32cm (f) 1943–44) Artillery regiment 679, Aug 1944 |
| Battery 696 | 28cm (11in) *Kurze Bruno* | 2 | Artillery regiment 676, Aug 1944 |
| Battery 721 | 28cm (11in) *Kurze Bruno* | 2 | (Qty 1 in 1940, Qty 2 in 1943–44) Artillery regiment 780, combined with regiment 640 in Aug 1944 |
| Battery 692 | 27.4cm (10.8in) 592 (f) | 3 | Artillery regiment 640 combined with regiment 780 in Aug 1944 |
| Battery 691 | 24cm (9.4in) 651 (f) | 3 | Artillery regiment 646, Aug 1944 |
| Battery 722 | 24cm (9.4in) *Th. Bruno* | 4 | Coastal |
| Battery 674 | 24cm (9.4in) *Th. Bruno* | 2 | Artillery regiment 780 combined with regiment 640 in Aug 1944 |
| Battery 664 | 24cm (9.4in) *Kurze Th. Bruno* | 2 | Artillery regiment 780 combined with regiment 640 in Aug 1944 |
| Battery 749 | 28cm (11in) K5 | 2 | Artillery regiment 640 combined with regiment 780 in Aug 1944 |
| Battery 725 | 28cm (11in) K5 + 28cm (11in) *N. Bruno* | 2 + 2 | Artillery regiment 646, N. Bruno split off Aug 1944 |
| Battery 459 | 37cm (14.6in) 651 (f) | 3 | Artillery regiment 646, Aug 1944 |
| Battery 693 | 40cm (15.8in) 752 (f) | 4 | Artillery regiment 646, Aug 1944 |
| Battery 698 | 38cm (14.9in) *Siegfried* | 2 | (Qty 1 in 1944 with 1 Siegfried going to 679) Artillery regiment 640 combined with regiment 780 in Aug 1944 |

(Courtesy of www.one35th.com)

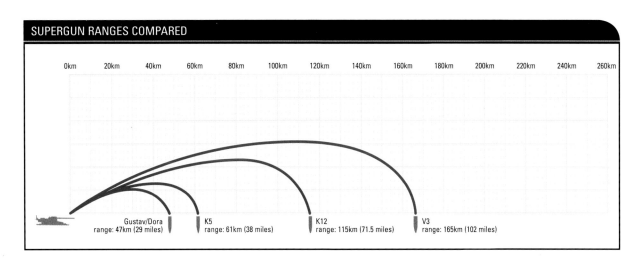

SUPERGUN RANGES COMPARED

| 0km | 20km | 40km | 60km | 80km | 100km | 120km | 140km | 160km | 180km | 200km | 220km | 240km | 260km |

Gustav/Dora
range: 47km (29 miles)

K5
range: 61km (38 miles)

K12
range: 115km (71.5 miles)

V3
range: 165km (102 miles)

■ The extended ranges of the heaviest German artillery potentially threatened not only rear areas but also troop and munitions concentrations and even Allied population centres. The Dora and K5 guns could theoretically hit targets 47km (29 miles), or more, distant from their positions. The 210mm (8.3in) K12 was originally conceived as an updated version of the Paris Gun, which shelled the French capital city during World War I. The K12 was fired from a position along the coast of the English Channel, and shell fragments were recovered in Kent, more than 80km (50 miles) away.

# Artillery Brigades

*On 30 August 1944, a dozen independent artillery brigades were ordered to be formed from existing artillery battalions and some of the artillery regiments which had already been assigned to specific army-level units from the general headquarters pool.*

These brigades were all motorized and organized between 25 September and 20 November 1944. The actual organization and nomenclature of these brigades varied widely, loosely based on one of two organizational tables. At the end of October 1944, the 595th Artillery Brigade included three battalions, the first and second equipped with two batteries of six 150mm (5.9in) guns and a single battery of six 105mm (4.1in) cannon, while the third battalion included

three batteries of three 210mm (8.3in) mortars.

### *Volks* Artillery Corps

In the autumn of 1944, the new *Volks* Artillery Corps were organized in two types. Numbered 166th, 401st to 410th, 704th, 732nd, 766th and 959th, their strength was actually slightly greater than a standard artillery regiment, each containing either five or six battalions with half of these equipped with light weapons and the others

with heavy weapons. The Type I *Volks* Artillery Corps included three 170mm (6.7in) guns, six 210mm (8.3in) mortars, 12 150mm (5.9in) howitzers, 12 122mm (4.8in) howitzers, 18 105mm (4.1in) howitzers, 18 88mm (3.5in) flak guns, and 18 75mm (2.95in) field guns.

The Type II *Volks* Artillery Corps consisted of a battalion of three batteries of 210mm (8.3in) mortars, each with nine weapons, 12 150mm (5.9in) howitzers, 12 122mm (4.8in) howitzers, 18 105mm (4.1in) howitzers,

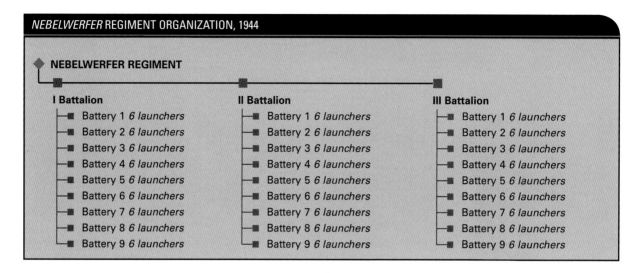

**NEBELWERFER REGIMENT ORGANIZATION, 1944**

NEBELWERFER REGIMENT

| I Battalion | II Battalion | III Battalion |
|---|---|---|
| Battery 1 *6 launchers* | Battery 1 *6 launchers* | Battery 1 *6 launchers* |
| Battery 2 *6 launchers* | Battery 2 *6 launchers* | Battery 2 *6 launchers* |
| Battery 3 *6 launchers* | Battery 3 *6 launchers* | Battery 3 *6 launchers* |
| Battery 4 *6 launchers* | Battery 4 *6 launchers* | Battery 4 *6 launchers* |
| Battery 5 *6 launchers* | Battery 5 *6 launchers* | Battery 5 *6 launchers* |
| Battery 6 *6 launchers* | Battery 6 *6 launchers* | Battery 6 *6 launchers* |
| Battery 7 *6 launchers* | Battery 7 *6 launchers* | Battery 7 *6 launchers* |
| Battery 8 *6 launchers* | Battery 8 *6 launchers* | Battery 8 *6 launchers* |
| Battery 9 *6 launchers* | Battery 9 *6 launchers* | Battery 9 *6 launchers* |

12 100mm (3.94in) guns, and 18 75mm (2.95in) field guns. Two types of motorized and partially-motorized corps were also formed. The Type I Motorized Corps included more than 400 trucks and 100 prime movers, while the Type II Motorized Corps included 294 trucks and 84 prime movers.

**Nebelwerfer**

At the outbreak of World War II, the *Feldheer* included three battalions of 105mm (4.1in) *Nebelwerfer* rocket launchers. Their deployment proved so successful that the number of battalions increased to eight by the eve of the invasion of France and the Low Countries on 10 May 1940, and the calibre of the weapons was increased to 120mm (4.7in) the following year and eventually to 210mm (8.3in), 280mm (11in) and 300mm (11.8in) in 1942. By early 1941, nine independent *Nebelwerfer* battalions and four regiments had been formed. Eight of the battalions included three motorized batteries of

six launchers each, a motorized signals and headquarters platoon, a meteorological platoon and a light munitions supply column. One battalion's three batteries were equipped with eight launchers each. The regiments consisted of three battalions of six launchers each, along with supporting formations.

As the war progressed, the number of *Nebelwerfer* formations steadily increased. During a 12-month period from the autumn of 1942, four new regiments, two battalions, two independent batteries and a mountain *Nebelwerfer* battalion were created. In the spring of 1944, four *Nebelwerfer* brigades were formed, and two others followed in September. In the final two years of the war, the *Nebelwerfer* formations included three fixed-position regiments, 20 standard regiments, and 11 heavy regiments. These regiments consisted of three battalions organized in nine batteries. The six launchers in each battery provided an aggregate firepower of

324 rocket-launching tubes. In 1943, some 150mm (5.9in) *Nebelwerfer* were mounted on armoured chassis or halftracks for the first time, and some formations were supplemented with one or two additional batteries.

The *Nebelwerfer* formations served on all fronts with the *Feldheer* during World War II. Elements of one were lost with the capitulation of *Panzerarmee Afrika* in Tunisia in 1943, while three were destroyed during the debacle at Stalingrad on the Eastern Front. In January 1944, the prowess of the *Nebelwerfer* as a defensive weapon which could deliver heavy concentrated fire was recognized with the formation of six brigades from the existing regiments. The brigades included two *Nebelwerfer* regiments equipped with launchers ranging from 150mm (5.9in) to 300mm (11.8in).

During the final four months of 1944, up to 10 new *Nebelwerfer* brigades were created, each with two regiments of three battalions. The battalions included three batteries of

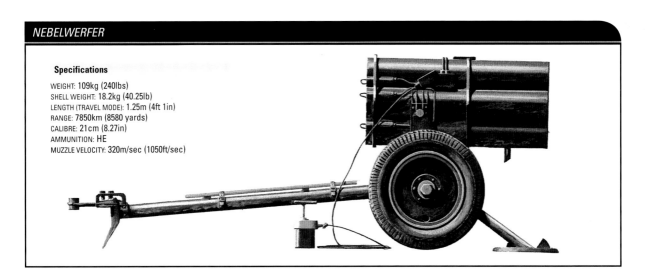

**Specifications**

WEIGHT: 109kg (240lbs)
SHELL WEIGHT: 18.2kg (40.25lb)
LENGTH (TRAVEL MODE): 1.25m (4ft 1in)
RANGE: 7850km (8580 yards)
CALIBRE: 21cm (8.27in)
AMMUNITION: HE
MUZZLE VELOCITY: 320m/sec (1050ft/sec)

six launchers, and four of the battalions were equipped with 150mm (5.9in) launchers, one with 210mm (8.3in) and one with 300mm (11.8in). Motorized brigades were formidable units, with a complement of 2933 men, 276 trucks, 109 prime movers, 18 300mm (11.8in) launchers, 18 210mm (8.3in) launchers, and 72 150mm (5.9in) launchers. The fixed-position *Nebelwerfer* brigades consisted of 1966 soldiers, 18 prime movers, 56 trucks, 36 300mm (11.8in) launchers and 72 150mm (5.9in) launchers. Numerous *Nebelwerfer* brigades were heavily engaged during the Ardennes offensive of December 1944, including several designated as *Volks Werfer* brigades, some of which were fully- or partially-motorized.

### Sturmgeschütze

In more than one way, the *Sturmgeschütze*, or assault guns, were an anomaly in the *Feldheer*. Although they operated in close support of the infantry and as anti-tank weapons, and were tracked and

self-propelled, these weapons were under the direct control of the Artillery Weapons Department rather than the panzer commanders who controlled virtually all other armoured fighting vehicles.

The purpose of the *Sturmgeschütz* was well defined when the vehicle was first conceived in the early 1930s, and the demand for it was reflected in steadily-climbing production numbers which topped 50 per month by 1940, four years after the first order was placed with German armaments manufacturers.

The *Sturmgeschütze* participated in the invasion of France and the Low Countries in limited numbers, and as the war widened, the vehicles provided other tangible advantages. They were fulfilling their combat missions while proving much more economical to produce than a medium or heavy tank. No turret was needed, and the chassis was that of the workhorse PzKpfw III tank, which had been in production for some time.

Eleven independent *Sturmgeschütz* battalions and six independent batteries were in service with the *Feldheer* in February 1941. Just five months later, 19 battalions had been formed. The battalion structure included a staff or headquarters battery along with three assault gun batteries of six vehicles each. In the spring of 1941, a seventh assault gun was added to each battery. The vehicles typically mounted variants of the 75mm (2.95in) gun, which was effective against fixed targets and armour at reasonable range. In 1943, the *Sturmgeschütz* battalions were renumbered and substantially increased with a staff battery and three companies, each fielding 10 *Sturmgeschütze*.

In the autumn of 1943, the *Sturmgeschütz* battalions were revamped considerably to facilitate a degree of independent operations. The headquarters and staff batteries included 164 soldiers, 43 non-commissioned officers, a civil service member and four officers. Of these, 24

## *STURMGESCHÜTZ* BATTALION ORGANIZATION, 1943

*From November 1943, StuG battalions consisted of three, 14-vehicle companies, giving the battalion a total strength of 42 assault guns. From the Kursk offensive onwards, the StuG III had evolved from a pure infantry support AFV into a potent 'all-rounder', which was equally effective as a tank destroyer. Although its main armament lacked all-round traverse, its low silhouette, thick frontal armour and powerful gun made it one of the most formidable German AFVs.*

1 Company

2 Company

3 Company

soldiers performed command and signals functions and were equipped with three PzKpfw III command vehicles. Other troops included a self-propelled flak platoon of quadruple-mounted 20mm (0.79in) flak guns and 41 soldiers, a 48-man reconnaissance and pioneer platoon, a maintenance troop, supply troop, and field train totalling 100 men, a six-man administrative unit and a baggage train handled by four men.

Within each company a command staff of 12 soldiers was equipped with two assault guns, while the three combat platoons included four assault guns and 16 soldiers. Another 53 soldiers took care of the baggage train, field train and light vehicle duties. Total company strength was three officers, 51 non-commissioned officers, and 59 other ranks. Aggregate battalion strength totalled 36 *Sturmgeschütze*, three command vehicles, 13 officers, 196 non-commissioned officers, one civil service employee, and 341 other troops. This was one of several reorganizations which occurred during the war, some of which were minor in nature.

By January 1944, a total of 46 *Sturmgeschütz* battalions had been formed. In early summer an escort company motorized in halftracks and a pioneer platoon were added, and in November the battalion staffs of all German armoured units were standardized. In each *Sturmgeschütz* battalion was a staff of 15 troops, while the headquarters company included 26 men, a combined reconnaissance and pioneer platoon had a seven-man HQ, with 20 soldiers organized in four reconnaissance

| STURMGESCHÜTZ BATTALION, NOVEMBER 1943 | | |
|---|---|---|
| Unit | Equipment | Strength |
| Headquarters and Staff Battery | Men | 164 |
| | Non-commissioned officers | 43 |
| | Civil service member | 1 |
| | Officers | 4 |
| | PzKpfw III | 3 |
| Self-propelled Flak Platoon | Men | 41 |
| | 20mm Flak Gun | 4 |
| Reconnaissance and Pioneer Platoon | Men | 48 |
| Maintenance, Supply and Field Train | Men | 100 |
| Administration | Men | 6 |
| Baggage Train | Men | 4 |
| Company Command Staff | Men | 12 |
| | Assault guns | 2 |
| Combat Platoon x 3 | Men | 16 |
| | Assault guns | 4 |
| Baggage Train | Men | 53 |
| Company | Officers | 3 |
| | Non-commissioned officers | 51 |
| | Other ranks | 59 |
| Battalion | Sturmgeschütze | 36 |
| | Command vehicles | 3 |
| | Officers | 13 |
| | Non-commissioned officers | 196 |
| | Civil service employee | 1 |
| | Troops | 341 |

troops of five soldiers each, and three pioneer troops of 12 men. The flak platoon included 35 soldiers. The company structure was also rearranged and included a total of 63 officers and men. From early 1943, some *Sturmgeschütz* battalions were assigned to panzer and panzergrenadier regiments to provide additional anti-tank capability.

## Tank destroyers
With only a few notable exceptions, the tank destroyer formations of the *Feldheer* were relatively small, rarely larger than a battalion until late in the war. Although the *Feldheer* planned to raise 20 battalions of the tank

destroyer variants of the PzKpfw V Panther and PzKpfw VI Tiger tanks, only about 150 of the so-called Jagdtiger, which mounted a 128mm (5.04in) cannon, were built. During the course of the war, the *Feldheer* deployed several lighter anti-tank weapons which doubled as assault guns, such as the Marder and Hetzer, the SdKfz 164 Nashorn equipped with an 88mm (3.5in) cannon, and the Jagdpanzer IV.

In the spring of 1944, the 560th *Jagdpanther* Battalion was formed and included a staff company with three Jagdpanthers, three Jagdpanther companies of 14 vehicles each and armed with 88mm

## JAGDPANZER, JAGDPANTHER AND ELEFANT COMPARED

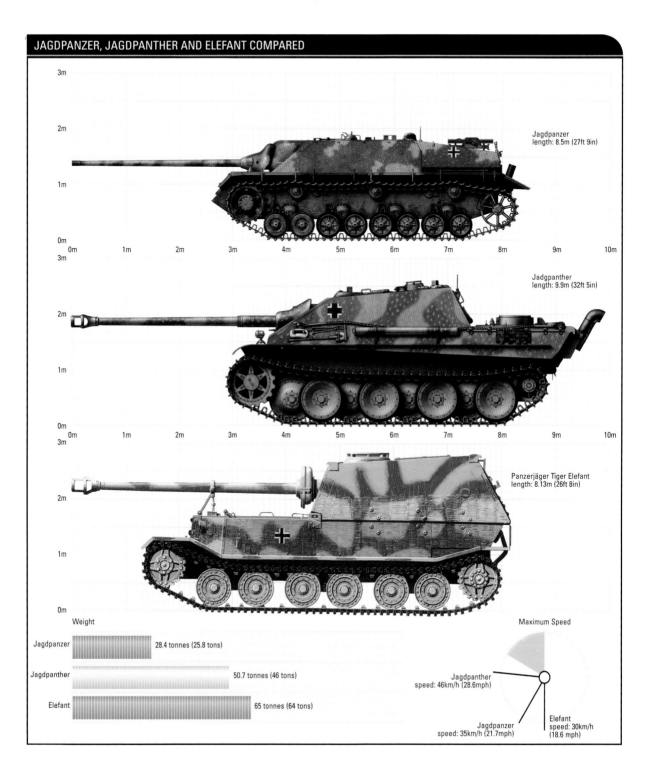

Jagdpanzer
length: 8.5m (27ft 9in)

Jadgpanther
length: 9.9m (32ft 5in)

Panzerjäger Tiger Elefant
length: 8.13m (26ft 8in)

Weight

Jagdpanzer — 28.4 tonnes (25.8 tons)

Jagdpanther — 50.7 tonnes (46 tons)

Elefant — 65 tonnes (64 tons)

Maximum Speed

Jagdpanther
speed: 46km/h (28.6mph)

Jagdpanzer
speed: 35km/h (21.7mph)

Elefant
speed: 30km/h
(18.6 mph)

(3.5in) main cannon, and a pair of flak platoons, one armed with four 37mm (1.45in) guns and the other with 20mm (0.79in) weapons. During the Battle of Kursk in July 1943, the 653rd and 654th *Panzerjäger* Battalions were equipped with the massive Porsche Elefant, which mounted an 88mm (3.5in) cannon and weighed 71 tonnes (70 tons). These battalions were decimated during the largest tank battle in history, and the Elefant performed poorly. Subsequently, the 653rd was issued the Jagdtiger and the 654th the Jagdpanther.

# Weapons

*Between the world wars, the Nazi rise to power was supported by the two major German armaments manufacturers, Krupp and Rheinmetall, both of which had survived World War I and the Treaty of Versailles relatively intact despite severe restrictions on the types of weapons which could be produced for the German armed forces and for export to other countries.*

A period of research and development begun during the 1920s produced some effective artillery weapons as well as some noble and progressive experiments which proved disappointing. At the same time, holdover designs from World War I and weapons of foreign manufacture were liberally placed in service with the *Feldheer* during wartime.

**Flak guns**
Arguably the most famous artillery weapon of World War II was the German 88mm (3.5in) flak gun, which was developed in response to a request for a weapon which was heavier than the 75mm (2.95in) gun which Krupp engineers had gone to Sweden to develop in the early 1930s in cooperation with technicians of the Bofors firm. The 88mm (3.5in) Flak

18 debuted in 1933 and was praised for its performance during the Spanish Civil War. Its shell weighed 9.2kg (20.3lbs), and the weapon's effective ceiling was 8000m (26,245ft) with a muzzle velocity of 820m (2690ft) per second.

Improvements to the weapon, allowing worn sections of the rifling to be changed rather than necessitating the replacement of the

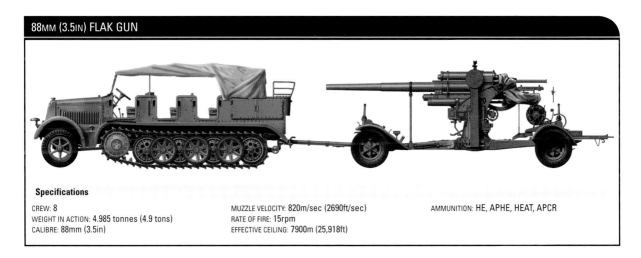

**88MM (3.5IN) FLAK GUN**

**Specifications**

CREW: 8
WEIGHT IN ACTION: 4.985 tonnes (4.9 tons)
CALIBRE: 88mm (3.5in)

MUZZLE VELOCITY: 820m/sec (2690ft/sec)
RATE OF FIRE: 15rpm
EFFECTIVE CEILING: 7900m (25,918ft)

AMMUNITION: HE, APHE, HEAT, APCR

whole barrel, resulted in the Flak 36, which was followed by the Flak 37 with its improved fire-control system. Rheinmetall developed the 88mm (3.5in) Flak 41 as an anti-tank and anti-aircraft weapon, but the system proved something of a disappointment and should not be confused with the iconic Flak 18, 36 and 37 series.

Rommel is largely credited with deploying the 88mm (3.5in) gun in an anti-tank role, particularly at the Battle of Arras during the campaign against France in 1940 and again with *Panzerarmee Afrika* during the Desert War. Rommel once noted, 'The struggle in the desert is best compared to a battle at sea. Whoever has the weapons with the greatest range has the longest arm. The longest arm has the advantage. We have it in the 88mm gun.'

True enough, the versatile '88' could outrange Allied tanks and destroy them from stand-off distances. With a rate of fire of 25 rounds per minute, a well-placed battery was capable of shredding enemy armoured formations swiftly.

The weapon was so successful that it took its toll on the Allies from a psychological perspective as well. More than 1100 of the Flak 18 and 36 were allocated to the *Feldheer* from 1939 to 1945, while nearly 14,000 were produced for *Luftwaffe* flak units.

**Infantry guns**

Organic to the infantry divisions of the *Feldheer* were artillery pieces which could provide direct and indirect fire support to the infantry formations and were maintained in the field, while other artillery was

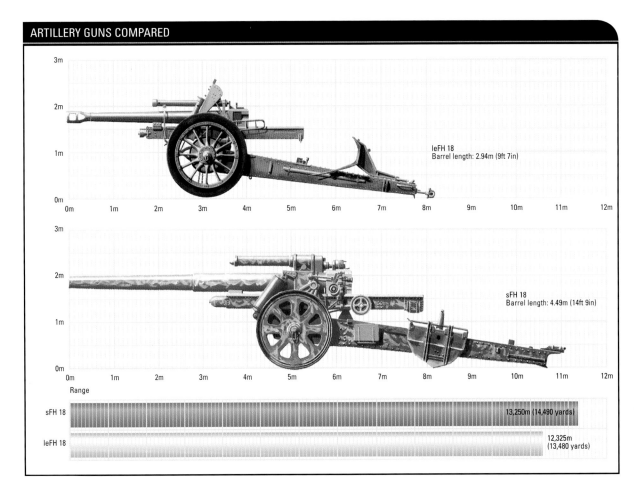

**ARTILLERY GUNS COMPARED**

leFH 18
Barrel length: 2.94m (9ft 7in)

sFH 18
Barrel length: 4.49m (14ft 9in)

Range

sFH 18     13,250m (14,490 yards)

leFH 18     12,325m (13,480 yards)

allocated as needed through the reserve pool. The most common infantry guns included the towed 75mm (2.95in) FK 16 nA and the 150mm (5.9in) sIG 33.

After World War I, the Germany Army abandoned its standard 77mm (3.03in) field gun for a 75mm (2.95in) design. The old World War I-vintage weapons were rebarrelled to the new calibre and entered service with the Army in 1934. Although this weapon was antiquated when war broke out, it was still in service in 1945. A lighter 75mm (2.95in) gun, the Krupp leFK 18, was designed in 1930 and entered service in 1938. However, only limited numbers were produced as an emphasis was shifted toward the 105mm (4.1in) guns of the pool artillery. The FK 16 fired a 5.8kg (12.8lb) projectile up to 12,875m (14,080 yards), while the range of the leFK 18 was slightly shorter at 9427m (10,310 yards). More than 4000 of the 150mm (5.9in) sIG 33 were produced from 1939 to 1945, and the weapon was the standard German heavy infantry gun of World War II. With a rate of fire of up to three rounds per minute, its maximum range was 4700m (5100 yards).

## Field and heavy artillery

The workhorse of the German field artillery during World War II was the 105mm (4.1in) leFH 18, which was produced by Rheinmetall in response to a request by the German Army for a heavier field howitzer than the old 77mm (3.03in) weapon of World War I. The weapon was popular on the world export market, but when war broke out it was quickly determined that a more powerful

shell was needed to achieve greater range. This resulted in the addition of a muzzle brake and the new designation of leFH 18(M). The standard weapon fired a 14.8kg (32.6lb) shell up to 12,324m (13,478 yards), and its primary drawback was its significant weight of 1955kg (4310lbs), which meant that it relied heavily on motorized transportation in what was only a semi-mechanized army.

■ The crew of a 210mm (8.3in) MRS 18 artillery piece load a huge 113kg (250lb) shell during the eight-month-long siege of Sevastopol, June 1942.

When a new 150mm (5.9in) howitzer was requested by the German Army, both Krupp and Rheinmetall produced outstanding designs, and the result was the placement of the Rheinmetall gun

## ANTI-TANK GUNS COMPARED

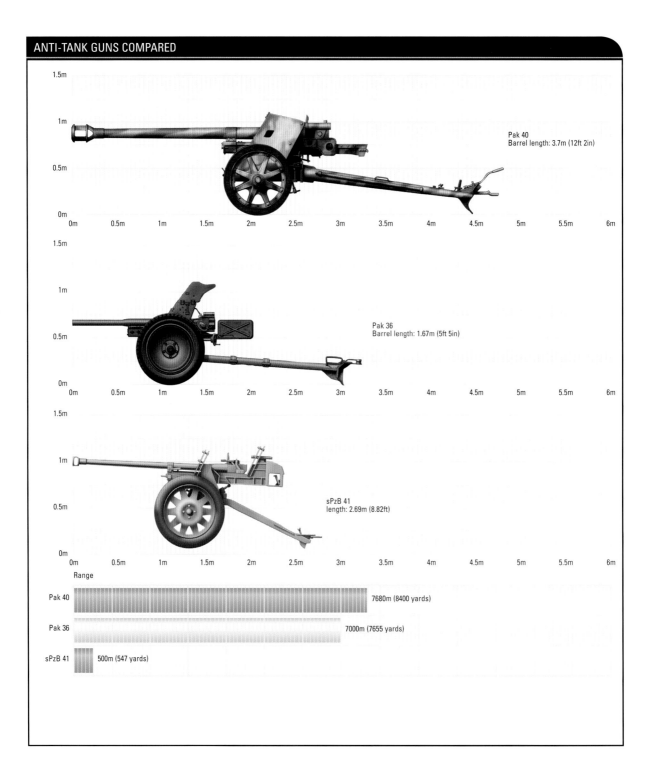

Pak 40
Barrel length: 3.7m (12ft 2in)

Pak 36
Barrel length: 1.67m (5ft 5in)

sPzB 41
length: 2.69m (8.82ft)

Range

Pak 40    7680m (8400 yards)

Pak 36    7000m (7655 yards)

sPzB 41   500m (547 yards)

atop the Krupp carriage in the sFH 18, which was actually a 149mm (5.86in) howitzer. Nearly 6000 examples of the gun, which was initially designed to be horse-drawn, were produced from 1939 to 1945, and the sFH 18 became the primary heavy artillery weapon of the *Feldheer* throughout the war. Its 43.5kg (95.9lb) shell travelled a maximum range of 13,323m (14,570 yards).

Other 150mm (5.9in) weapons (both actually 149.1mm/5.87in) in use during World War II included the Rheinmetall Model 18, which proved difficult to transport due to its long barrel which had to be detached from the carriage for movement of any great distance, and the Krupp 150mm (5.9in) howitzer which had originally been developed for the Turkish Army. Transportation and ammunition issues relegated the Krupp howitzer to training and coastal defence roles. Larger-calibre weapons were fairly common in the *Feldheer*, including 170mm (6.7in), 210mm (8.3in) and 240mm (9.4in) guns. A mountain howitzer, the 75mm (2.95in) Geb G 36, could be broken down into several components and carried by pack animals. More than 1200 of these were constructed during the war.

### Anti-tank guns
From 1939 to 1945, at least 21 variants of anti-tank gun were produced for the *Feldheer*. These ranged in calibre from 37mm (1.45in) to 88mm (3.5in). By far the greatest production weapon of this type was the 75mm (2.95in) Pak 40. The Pak 40 was significantly heavier than its predecessor, the Pak 38, primarily due to a shortage of lighter steel

alloys by the time the weapon entered mass production in 1942. By the end of the war, more than 23,000 had been produced. Considered the best weapon of its kind by many of the soldiers who served it, the Pak 40 fired a 5.7kg (12.6lb) round a distance of up to 7680m (8400 yards). The earlier 37mm (1.45in) Pak 35/36 had seen service during the Spanish Civil War, and the 50mm (1.97in) Pak 38 had arrived too late on the Eastern Front for the commencement of Operation 'Barbarossa' but did perform well against the thick armour of the Soviet T-34 medium tank.

### Railway guns, mortars and rocket launchers
A relative handful of heavy and costly railway guns were produced during the war, and in addition to the famed 800mm (31.5in) 'Gustav' and 'Dora' weapons which were used against the Red Army on the Eastern Front primarily as siege weapons, 203mm (8in), 210mm (8.3in), 280mm (11in), 283mm (11.1in), 310mm (12.2in) and 380mm (14.9in) railway guns were produced. At the embattled Anzio beachhead, the fire of heavy 283mm (11.1in) railway guns created a literal hell on earth for Allied soldiers, compelling them to remain under cover during daylight and move only at night, even to take rations.

Heavy mortars ranging from 210mm (8.3in), 240mm (9.4in) to 355mm (13.9in), and a single 420mm (16.5in) example, were also fielded. Among the most significant mortars was the 210mm (8.3in) Mörser 18, a towed weapon of which slightly more than 700 were manufactured. The Mörser 18 fired a 113kg (250lb) shell up to 14,500m

(15,857 yards). It was produced to provide effective plunging fire against fixed fortifications, and the last came off the assembly line in 1942, the gun having been discontinued in favour of a lighter 170mm (6.7in) version. Two mammoth mortars of the 'Karl' series were the 600mm (23.6in) Gerät 040 and the 540mm (21.3in) Gerät 041.

The multiple-tube Nebelwerfer 41 150mm (5.9in) rocket launcher fired high-explosive and smoke rockets a distance of 7000m (7655 yards), while the heavier Nebelwerfer 42 fired 210mm (8.3in) rockets. Later variants of these weapons fired 280mm (11in) and 310mm (12.2in) rockets. The Wurfgerät 40 and 41 fired incendiary rockets, while the six-tube Wurfrahmen 40 came in both 280mm (11in) and 320mm (12.6in) versions.

### Self-propelled artillery
In addition to the well-known Sturmgeschütz III and IV assault guns, and the Jagdtiger and Jagdpanther tank destroyers, the Germans developed a number of self-propelled assault guns to provide mobile firepower in direct support of infantry operations and to take on enemy armoured vehicles. Among the most prominent self-propelled artillery pieces were the 105mm (4.1in) leFH 18 Wespe (Wasp), 150mm (5.9in) Stu. Panzer 43 Brummbär (Grumbler), 150mm (5.9in) Hummel (Bumblebee), 88mm (3.5in) PzJ III and IV Nashorn (Rhinoceros), and K43 Elefant, or Ferdinand. The Marder II and III mounted the anti-tank 75mm (2.95in) Pak 40, while the Hetzer was armed with a 75mm (2.95in) Pak 39 cannon mounted atop the 38(t) chassis of Czech design.

# CHAPTER 7

# Support and Auxiliary Services

*The vast array of support, logistics and specialized functions required to keep an army in the field on the move and supplied with the matériel of war were undertaken by a number of auxiliary and support services within the Heer.*

*Additionally, specialized units within the combat formations conducted operations to facilitate movement, maintain communications, render medical aid to the sick and wounded, provide veterinary care to the horses and mules upon which the Feldheer was largely dependent for transportation, gather and interpret intelligence, and perform other functions.*

*As might be expected, for every man who shouldered a rifle and went into battle there were several in non-combat formations who served as logistical support to keep them fighting.*

■ German pioneers lay telephone lines in a town somewhere in western Russia during the invasion of the Soviet Union, summer 1941.

# The Engineers

*The engineers of the German Army are perhaps the best known of its specialized troops. Logically, this conclusion stems from the fact that combat engineers, or pioneers, were quite similar in general function and assignment to infantrymen. Actually,* Heer *engineers included combat, fortress and construction subspecialisms.*

At the divisional level, the engineer battalions were considered true engineer troop formations. These troops were organized into regiments and allocated to battle groups and other formations as needed. The administration and deployment of these divisional engineers was dictated by the circumstances of the battlefield, whether offensive or defensive in nature. However, those engineers which were organic to lower-level formations, such as the infantry company, were actually combat soldiers who performed specific battlefield tasks and were under the command of the unit in which they served. Therefore, the designation of these soldiers as 'engineer troops' is only partially correct.

Combat engineers performed a variety of tasks, including the clearing of minefields, demolition of fixed fortifications such as bunkers and pillboxes, use of flamethrowers and deployment of small boats for river crossings. Engineers prepared forward operating bases for the *Luftwaffe* and were routinely engaged in the construction of defensive positions in the field. An engineer battalion was organic to each infantry division of the *Feldheer* and included a headquarters company and three additional companies. The later *Volksgrenadier* divisions included engineer battalions of two companies. Motorized infantry divisions included an armoured engineer battalion, while mountain and parachute engineer battalions were also organized. Each of these was equipped according to the anticipated needs of the type of division in which the troops served.

Another primary function of the engineers was the construction of bridges. Prior to 1943, bridging detachments or columns were included in all engineer battalions.

## PIONEER COMPANY (PANZER DIVISION), 1944

*The pioneer company of the Type 1944 panzer division included panzergrenadiers who had been specifically trained to perform the functions of combat engineers, removing obstacles such as mines, reducing fixed fortifications and deploying flamethrowers on the battlefield. The pioneer company included command and staff troops, a halftrack platoon, a pair of engineer platoons and a mortar platoon transported by truck.*

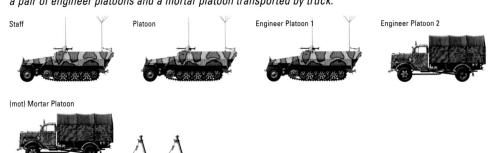

Staff

Platoon

Engineer Platoon 1

Engineer Platoon 2

(mot) Mortar Platoon

However, substantial reorganizations of the *Feldheer* divisions in 1943 and 1944 resulted in the bridging units being withdrawn from infantry divisions and consolidated within a general headquarters pool at the corps or army level. Each engineer bridging battalion then consisted of about 900 soldiers organized in four companies with an additional engineer park company which was directly responsible for the bridging equipment.

While bridging units were removed from the table of organization and equipment in the infantry divisions, they remained with the panzer divisions for the duration of the war. At the same time, the construction engineers, whose primary tasks were road construction, bridge repair and the construction or demolition of obstacles, had been designated as simply construction troops prior to

## PIONEER BATTALION (PANZER DIVISION) , 1944

*The pioneer battalions assigned to Type 1944 panzer divisions were considered true combat engineers and were allocated to combat units as needed from regiments located in a central pool. Following a reorganization in 1943, bridging units were removed from infantry divisions. However, due to the need to facilitate the cross-country manoeuvre of armoured formations the panzer divisions retained their bridging columns.*

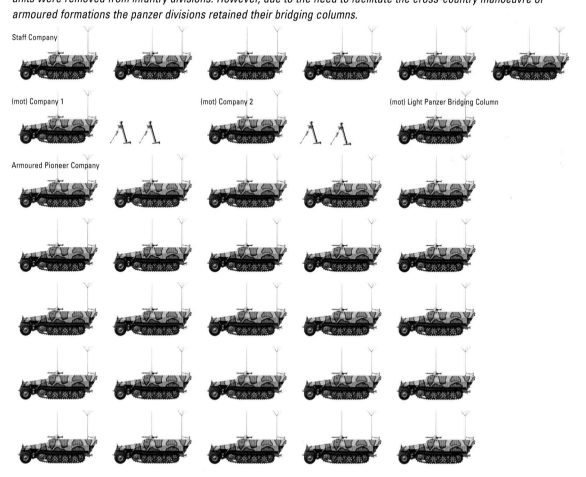

Staff Company

(mot) Company 1    (mot) Company 2    (mot) Light Panzer Bridging Column

Armoured Pioneer Company

## PIONEER ELEMENT ORGANIZATION, TYPE 1944 PANZER DIVISION

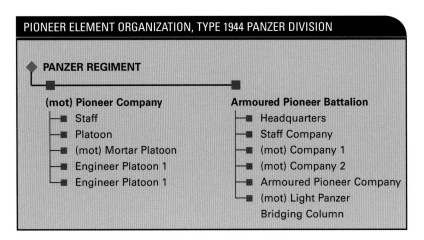

**PANZER REGIMENT**

**(mot) Pioneer Company**
- Staff
- Platoon
- (mot) Mortar Platoon
- Engineer Platoon 1
- Engineer Platoon 1

**Armoured Pioneer Battalion**
- Headquarters
- Staff Company
- (mot) Company 1
- (mot) Company 2
- Armoured Pioneer Company
- (mot) Light Panzer
  Bridging Column

constructed railway lines for the movement of troops and supplies.

The standard Type 1944 panzer division included a motorized pioneer company and an armoured pioneer battalion. The company was composed of its staff complement, a single platoon transported by halftrack and armed with six flamethrowers and six light machine guns, a truck-borne motorized mortar platoon with two heavy machine guns and two 81mm (3.2in) mortars, and two specifically-identified engineer platoons, one transported by halftrack and the other by truck. The truck-borne platoon was armed with eight light machine guns and 12 flamethrowers, while the halftrack platoon included a 20mm (0.79in) gun, six flamethrowers and 12 light machine guns.

■ German pioneer troops use the directional outboard motor to steer a *Sturmboot* over the river Bug during the invasion of the Soviet Union, summer 1941. The soldier on the left has slung on his back a metal case containing a spare MG34 barrel.

the autumn of 1943, when these units were reclassified as engineers and assigned directly to the units which they supported. Separate railway engineering regiments, consisting of two battalions of four companies each, repaired, maintained and

The heavier armoured pioneer battalion included the staff and a staff company with six halftracks and 14 light machine guns, two motorized companies with a pair of heavy machine guns, 18 light machine guns and two 81mm (3.2in) mortars each, an armoured pioneer company of 25 halftracks mounting light machine guns, two heavy machine guns, three 20mm (0.79in) flak cannon, 18 additional light machine guns, six flamethrowers, two 81mm (3.2in) mortars, and a motorized light panzer bridging column.

By 1945, the panzer division's complement of pioneers was greatly diminished to a single armoured battalion of 716 soldiers organized in staff elements with nine light machine guns, a motorized staff and supply company with four light machine guns, two motorized pioneer companies with a pair of 81mm (3.2in) mortars, 18 light machine guns and two heavy machine guns each, an armoured pioneer company with 19 light machine guns and two heavy machine guns, and a bridging column.

The *Feldheer* deployed several types of bridging units, which were designated by a specific letter corresponding to the type of bridging equipment in use. Among these were the Type B bridge, which was constructed of pontoons with a steel superstructure and a wooden roadway sufficient in strength for the passage of a load weighing up to 20.3 tonnes (20 tons) depending on the number of pontoons allocated, the Type K bridge which was constructed of steel girders and could support up to 27.4 tonnes (27 tons) and was sufficient for

light tanks to cross distances of nearly 20m (22 yards), and the infantry assault bridge, supported by inflatable boats with a narrow walkway which allowed infantry to move across a stream in single file and could hold up against a current of just over 3.7km/h (two knots).

The pioneers deployed inflatable, wooden and steel assault boats of various sizes, depending on the demands of combat and the strength of the forces engaged. One of the largest of these was a 16.2-tonne (16-ton) amphibious tractor with twin propellers powered by a 224kW (300hp) Maybach HL 120 engine. The tractor could transport up to 16 soldiers and was also used in the construction of small bridges or for towing in calm waters.

Inflatable boats were capable of supporting up to 13.7 tonnes (13.5 tons), and some were more than 7.93m (26ft) long. The standard

■ A Goliath remote-controlled demolition vehicle is guided by German pioneers towards a captured Soviet assault gun somewhere on the Eastern Front. While a very original idea, the Goliath proved to be ineffective in combat.

motorized assault boat was constructed of wood and carried a crew of two and up to seven additional soldiers. Its length was just under 6.09m (20ft).

Another specialized engineer detachment worthy of note was the 35-man armoured engineer platoon, Goliath, which was equipped to deploy a small tracked bomb or mine. The Goliath was controlled by a stick which was manually manipulated and attached to the tracked bomb by telephone cable. The Goliath was used in a demolition and anti-tank role and was 1.2m (4ft) long and 0.3m (1ft) tall.

# Supply and Logistics

*A centralized production and distribution programme was developed in Germany prior to the beginning of World War II.*

Three Reich ministries controlled the actual production and distribution of war matériel and supplies to the *Feldheer* and the Replacement Army, the other branches of the *Wehrmacht*, and the *Waffen-SS*. From February 1942, Hitler's personal architect, Albert Speer, served as Reich Minister of Armaments and War Production, whose ministry controlled the production of weapons, ammunition and other supplies critical to the war effort. The Ministry of Economic Affairs was responsible for all other aspects of industrial production in Nazi Germany, while the Ministry for Food and Agriculture was charged with the production of foodstuffs.

Each of these ministries was functionally a component of the General Staff, and the needs of the armed forces at any given time were coordinated and fulfilled through the orders of the high command, which issued requisitions for supplies to the appropriate ministry in quantity. Equally important was the planning role of the General Staff, which influenced the future production needs in relation to upcoming operations and the capacity of German industry to meet those needs.

A system of large supply depots, often with extensive storage and warehouse structures underground, was established throughout Germany to facilitate distribution via roads,

waterways and air transport. The Army high command (OKH) was responsible for the procurement and distribution of much of the supplies allocated to the *Waffen-SS*, although the command structures of the two were entirely separate.

The supply function within OKH involved two separate areas of responsibility. The Chief of Army Equipment and Commander of the Replacement Army supervised the function within the Zone of the Interior, or within the national borders of Germany. His purview included the requisitioning of supplies, marshalling and storage in the various depots located throughout the country, and their distribution to Army units in Germany and in the field abroad. Interpreting the directives of the high command, he allocated supplies based on the needs of training, garrison and administrative units in Germany and followed with the available allotment for the *Feldheer* troops fighting on the front lines. He was also responsible for determining which supply depots were in the locations which were most advantageous for economical and rapid distribution.

The second area of responsibility was with the Chief of *Feldheer* Supply and Administration, or General Quartermaster, who sent requisition orders to the various supply depots and was responsible for receiving,

storing and distributing supplies to *Feldheer* units.

## Matériel of war

From production to distribution and allocation, the volume of supplies, including food, ammunition, fuel, clothing, and other essentials, was tremendous within the *Feldheer*. According to the US War Department Technical Manual, *TM-E 30-451: Handbook on German Military Forces*, which was published in 1945, the expenditure of supplies in a panzer division on the Eastern Front in 1941 amounted to 30.4 tonnes (30 tons) per day while inactive and up to 711.2 tonnes (700 tons) per day when engaged in heavy combat. Infantry divisions were estimated to consume up to 81.2 tonnes (80 tons) and 1117.6 tonnes (1100 tons) respectively. When engaged in offensive or heavy defensive fighting, each German soldier was believed to consume up to 22.6kg (50lbs) of supplies per day. Even when inactive, the per-soldier daily estimate was up to 4.5kg (10lbs).

The average German soldier received enough rations for three meals a day with one-half the regular daily allotment consumed at mid-day, one-third in the evening, and one-sixth at breakfast the following morning. Four classes of rations were issued depending on the location and type of duty in which the individual was engaged. The standard ration

## SUPPLY VEHICLES COMPARED

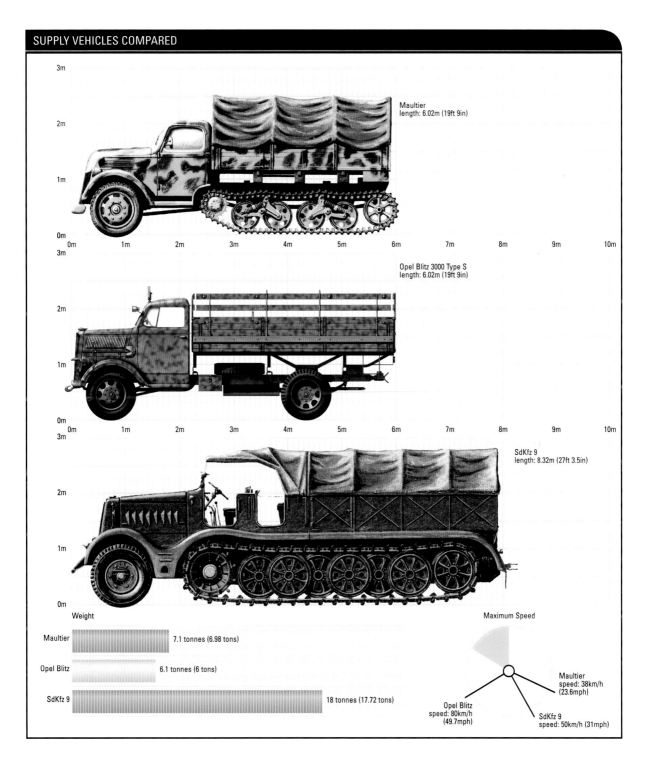

Maultier
length: 6.02m (19ft 9in)

Opel Blitz 3000 Type S
length: 6.02m (19ft 9in)

SdKfz 9
length: 8.32m (27ft 3.5in)

Weight

Maultier          7.1 tonnes (6.98 tons)

Opel Blitz        6.1 tonnes (6 tons)

SdKfz 9           18 tonnes (17.72 tons)

Maximum Speed

Maultier
speed: 38km/h
(23.6mph)

Opel Blitz
speed: 80km/h
(49.7mph)

SdKfz 9
speed: 50km/h (31mph)

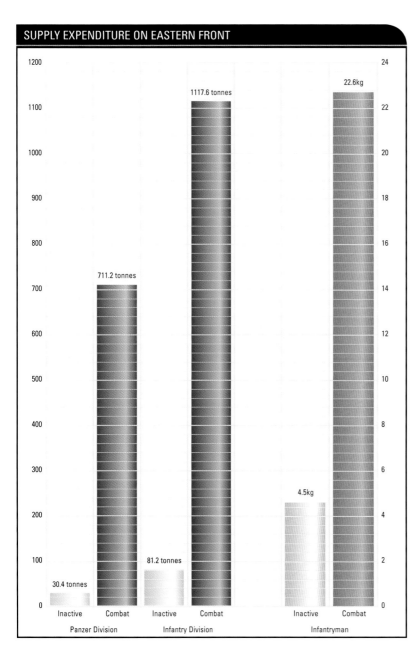

SUPPLY EXPENDITURE ON EASTERN FRONT

kitchen, or in a supply dump. Soldiers were encouraged to live off the land as much possible. Special march, iron, combat and close combat rations were also issued. These were not usually distributed unless combat conditions or supply restrictions prevented the delivery of full rations.

Rations for animals were distributed based upon the type of animal and generally considered to be the amount a single horse, dog, draft ox or carrier pigeon would consume in one day. Horses were divided into four groups, namely small horses, light draught horses and saddle horses, draught horses of heavy breed and draught horses of heaviest breed. Each of these received corresponding rations, with the draught horses of heaviest breed fed the most. On the Eastern Front these received a daily allowance of 5.3kg (11.6lbs) of hay, 5.75kg (12.8lbs) of straw and 5.65kg (12.5lbs) of oats.

**Ordnance department**
The ordnance department of the *Heer* was responsible for the storage, replacement allocation, and repair of equipment and weapons. The *Feldheer* maintained equipment parks, which were essentially maintenance and repair facilities which also held up to 200 new or replacement vehicles or specifically served infantry, artillery, signals and engineer units with supplies, spare parts and replacement equipment.

Replacement equipment and clothing were distributed according to an allotment at unit and individual levels based on a prescribed table, while fuel allotments were calculated on a consumption basis required to

weighed about 1.5kg (3.3lbs). It included 700 grams (1.5lbs) of rye bread, up to 136 grams (0.3lbs) of fresh meat, 320 grams (0.7lbs) of potatoes, and portions of other staples. The Army on the move generally maintained 10 days of field rations per soldier, either with the individual, stored on a combat vehicle, with the supply train or field

move a vehicle in its formation a distance of 100km (62 miles). Theoretically, as the fuel was expended it was replaced, while three consumption units were stored at fuel dumps and each panzer formation carried an additional four units. Reconnaissance units carried six and one-half units, and all other formations carried five.

The initial issue of ammunition for a given unit was the total amount carried by the specific formations within the unit by supply trains, by the troops themselves, and positioned in ammunition dumps. As it was expended, the initial issue was to be systematically replaced as levels of available ammunition were reported through the various levels of command.

Each initial issue was based on the number and types of weapons within a given formation, and each weapon was allocated a specific number of rounds. Two units of issue for each weapon were carried within a division, while a reserve unit was on hand in the supply column. The allocation toward the front of the combat formation amounted to somewhat more than a full unit, while the rest was held in a ready reserve further to the rear.

A standard infantryman in a *Volksgrenadier* division would receive a forward issue of 720 rounds of 7.92mm (0.31in) ammunition with 540 rounds in division reserve, allocated from a unit of issue of 630 rounds. Since two units of issue were carried within the division, the total number of rounds available per weapon was 1260. The 120mm (4.7in) mortar ammunition allocation

included 150 rounds in forward issue, 90 in division reserve and a unit of issue of 120 rounds. The 105mm (4.1in) and 150mm (5.9in) howitzers were issued 125 rounds each, and

the 88mm (3.5in) flak gun received 300 rounds. The *Feldheer* estimated that three units of issue were sufficient to sustain combat formations in action for up to 10 days.

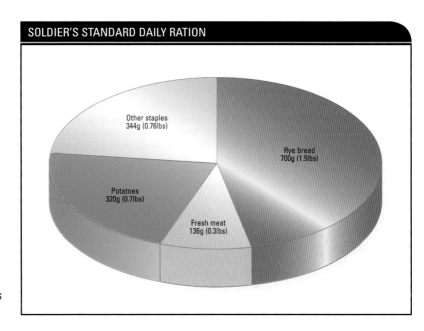

SOLDIER'S STANDARD DAILY RATION

Other staples
344g (0.76lbs)

Rye bread
700g (1.5lbs)

Potatoes
320g (0.7lbs)

Fresh meat
136g (0.3lbs)

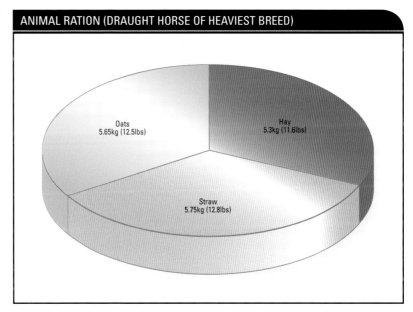

ANIMAL RATION (DRAUGHT HORSE OF HEAVIEST BREED)

Oats
5.65kg (12.5lbs)

Hay
5.3kg (11.6lbs)

Straw
5.75kg (12.8lbs)

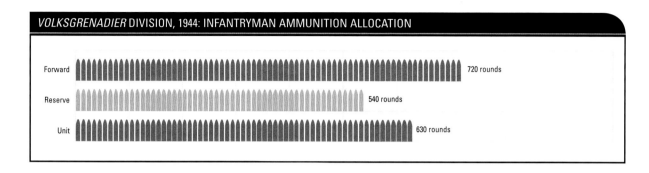

VOLKSGRENADIER DIVISION, 1944: INFANTRYMAN AMMUNITION ALLOCATION

Forward — 720 rounds
Reserve — 540 rounds
Unit — 630 rounds

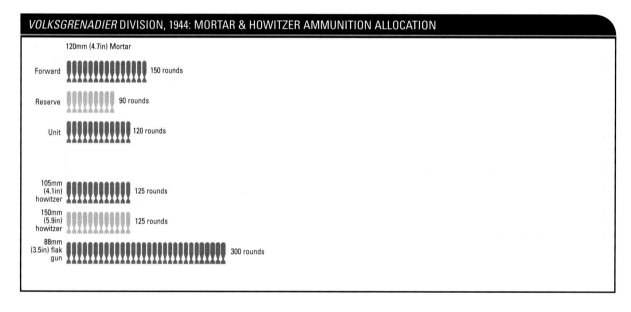

VOLKSGRENADIER DIVISION, 1944: MORTAR & HOWITZER AMMUNITION ALLOCATION

120mm (4.7in) Mortar
Forward — 150 rounds
Reserve — 90 rounds
Unit — 120 rounds

105mm (4.1in) howitzer — 125 rounds
150mm (5.9in) howitzer — 125 rounds
88mm (3.5in) flak gun — 300 rounds

# Transportation

*The transportation of troops, equipment and supplies was generally under the control of the OKW Chief of Transportation, who coordinated movement with regional transportation headquarters and the civil railway and water transportation organizations.*

Military transport was always of the highest priority, particularly when it involved the use of an extensive and efficient system of railways which functioned well even under the strain of Allied bombing as the war wore on.

The German railway system, in double-tracked configuration of standard gauge, was capable of handling up to 30 military trains in each direction per day. A single line could carry up to 10 trains. For long

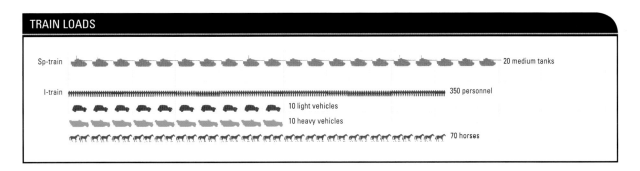

**TRAIN LOADS**

| | |
|---|---|
| Sp-train | 20 medium tanks |
| I-train | 350 personnel |
| | 10 light vehicles |
| | 10 heavy vehicles |
| | 70 horses |

distance movement, the *Feldheer* relied heavily on rail transportation, particularly to reach the most distant or remote areas where German troops were stationed, such as Scandinavia and southern Italy.

**Train types**

The standard troop train was capable of transporting units as large as a battalion with all supporting personnel and equipment. Certain types of trains were identified based upon specialized function or capacity. The K-train, or motor vehicle train, included up to 51 cars per train carrying 250 soldiers, 20 heavy vehicles weighing up to 22.3 tonnes (22 tons) each, 20 light vehicles and other equipment. These estimates could vary depending on the type of equipment and the number of soldiers to be transported, with lighter equipment allowing a larger number of personnel to board. The S-train, or special train, was designed to carry heavy tanks and assault guns, usually up to six PzKpfw VI Tiger tanks or eight PzKpfw V Panther tanks along with

■ **A German armoured train makes a stop somewhere in the Reich.**

lighter equipment, and up to 125 soldiers aboard as many as 35 cars.

Other specialized trains included the Sp-train, or special tank train, which could transport up to 20 medium tanks along with assigned personnel and equipment aboard 33 cars, and the I-train, or infantry train, which included 55 cars transporting 350 personnel, 10 light vehicles, 10 heavy vehicles weighing up to 22.4 tonnes (22 tons) each, 70 horses and various items of light equipment. With fewer vehicles aboard, the I-train could carry as many as 800 soldiers. The replacement troop train was intended to carry up to 2000 replacement soldiers in as many as 60 cars. From 35 to 40 trains were typically required to transport a fully-equipped infantry division, while a panzer division would require up to 80.

Combat supply trains carried fuel, food and ammunition to the front and often included up to 40 cars with more than 457.2 tonnes (450 tons) of rations or supplies and 529,000 litres (116,366 gallons) of fuel. Horse supply trains were up to 55 cars long, each of which carried as many as eight standard or six heavy draught horses, with a total capacity of up to 440 animals.

Armoured trains operated frequently to keep railway lines open, combat partisans, provide anti-aircraft defence and maintain communications. These often included as many as six armoured railway cars with more than 100 soldiers. The armoured trains regularly carried light tanks or armoured cars to perform reconnaissance duties or establish perimeter defences in combat situations, while a pair of cars served as platforms for 20mm (0.79in) flak guns or a combination of flak and anti-tank weapons. Two other cars carried a complement of infantry armed with 105mm (4.1in) howitzers, up to 22 light machine guns, a heavy machine gun and at least two mortars, probably 81mm (3.2in).

### The road march

Across Germany and the occupied territories, certain roads were designated by the high command as primary military routes. These included main thoroughfares and the Autobahn. When military transportation was to take place along these routes, civilian traffic was re-routed or suspended completely. The standard infantry division was capable of marching

about 32km (20 miles) per day, although this distance was influenced by incidences of combat, weather conditions and the number of trucks and pack animals available to assist. Panzergrenadier divisions normally were capable of moving 145–241km (90–150 miles) per day, and panzer divisions 97–145km (60–90 miles). Combat conditions might decrease daily distances to 24km (15 miles) or less for infantry units on foot and 48km (30 miles) for motorized units.

An infantry division marching at 4.8km/h (3mph) would extend a length of approximately 48km (30 miles). A panzer division travelling at 19.3km/h (12mph), the average speed of its tanks, extended about 113km (70 miles), and a panzergrenadier division roughly 129km (80 miles) while travelling at 26km/h (16mph).

### Waterborne movement

Measured in gross registered tons, or one ton per 2.83 cubic metres (100 cubic feet) of the total enclosed space of a vessel, an infantry division required up to 70,000 gross registered tons, approximately six tons per soldier, for efficient movement of any great distance. The loading time of a ship of 2000 gross registered tons

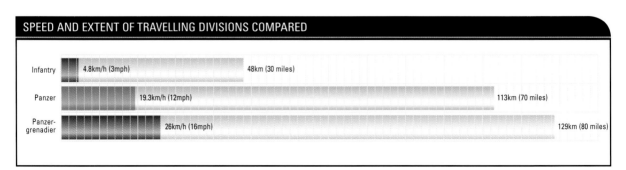

**SPEED AND EXTENT OF TRAVELLING DIVISIONS COMPARED**

Infantry — 4.8km/h (3mph) — 48km (30 miles)

Panzer — 19.3km/h (12mph) — 113km (70 miles)

Panzer-grenadier — 26km/h (16mph) — 129km (80 miles)

was approximately 16 hours. Heavier formations required much longer times for loading and unloading, as well as greater gross tonnage. The average distance covered by a fully-loaded ship was estimated at 370km (200 nautical miles) per day.

Long-distance movement by water was uncommon in the *Feldheer*. However, some operations were undertaken in Norway, the Crimea and North Africa. One major hindrance to the execution of Operation 'Sealion', the planned invasion of England which was scrapped, was the lack of any real capability to conduct a large-scale amphibious assault. Transiting canals, rivers, lakes and other inland bodies of water was often accomplished by barges or smaller craft whose tonnage requirements were not necessarily as rigid as those of ocean-going vessels.

For longer voyages, the gross registered ton could also be translated into its volume equivalent of 2.83 cubic metres (100 cubic feet). From there, a man was allocated two gross registered tons, a medium tank 25, a horse eight, a light vehicle 10, and a medium vehicle or artillery weapon 20 tons.

# Medical Services

*In Nazi Germany, the Armed Forces Surgeon General was chiefly responsible for the highly-organized administration of medical services within the* Wehrmacht. *Directly subordinate to the Armed Forces Surgeon General was the Chief Army Medical Inspector, who was stationed in Berlin at the headquarters of the Replacement Army but was not subordinated to it.*

The Armed Forces Surgeon General supervised a staff known as the Army Medical Inspectorate and was responsible for the medical services of the *Feldheer* and the Replacement Army, which included the training of medical personnel, oversight of sanitation and hygiene within the *Heer*, the evacuation and hospitalization of combat casualties, the administration of military hospitals, and the supplies of pharmaceuticals and medical equipment for the *Heer*. In the Replacement Army, a corps area surgeon was responsible for both personnel and territorial matters.

Permanent medical installations in Germany included medical units, hospitals and supply depots. The medical units were under the control of the corps area surgeons and included the medical replacement battalions, which supplied the *Feldheer* with qualified medical personnel, and the medical battalions in which all medical personnel in the Replacement Army or in hospitals served, except those who were in training. A corps area included three medical battalions, each in a separate garrison city and composed of smaller units. Each medical section was commanded by a garrison surgeon who also was responsible for the nearby military hospitals.

Hospitals consisted of general facilities, tuberculosis and sanatorium facilities, convalescent facilities and hospitals for prisoners of war. Due to the great need during wartime, a number of buildings such as schools or hotels were converted to hospitals, and the general hospitals were recognized by the name of the town in which they were located, followed by Roman numerals in the event that more than one hospital was located in the area. Most hospitals dealt with a wide array of casualties, and the most common of these were designated by numbers 1 to 21, which allowed the distribution of patients to the few facilities which might be better equipped to treat a certain type of injury.

All general hospitals were components of the Replacement

Army, and initially all patients transferred to such facilities were in effect transferred from the *Feldheer* to the Replacement Army.

However, as the war progressed and the combat zones crept closer to Germany, patients were not transferred to the Replacement Army until after they had spent eight weeks in the general hospital. This directive was also applied to field hospitals.

Hospitals submitted daily reports which detailed the number of available beds to local distribution centres. A medical liaison officer assigned to a local transportation section supervised the assignment of patients to hospitals in the local district.

**Medical services organization**

During the course of the war, more than four million German military personnel were wounded and survived. This was due in many cases to the medical attention provided on the battlefield and in hospitals and aid stations located near the front lines. The *Feldheer* medical services

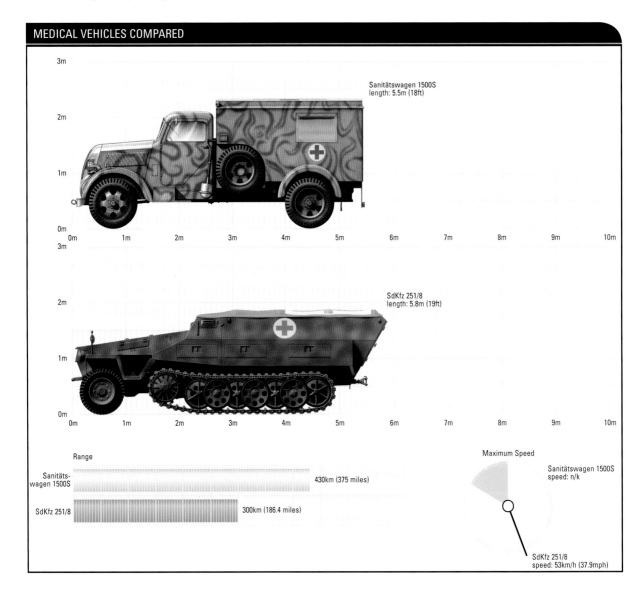

MEDICAL VEHICLES COMPARED

Sanitätswagen 1500S
length: 5.5m (18ft)

SdKfz 251/8
length: 5.8m (19ft)

Range

Sanitäts-wagen 1500S      430km (375 miles)

SdKfz 251/8      300km (186.4 miles)

Maximum Speed

Sanitätswagen 1500S
speed: n/k

SdKfz 251/8
speed: 53km/h (37.9mph)

organization included a medical battalion assigned to each field army. Each battalion numbered about 470 personnel and controlled as many as four field hospitals.

Those companies that made up the battalions were often assigned to a division and supervised a single field hospital. Platoon-sized formations included a mobile ambulance detachment and personnel which treated casualties at the aid stations. Until 1943, field hospitals were allocated at the division level. From then on, they were under the direct control of the army-level administration.

A battlefield casualty was first evacuated on foot or by stretcher to a battalion aid station. This was followed, if necessary, by a referral to the regimental aid station situated little more than 457m (500 yards) behind the lines. At a larger regimental medical facility, more extensive stabilization efforts were carried out along with surgery, suturing, amputations and other procedures. From there, the seriously wounded were collected at a casualty clearing point for transportation to a medical facility in Germany or the occupied territories. Often at the regimental level, a doctor

determined whether a soldier required additional medical treatment or could be returned directly to his unit. Certain facilities were also designated for the treatment of those deemed slightly wounded.

Medical supplies and equipment were allocated through a large medical park in Berlin and at corps level medical parks throughout Germany. The Berlin medical park was also responsible for the development and implementation of general medical policy, the testing and authorization of new treatments and drugs, and the distribution of most captured medical supplies.

# Veterinary Services

*The Veterinary Inspector was responsible for the veterinary services in both the* Feldheer *and the Replacement Army, subordinate to the commander of the Replacement Army but receiving his orders directly from the Commander-in-Chief of the Army.*

Throughout World War II, the *Heer* remained dependent upon the horse for 80 per cent of its transportation requirements. Indicative of that dependency is the fact that up to 750,000 horses were deployed on the Eastern Front during Operation 'Barbarossa', the German invasion of the Soviet Union. Of these, more than half died of overwork, the effects of the harsh climate, or sheer exhaustion in the mud and snow of the Russian winter.

The Veterinary Service was responsible for the selection and health of thousands of animals during

the war. Veterinary officers were an integral component of the major Army headquarters and were routinely detailed to units which maintained horses. The number of horses required to provide transportation for a single infantry division varied from slightly more than 4000 to over 6000, and these were continually in need of medical care and treatment for injuries and wounds.

### Veterinary Inspector
The Veterinary Inspector was responsible for all veterinary personnel and farriers and supervised

| HORSES PER DIVISION | |
| --- | --- |
| Unit | Horses |
| Infantry Division | 4–6000+ |
| *Volksgrenadier* Division | 2700 |
| Mountain Division | 3000 |

the activities of Army veterinarians in the treatment, evacuation and replacement of horses and equipment. With respect to the Replacement Army, he was responsible for the training of veterinary personnel and the distribution of equipment. Within

■ A German Army baggage train moves along a road somewhere in the Ukraine during the invasion of the Soviet Union, July 1941.

for its two regiments. Mountain divisions utilized at least 3000 horses and mules for carrying supplies and equipment across rugged terrain.

Within each corps area at least one home horse hospital operated, caring for injured horses which had been evacuated from the *Feldheer* treatment facilities and horses of the Replacement Army which required treatment. These hospitals were numbered the same as their corps area, and if more than one hospital were present these would be followed sequentially by a three-digit suffix beginning with 100. When horses were deemed fit for a return to duty, they first were transported from the home horse hospital to the home horse park within the corps area. Subsequently, the corps veterinarian determined which horses were to be sent to the *Feldheer* and which were assigned to the Replacement Army.

When a horse was injured or became ill near the front, it received initial treatment at a field station. If further treatment was required, it was transported to a divisional facility which could care for up to 150 horses at a time. Field or Army horse hospitals would later receive horses requiring additional treatment in groups of up to 40. A number of these hospitals existed outside Germany and were capable of treating up to 500 horses. Veterinary officers were easily distinguished from other officers of the *Heer* by the snake insignia on the shoulders of their tunics.

## VETERINARY COMPANY ORGANIZATION, 1942

- Horse Collecting Platoon
- Fodder Platoon
- Hospital Platoon

Germany itself, veterinary personnel and facilities were under the command of the corps area veterinarian, also known as the deputy corps veterinarian, and a member of the staff of the deputy corps commander.

Infantry divisions in the field generally included a veterinary company with more than 150 officers and soldiers organized in three platoons with horse collecting, fodder, and horse hospital functions. As mentioned above, throughout the war, the table of organization and equipment of the German infantry division required at least 4000 horses; a *Volksgrenadier* division was slated with a complement of more than 2700

# Signals and Communications

*Signals troops were responsible for the effective and efficient communications which were essential to victory on the battlefield. Each German division contained a signals battalion which included a telephone company, a radio company, and a light signals column or a battalion supply platoon.*

The infantry division's signals battalion usually included 379 soldiers, while a panzer division signals battalion numbered more than 500. Similar to the pioneer units, those signals troops which served in platoons and organic divisional units were assigned to the units in which they served and performed basic signals functions. The troops of the designated signals battalion were more specialized.

### Functions

Signals troops were involved in the operations of the *Heer* at the highest level, relaying information to and from OKW, Hitler's far-flung headquarters, and the various levels of command from administration to field units. The functions of the signals troops included radio, telephone, telegraph and flag communications along with message

## ARMOURED SIGNAL BATTALION, TYPE 44 PANZER DIVISION

*The organization of a Type 1944 panzer division included an armoured signals battalion, which consisted of the battalion staff, an armoured telephone company with six halftracks, each mounting a light machine gun along with five additional light machine guns, an armoured radio company with two PzBefWg IV medium command tanks, eight halftracks mounting 14 light machine guns and five additional light machine guns, and one motorized signals supply column with two light machine guns.*

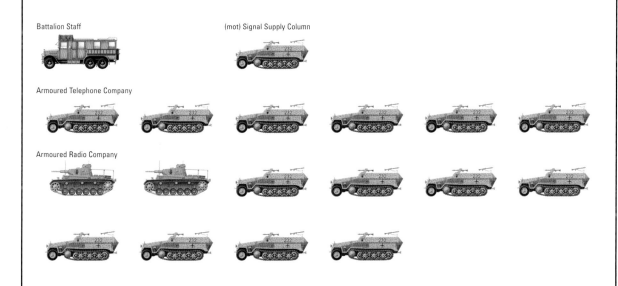

Battalion Staff

(mot) Signal Supply Column

Armoured Telephone Company

Armoured Radio Company

Die
Wehrmacht
HERAUSGEGEBEN VOM OBERKOMMANDO DER WEHRMACHT

Nach 25 Tagen!

■ Launched by the Nazi Party, *Die Wehrmacht* was published from 1936 to 1944 as a propaganda organ for the German Army. It promoted the German armed forces and was aimed at young readers. From February 1938 onwards, the official editor was the new *Oberkommando der Wehrmacht*.

transmission via dispatch riders on bicycles or motorcycles or by dogs or homing pigeons. These troops were also responsible for encoding and decoding secure messages and jamming or intercepting enemy radio traffic and communications.

During World War II, the *Feldheer* used more than 20 types of sturdy radios mounted on vehicles. Their ease of maintenance kept such equipment in service during harsh conditions. A variety of battery-powered radios were carried by infantrymen in backpacks, and electrical power for the vehicle-mounted radios was delivered by converters which were charged by the vehicle batteries. The range capabilities of the equipment varied widely. Larger equipment allowed headquarters to communicate with troops in the field across great distances. Armoured vehicles, particularly halftracks and armoured cars, were often outfitted for command and control and facilitated coordination of units in combat.

## Field telephones

The most common field telephone was the Type 33, which was battery-powered and often used to establish communications between fixed front-line positions and higher echelons of command toward the rear. Switchboard interchanges could accommodate up to 300 field lines. Among the *Feldheer*'s most important means of communication was the well-known encrypting machine called Enigma. Using a system of rotors and a battery-powered keyboard, the machine substituted one character for another based on settings which had previously been established.

## Propaganda operations

Early in 1943, propaganda troops were formally separated from the signals organization and constituted their own specialized arm of the *Feldheer*. A propaganda company was usually composed of a headquarters along with three war reporter platoons, a propaganda platoon and a support formation. The primary function of these troops was to report on and document the war while dispensing propaganda both directed at the enemy and at their own troops. These personnel included news print reporters, film camera operators, photographers, and radio broadcasters.

The propaganda platoon included 310 personnel, more than 50 vehicles and 26 motorcycles. The propaganda arm of the *Wehrmacht* was responsible for the production of *Signal* magazine, one of the first publications in the world to extensively make use of colour photography.

Other propaganda dealt with the overarching themes of defending the Fatherland, Nazi ideology and the rationale for offensive operations, such as the hugely costly invasion of the Soviet Union.